T0372859

Far-Right Extremism Online

By imparting crucial insights into the digital evolution of far-right extremism and its challenges, this book explores how far-right extremism has transformed, utilising digital spaces for communication and employing coded language to evade detection.

Far-right extremism has spread extensively across online platforms. Flourishing within echo chambers, these groups propagate different types of online and offline actions and advance their hateful ideologies to a wide-ranging audience. This book highlights the issues surrounding far-right extremism, which distinguishing it from terrorism and examining its contemporary digital manifestations. Importantly, it sheds light on how far-right groups utilise online platforms for communication, radicalisation, and on-ground actions, relying on alternative truths, misinformation, conspiracy theories, fashion, and memes to connect with like-minded individuals. The book also addresses content moderation challenges and the impact of rising populism in today's political climate, which fuels societal divisions and uncertainty.

Far-Right Extremism Online is a valuable resource for academics, students, analysts, and professionals working in counter-extremism, cybersecurity, digital communication, and national security. It is also an indispensable guide for those concerned about far-right extremism in the digital age.

Tine Munk is a Senior Lecturer in the Criminology and Criminal Justice Department at Nottingham Trent University, UK. Tine is predominately teaching and researching cybercrime and cybersecurity. Her overarching research interest is cybercrimes in a political context focusing on these crimes' power, responses, and impacts.

Routledge Studies in Digital Extremism

Far-Right Extremism Online
Beyond the Fringe
Tine Munk

Far-Right Extremism Online

Beyond the Fringe

Tine Munk

Routledge
Taylor & Francis Group

LONDON AND NEW YORK

First published 2024
by Routledge
4 Park Square, Milton Park, Abingdon, Oxon OX14 4RN

and by Routledge
605 Third Avenue, New York, NY 10158

Routledge is an imprint of the Taylor & Francis Group, an informa business

British Library Cataloguing-in-Publication Data
A catalogue record for this book is available from the British Library

Library of Congress Cataloging-in-Publication Data
Names: Munk, Tine, 1970- author.
Title: Far-right extremism online: beyond the fringe / Tine Munk.
Description: New York: Routledge, 2024. |
Series: Routledge studies in digital extremism | Includes bibliographical
references and index.
Identifiers: LCCN 2024011223 (print) | LCCN 2024011224 (ebook) |
ISBN 9781032286624 (hbk) | ISBN 9781032286648 (pbk) |
ISBN 9781003297888 (ebk)
Subjects: LCSH: Right-wing extremists. | Radicalism–Technological
innovations.
Classification: LCC HN49.R33 M86 2024 (print) | LCC HN49.R33 (ebook) |
DDC 303.48/4–dc23/eng/20240313
LC record available at https://lccn.loc.gov/2024011223
LC ebook record available at https://lccn.loc.gov/2024011224

ISBN: 9781032286624 (hbk)
ISBN: 9781032286648 (pbk)
ISBN: 9781003297888 (ebk)

DOI: 10.4324/9781003297888

Typeset in Times New Roman
by Deanta Global Publishing Services, Chennai, India

Inge Højsgaard Munk
22.11.1942 - 06.01.2018

Contents

List of Tables

Acknowledgements

Embarking on a research journey through the intricate and often shadowy world of far-right extremism has been fascinating and daunting. This book aims to capture a snapshot of this rapidly evolving area, notably the far-right's actions and communications in the less visible realms of the Internet.

My deepest gratitude goes to my editorial team, particularly Medha Malaviya, whose unwavering support and guidance were pivotal, especially in allowing me to author another book during this challenging research. Morwenna Scott, your support and encouragement have been instrumental in finishing this project. I am immensely thankful to Pradiksha Dharsini (Deanta) for their production work and for their expertise in copyediting. I appreciate the reviewers who provided insightful feedback and constructive criticism: Senior Lecturer Elliot Doornbos from NTU, Professor Tim Owen from UCLan, and the third anonymous reviewer whose perspectives have been invaluable.

Submitting three books in 28 months takes its toll. This book reflects my research, but it is also a testament to the collective effort and belief of all those who stood by me throughout this period. A huge thanks to 'Blå Gruppe' in Denmark for always supporting me no matter which project I embark on: Maibritt and Jan Falkesgaard, Inge and John Ankjær Betz, Laura and Jesper Munk – and Version 2.0, Marcus and Sarah Ankjær Bertz, and Emma, Emil and Jeppe Munk. Also, thanks to Evald Munk and Ruth Rousing.

It is great to have several people who stand by me during the process – and, importantly, give me space when I disappear into my research mood and forget the world around me. Your patience, support and encouragement mean everything to me. Thank you for taking this journey with me: Tine Lee Senft, Bettina Jackobsen, Lene Dam, Dr Magali Peyrefitte, Sara Rodriguez, Juan Ahmad, Professor Angus Nurse, Elliot Doornbos, Dr Ian Mahoney, Dr Morag Kennedy, Dr Graham Smith, Becs Watermann, Georgia Mouskou, Dr Vicky Kemp, Teresa Yates, Nicks Yates, Anne Philips, Liz Newton.

I thank all my colleagues and students at the NTU Criminology and Criminal Justice Department 2022–2023 and 2023–2024. Especially, the academic and professional network that is instrumental in my work. I would like to highlight the cybercrime group: Dr Thais Sardá, Philip Wane, and Martin Tangen. Thank you for your support and inspiration!

List of Abbreviations

2YT4U – Too white for you
AfD – Alternative for Deutschland
AI – artificial intelligence
AWD – Atomwaffen Division
CoE – the Council of Europe
Dotr – Day of the Rope
EU – the European Union
GI – Generation Identity
GIFCT – the Global Internet Forum to Counter-terrorism
HIAS – the Hebrew Immigrant Aid Society
Incel – Involuntary Celibate KKK – Ku Klux Klan
LGBTQ+ – Lesbian, gay, bi, trans, queer, questioning and ace
ML – Machine learning
ND – European new Right
NDP – the National Democratic Party of Germany
NPC – Non-playable character
NSDAP – Nationalsozialistische Deutsche Arbeiterpartei/ the National Socialist German Workers' Party
OSCE – the Organization for Security and Co-operation in Europe
SJW – Social Justice Warrior
TAT – Tech against Terrorism
TCAT – Terrorist Content Analytics Platform
TOR – The Onion Router
UK – United Kingdom
UN – the United Nations
US – United States of America
VPN – Virtual private networks
WAR – White Aryan Resistance
WBS – White Boys Summer
WWII – World War II
WWG1WGA – Where We Go One We Go All

1 Introduction
Unveiling Far-Right Extremism Online

Introduction

The Pivotal Moment

Did anyone in the aftermath of the United States (US) Presidential Election 2020 imagine watching an angry crowd of people attack the US Capitol Hill building during a joint session of Congress on the 6th of January 2021? Probably not. This attack was a stark reminder of the growing far-right movement on democracy's fringe and its potential to disrupt peaceful power transitions (Sommerlad, 2022; BBC News, 2022; Cohen, 2021). Many attendees wore military-style clothing and gear at the rally, and this heightened the tension by demonstrating that groups and individuals came prepared for trouble (Brooks, 2022; Macfarlane & Mcdonald, 2022; Sommerlad, 2022).

The events leading up to the Capitol Hill insurrection on the 6th of January 2021 essentially began with the Save America/ Stop the Steal movement and their rally in support of then-President Trump at a location in Washington DC (Savage, 2021; BBC News, 2022; Cohen, 2021; Barry, 2021). This movement developed in the aftermath of the election, where Biden was declared the winner – this was challenged by the outgoing President Trump, who claimed that the election was fraudulent. While Trump initially advocated for a peaceful protest during his speech at the event, his tone quickly shifted to a more combative stance, urging his supporters to fight fervently (BBC News, 2022; Brooks, 2022; Macfarlane & Mcdonald, 2022; Sommerlad, 2022). Trump's early statement encouraged his supporters to protest, stating:

> I know that everyone here will soon be marching over to the Capitol building to peacefully and patriotically make your voices heard.
>
> (BBC News, 2022; Savage, 2021)

However, the outgoing president ended his speech on a harsher note:

> We fight. We fight like hell, and if you don't fight like hell, you're not going to have a country anymore. So let's walk down Pennsylvania Avenue.
>
> (BBC News, 2022; Sommerlad, 2022; Brooks, 2022; Macfarlane & Mcdonald, 2022)

DOI: 10.4324/9781003297888-1

As a result, rally attendees moved to disrupt the certification of election results at the US Congress, where President-elect Biden was to be confirmed the victor over President Trump (BBC News, 2022; Cohen, 2021). The crowd included several far-right factions, such as the Proud Boys, the Boogaloo Bois, and the Oath Keepers, in conjunction with other far-right extremist groups, QAnon followers, neo-Nazis, local government Republicans, and average citizens (Wong, 2022; Sommerlad, 2022; Brooks, 2022). The Save America/ Stop the Steal event was livestreamed on news outlets and social media, where Trump's tweets stoked further anticipation by hinting that the rally would be "wild" (Sommerlad, 2022; Savage, 2021; Barry, 2021).

Capitol Hill's security was compromised, resulting in confrontations with law enforcement and the subsequent invasion of the building. Congress halted the voter certification process, even though Vice President Pence opted not to. Rioters swarmed the Capitol, brandishing Trump and American flags, as the House debate was interrupted. Those inside took refuge and put on gas masks as the situation was severe (BBC News, 2021; Brooks, 2022; Macfarlane & Mcdonald, 2022; Viala-Gaudefroy, 2022). Evacuation procedures were initiated, and additional security measures were employed to protect top officials. For example, the Secret Service ensured Vice President Pence's and Speaker Pelosi's safety. Following the chaos, President-elect Biden labelled the attack as an unprecedented assault on democracy. He urged President Trump to call off his supporters and emphasised the importance of upholding democratic values (Brooks, 2022). This severe disruption of peaceful power transition showcased the critical need for unity and vigilance in upholding democratic norms. It raised serious concerns about political polarisation, the spread of misinformation, and the state of American democracy.

The Online Environment and Amplification of the Event

The US Capitol insurrection emphasised how real-world events are closely linked to online activities. Social media played a critical role in planning and intensifying the attack, leaving digital evidence that authorities later used for identification and prosecution (Kunzelman, 2021). This incident reignited debates over tech companies' responsibilities to protect free speech and limit harmful content (Chapter 2). Key platforms like X/Twitter, Facebook, and Parler were hubs for misinformation about the election and instrumental in planning the Save America Rally (Culloty & Suiter, 2021, p. 11).

The rise of digital platforms has contributed to the echo chamber effect. These echo chambers are crucial to reinforcing far-right extremist ideologies. The 6th of January Capitol Hill attack is a vivid example of these powerful echo chambers usefulness to spread a particular narrative and hold people in a bubble with like-minded online users (Chapter 3) (Stanton, 2021; Hughes & Krill, 2022). The event was not solely the work of organised far-right extremist groups like the Proud Boys or the Oath Keepers but also involved individuals who subscribed to a mixture of far-right streaming services and online platforms based on extremist ideologies and conspiracy theories. These entities have been persistently active online and at pro-Trump rallies during the presidency and during the 2020 election (Hughes & Krill, 2022; BBC News, 2021; European Parliament, 2021a). The participants were emboldened by a hostile environment, stressed by the COVID-19 pandemic, and polarised by divisive figures, notably former President Trump (Stanton, 2021). Anonymity on these platforms encourages users to explore extremist content without immediate repercussions. After the attack on Capitol Hill, participation in similar events declined, which possibly indicated regret. However, the threat of far-right extremism persists, as shown by a lone white supremacist's tragic 2022 attack in a Buffalo supermarket attack and others afterwards (Chapter 3) (Hughes & Krill, 2022; AP, 2023; McKinley et al., 2022). The riot showed the powerful impact of online culture on real-world beliefs and actions. Online platforms are not merely passive conduits for extremist ideologies but act as active tools in shaping a new form of extremism that thrives on anonymity, leverages disinformation, and capitalises on societal vulnerabilities. Far-right extremism defies easy categorisation by being adaptive and ever-evolving, making it even more challenging to counter groups and individuals effectively (Chapters 2 and 3).

Digital Platforms and the Echo Chamber Effect

Online echo chambers can foster extremism by amplifying existing beliefs as demonstrated by the Capitol Hill attackers (Erickson et al., 2023; Nguyen, 2020). Individuals with moderate views can quickly be radicalised when individuals become deeply involved in such communities. The desire for social belonging often draws people closer to extremist ideologies (Brown et al., 2022). However, these echo chambers might also have another role in amplifying political identities instead of solely radicalising members. This suggest that these spaces may intensify shared oppositional stances rather than promote extreme ideologies (Chapter 3) (Klein, 2020; Törnberg et al., 2021).

The disinformation campaigns that gained footing during the 2020 Presidential Election increased the complexity (European Parliament, 2021a, pp. 2–3; Pennycook & Rand, 2021). Mainstream media outlets like Fox News spread Trump's baseless claims of Election fraud, laying the groundwork for the Capitol riot (Darcy, 2020; Pennycook & Rand, 2021). The Stop the Steal movement prospered on Facebook since its creation in November 2020, even after bans were implemented on key social media sites (Bond & Allyn, 2021). The falsehoods have become so pervasive that they have united disparate extremist groups under a common disinformation umbrella, from the Proud Boys to QAnon (Chapter 3) (European Parliament,

2021a, pp. 2–3). Despite regulation attempts, disinformation surged on Facebook and Twitter during the insurrection. Facebook saw nearly 40,000 false news claims hourly, while Instagram's most reported violent account was @realdonaldtrump (Chapter 4) (Timberg et al., 2021).

The Role of Online Forums in Far-Right Extremism

Weeks before the Capitol attack, Trump supporters openly discussed plans on platforms like Parler, Telegram, and TheDonald.win. This raises questions about law enforcement's readiness. Leaders of the Stop the Steal movement signalled aggressive plans as early as the 23rd of December (Frenkel, 2021; McEvoy, 2021; Dilanian & Collins, 2021). Online spaces have also become arenas for explicit coordination and planning of extremist actions. Numerous posts suggested arming up for a Congress visit. Months in advance, there were vocal online urges to oppose Congress members and take back the Capitol. On boards.4chan.org/pol/, a user foreshadowed, "The storm is coming" (a QAnon conspiracy theory quote). Echoing this sentiment, TheDonald.win online users talked about infiltrating the Capitol (Talley & Levy, 2021). After being de-platformed, extremist groups like QAnon and the Oath Keepers turned to less-regulated amateur radio, often using coded language. A Massachusetts militia even published a code guide, suggesting phrases like 'going to dance' for training and 'tools' for guns (Fenton, 2022).

The Capitol Hill insurrection spotlighted how online subcultures, especially on far-right forums like 4chan, redefine symbols like Pepe the Frog and the Kek flag for darker purposes (Chapter 5) (Fernando, 2021; Simon & Sidner, 2021; The Washington Post, 2021). QAnon's symbols spread mainly via online conspiracy forums and social media groups (Chapter 3). This exemplifies how unchecked online information can incite actions like the Capitol Hill attack (Fernando, 2021; The Washington Post, 2021). Digital spaces transform these symbols and popularise slogans like Release the Kraken, often leading to real-world actions (Chapter 5) (Simon & Sidner, 2021).

Live streaming added to the existing online challenges (Karimi, 2021). The Capitol Hill insurrection was broadcast live across platforms, complicating tech companies' efforts to enforce real-time content moderation (Alexander et al., 2021). These streams were not just a window into the event but also propaganda tools for extremist ideologies (Karimi, 2021). Live streams during the event displayed a mix of viewpoints and intensified audience polarisation where global viewers see unfolding events and multiple perspectives being distributed across platforms like X/Twitter, Facebook, and Twitch (Chapter 4) (Alexander et al., 2021; Koebler, 2021). However, the widespread sharing also aided law enforcement in identifying participants, much like how social media was leveraged during the 2020 Black Lives Matter protests (Cole, 2021). Citizen groups like the Sedition Hunters helped the FBI identify attackers using digital tools such as facial recognition and social media analysis (Gross, 2021; Mak, 2021).

Rejection of Democracy

Far-right extremism fosters societal polarisation, advocating a divisive 'us versus them' mentality. This mindset weakens social cohesion and democratic institutions by perpetuating hatred and divisions between diverse groups. Far-right ideologies hinge on a hierarchical system that views its adherents as superior and all others as inferior (Miller-Idriss, 2022, p. 6). Such ideologies are founded on the principles of in-groups (the insiders) and out-groups (the outsiders), with the former drawing strength from shared values, norms, or even racially biased categories (Wodak, 2021, p. 100). These distinctions can be fluid, adapting to socio-political contexts and global ideological shifts. This enables the group members to see their in-groups as being positively distinct from others. At the same time, the out-groups are portrayed as weak in comparison. Often, these actors intensify this division, casting 'us' as the righteous masses and 'them' as corrupt elites or outsiders. This division aims to foster in-group pride while degrading out-groups (Magnus, 2022).

Peer Groups and Social Networks in Extremist Radicalisation

Peer groups and social networks are fundamental in radicalisation, and understanding their dynamics can shed light on recruitment into extremist factions. Typically, these ideologies challenge the foundational principles of global democracies, targeting their pillars like free elections, checks and balances, the rule of law, and fundamental freedoms (Miller-Idriss, 2022, p. 4). Extremist groups like the Proud Boys and Oath Keepers at the Capitol combined organised units and lone actors. Influenced by the unfounded Stop the Steal theory, they believed the election was rigged and this was instrumental in increasing their aggressive actions. They saw their assault on the Capitol as a justified defence of America's integrity against Democrats (Hughes & Krill, 2022).

Challenging Democratic Foundations through Extremist Ideologies

Extremism is closely associated with anti-constitutionalism and anti-democracy. Followers reject the core values, procedures, and principles inherent in a democratic society. This term is often used interchangeably with synonyms such as fanaticism, zealotry, bigotry, terrorism, and revolution, and its perception can vary depending on an individual's perspective

(Caiani & Parenti, 2016). What one may consider acceptable or extreme depends on their personal beliefs and views (Neumann, 2013, p. 876). Far-right extremists undermine democracy by promoting exclusionary policies and rejecting democratic values. Disillusionment with governance and detachment from mainstream politics fuel their rise (Miller-Idriss, 2022, p. 5).

Opponents of political correctness have increasingly turned to right-wing extremist groups that reject societal norms (Furendi, 2005, pp. 152, 154). Over the years,, European entities like Germany's People's Union (1987-2011) expressed neofascist leanings, and France's National Front (1972-2018) championed free markets and anti-welfare policies (Martin & Prager, 2019, p. 267). In the US, such extremism often finds a home in grassroots organisations rather than mainstream parties. The 2020 Capitol Hill attack and the rise of 'copycat terrorism' have shifted focus from religious terrorism to right-wing extremism, exacerbated by the pandemic and access to various online platforms (Schori Liang & Cross, 2020, p. 2). Far-right ideologies promoting discrimination threaten equality and human rights, often inciting violence and marginalising vulnerable groups. Europe has seen a surge in racism affecting minorities due to perceived cultural and religious differences (CoE, 2021, p. 8).

The Process of Radicalisation in Far-Right Extremism

Radicalisation is a step-by-step process leading to extreme ideologies. This process often starts with individuals in vulnerable situations. It follows distinct phases where targets, typically identified in vulnerable contexts, undergo psychological, doctrinal, and violent radicalisation (González et al., 2022; Horgan, 2009). The core issue is the divide between 'us' and 'them'. Far-right group members often feel marginalised from society. Therefore, they are motivated to take action to restore their social status. Key drivers include social pressure, exposure to extremist content, and radical affiliations. These groups offer alienated individuals a sense of identity and community (Youngblood, 2020). Online spaces are engaging for young people. These spaces are progressively used to, amplify traditional prejudices and contribute to radicalisation (Chapters 4 and 5) (Adams, 2022). Emotional and psychological states like anger or identity crises make individuals more open to extremist narratives. Extremist groups use psychological tactics that target cognition, emotion, and environment to unify members and justify violence. Therefore, it becomes vital to understand how these groups operate and what causes these societal divisions in a society where far-right extremist groups' ideologies and actions become normalised (González et al., 2022).

Theories and Ideological Directions

Accelerationism

Accelerationism drives the apocalyptic fantasies that motivate violent actions by extremists. Members of the accelerationist ideology believe the best way forward is to hasten the apocalypse by increasing polarisation, chaos, and social conflict to undermine the social order. The supporters think these radical actions will enable them to quickly reach a restorative rebirth of the dominant white group (Miller-Idriss, 2021). The foundation of accelerationism is linked to the idea that Western governments and systems are corrupt, and white supremacists must change quickly by collapsing the current order through chaos and tension. A new order based on white supremacy will emerge (Hardy, 2021; Europol, 2022, p. 53). Originally a Marxist theory, accelerationism proposed intensifying capitalist flaws to destroy the system. Far-right extremist groups repurposed this for their violent and divisive agenda (CEP, 2022a; New Statesman, 2016; Europol, 2022, p. 53).

Accelerationism in the Trump Era: Linking Extremist Groups to Capitol Hill Attack

Some view former President Trump's 2016 campaign and subsequent presidency as embodying the accelerationist ideology (Beckett, 2017). Accelerationists, believing in violence by lone actors or cells, seek to incite race wars. Groups like The Base emphasise that the current order must be dismantled through destabilising acts, intending to initiate a race war and government overthrow (CEP, 2022a; Byman, 2022, p. 130). Atomwaffen Division (AWD), a neo-Nazi organisation, originated from the Iron March online forum in 2015 has promoted similar views. With active cells operating primarily independently in various countries, the group has reached several groups and individuals, extending its influence and network (Garternstein-Ross et al., 2020; Byman, 2022, p. 132). Founded in 2016, the Proud Boys, mainly young white males, claim to defend Western culture but frequently hold racist, misogynistic, and anti-Semitic views (Hughes & Krill, 2022). Similarly, the Oath Keepers was formed in 2009, opposing government over-reach and later embracing far-right election fraud theories. By 2020, the group backed the Stop the Steal movement by rallying against left-wing activists (Hughes & Krill, 2022).

The Boogaloo Bois, emerging in 2019 and linked to sites like 4chan, anticipate a second American Civil War. The group often appears online alongside references to 'racewar' and 'dotr' meaning 'day of the rope'. They reference the Turner Diaries by Pierce, a neo-Nazi and the founder/chairman of National Alliance. The Turner Diaries from 1978 depicts mass lynchings of multiculturalism supporters and has inspired far-right extremist groups (Committee on Homeland Security, 2020). The term 'day of the rope' from this book symbolises executing 'race traitors'. The hashtag #Dayoftherope has also been used on Twitter/X to advocate violence against those considered traitors, including black people and journalists (CEP, 2022c; Wilson, 2018). The Turner Diaries even portrays a Capitol Hill attack reminiscent of the 6th of January, where rioters chanted about executing Vice-President Pence (Borger, 2021; Woodruff Swan & Cheney, 2022; CEP, 2022c; Wilson, 2018).

Global Variations of the Accelerationist Movement

Under the Trump administration, polarisation intensified within the US – but it was also a time when far-right populism spread across Europe. This world-wide surge in violence and extremism belief became a catalyst for change. Many groups view accelerationism as a solution and reaction to perceived existential threats to white civilisation, gaining supporters primarily from the Global North (Miller-Idriss, 2022, p. 15). ADW has ties to Germany, Canada, England, Poland, the Czech Republic, and Ukraine. European groups such as Combat 18, Blood and Honor, Bloed, Bodem, Eer en Trouw, and Die Harte Kern also endorse this movement, with aspirations to ignite a race war through various plots and attacks (Byman, 2022, p. 132; BBC News, 2020; The Guardian, 2020; Diab, 2010). This violent embrace of accelerationism marks a transition from merely conceptualising an apocalypse to proactively fostering chaos with a vision for a white-dominated order (Miller-Idriss, 2021).

Accelerationism Online

Online, accelerationists have disseminated numerous conspiracy theories, disinformation, and hateful propaganda. They advocate for white power and call for the expulsion or extermination of Jewish people, ethnic and racial minorities, and white 'race traitors' (Garternstein-Ross et al., 2020). ADW, with members in several US states, has likely held paramilitary camps providing training in combat situations, survival skills, and physical fitness, according to their online propaganda (Garternstein-Ross et al., 2020). The dangers of accelerationist ideology online are multifaceted and far-reaching. They present significant challenges to societal cohesion, public safety, and democratic values. Efforts to counter online accelerationism must include law enforcement and intelligence agencies, technology companies, educators, community leaders, and mental health professionals. Coordination and collaboration across sectors and borders will be essential to understanding, monitoring, and mitigating the risks associated with this complex and evolving threat (Table 1.1).

Table 1.1 Summary of the Accelerationist Movement

Features	Characteristics
Recruitment and Radicalisation	Online platforms and encrypted apps enable recruitment and radicalisation. Share propaganda and guide inciting violence. Internet anonymity, using echo chambers, amplifying and normalising extremist views.
Coordination and Planning	Use online platforms to coordinate and plan attacks. The Internet's decentralisation allows lone actors to act autonomously, making detection by law enforcement challenging.
Disinformation and Propaganda	Spread conspiracy theories and disinformation to polarise communities and undermine trust in institutions. Exploiting current events to deepen divisions.
Encouraging and Glorifying Violence	Online content glorifies violence and offers practical guidance on committing violent acts, desensitising individuals. Promoting violence as a legitimate political tool.
Cross-Border Influence	Spread accelerationist ideologies globally, transforming local extremist views into transnational threats through online coordination and collaboration.
Impact on Vulnerable Populations	Prey on marginalised individuals, using the 'them' and 'us' rhetoric. Offer belonging and identity to those with similar viewpoints.

Identitarian

The Identitarian movement (also known as Generation Identity (GI)) is influenced by the European New Right (ND) in the 1960s. ND thinkers embedded left-wing ideas into ethnonationalist ideologies, emphasising Europeans' sole rights to their 'homelands'. The ND approach also encompassed 'metapolitics' to blend anti-capitalist and cultural dominance aims (Wilson, 2019). In the early 2000s, Génération Identitaire was formed as the youth wing of Bloc Identitaire in France. Over time, the movement has developed a formula involving provocative actions and slick promotional efforts that exploit social media – and over time, they have perfected their attention-grabbing activities and potent social media campaigns (Wilson, 2019; Gattinara, 2022).

Exploring the Identitarian Movement: The Great Replacement Theory, Its Roots, and the Global Impact

The movement endorses the Great Replacement theory. This theory was developed by Camus in 2012, suggesting non-European immigrants are replacing Europeans (CEP, 2022b; Miller-Idriss, 2022, p. 9). Far-right extremist groups often centre their arguments on three main theories: the Great Replacement (globally recognised), white genocide (mainly in the US), and Eurabia (mainly in Europe). These ideologies arise from a belief in the bleak future of the white race, attributing its perceived decline to immigrants, Muslims, and Jews in the Global North. Thus, they emphasise the need to defend and preserve their white heritage (Miller-Idriss, 2022, p. 9). Beyond ethnicity and cultural identity, some Identitarian groups also critique capitalism and globalism. They see these systems as undermining traditional cultures and contributing to unwanted immigration and cultural change. The Identitarian groups use mainstream topics like immigration control to amplify and legitimise their viewpoints, sometimes partnering with far-right political parties, such as Syriza in Greece, the Five Star Movement in Italy, and Podemos in Spain. These parties, capitalising on populist arguments, have gained significant vote shares and influence, contributing to their rising prominence (Mylonas & Tudor, 2021; Eschle, 2004, p. 72; Elsenhans, 2017; Vachudova, 2021; Font et al., 2021).

The GI brand was globally inaugurated in 2012 in Poitiers, France. The movement's emphasis on youth, actions, popular culture, and corporate identity was groundbreaking (Šima, 2021; Bruns et al., 2014, p. 56; Hume et al., 2021; Byman, 2022, p. 85). Identitarian entities cleverly leverage symbols from diverse sources, exemplified by the lambda symbol from the movie '300', to resonate with historical valour (Šima, 2021). Understanding the importance of image, Identitarian groups often focus on branding strategies, using recognisable symbols, slogans, clothing, and narratives that align with their target audience (Gaugele, 2019; Nilan, 2021).

Global Variations of the Identitarian Movement

GI movements often forge alliances with other far-right factions. Their international reach includes affiliates like Génération Identitaire (France), Generazione Identitaria (Italy), and Identitäre Bewegung Österreichs (Austria). 2016 Identity Evropa emerged in the US, targeting white college-aged men to champion white nationalism (SPLC, 2022; Beckett, 2017). After involvement in various protests, notably the Unite the Right rally in Charlottesville (2017), they rebranded as the American Identity Movement (SPLC, 2022; Beckett, 2017).

GI groups stage provocative actions like occupying mosques or hosting pork feasts to alienate Muslim communities. They seek media coverage to boost their anti-immigrant and ethnonationalist stances. Their activities, spanning numerous countries, often lead to confrontations, which gives them exposure in mass media – a part of the groups' strategy (Wilson, 2019; Byman, 2022, p. 91; The Economist, 2018). In 2021, the French government banned GI. It is unlikely that the group will be successful with their subsequent appeal of this decision. Members will possibly persist under a new name and leadership. However, this ban has reframed their narrative, and they now portray themselves as victims of political bias aiming to suppress them (Camus, 2021; Willsher, 2021).

Identitarian Online

GI has a solid online presence for recruitment and outreach, though its visibility can vary regionally and temporally. While GI is more active online than offline, they strategically align white supremacy views with mainstream political concerns, such as immigration and refugees – an ethno-national call for deporting European residents of immigrant backgrounds or non-white descent (Ebner, 2019; Byman, 2022, p. 85). Using social media, the groups circulate propaganda, enlist members, and connect with allies. Their digital content is often polished and contemporary, aimed at portraying a modern, appealing image.

These far-right groups are digitally savvy, using the online environment to distort public perception, promote their political agenda, and intimidate journalists (Ebner, 2019). They focus on white people's unique interests, using a branding strategy emphasising self-interest and challenging condemnation (SPLC, 2022). The Identitarian ideology extends beyond mere deportation and rejection of asylum seekers. It emphasises youthful authenticity and crisis in European civilisations, distinguishing itself from other far-right groups (Šima, 2021). The dangers of Identitarian ideology online are multifaceted and deeply concerning. They range from immediate threats like violence and harassment to broader societal issues based on polarisation and erosion of democratic values.

GI's online presence has been relatively visible, particularly among the target demographic (typically young, white Europeans). However, actions to counter their message, legal constraints, and platform policies may impact this visibility, potentially reducing their reach and influence online. The landscape is dynamic, and the situation can change as platforms and regulations evolve (Table 1.2).

Table 1.2 Summary of the Identitatiran Movement

Features	Characteristics
Spread of Hate and Discrimination	Advocates ethno-nationalism. Endorses exclusive territorial rights for specific ethnic groups. May incite hostility towards immigrants and minorities.
Incitement to Violence	Publicly reject violence while underlying beliefs may provoke violent actions. The Great Replacement theory may lead to violence against outsiders.
Manipulation and Radicalisation	Spreads misinformation online, bend reality and intensifying fears and biases. Recruits widely through online platforms. Attracts disaffected youth with polished online content, deepening radicalisation. Promotes the 'us versus them' narrative, heightening societal division and disrupting social harmony.
Mainstreaming of Extremist Views	Undermines pluralistic democratic values. Heightens fears about immigration and cultural change, fostering a reactionary society. Employs branding and self-interest to mainstream views. Normalises extremism, shifting political discourse.
Potential International Connections	The Identitarian movement's online presence fosters international connections. Sharing tactics and ideology. Online and offline tactics to amplify its global impact.

Theoretical Framework

Theoretical frameworks provide perspectives on far-right groups' structures, motivations, and strategies. These theories illuminate the multifaceted nature of far-right extremism, considering individual, group, and broader contextual influences in synergy with socio-political, economic, and historical factors (Saull, 2015a; Stewart, 2020). Delving into these interconnected dimensions is imperative to truly understand extremist ideologies' origin, resilience, and appeal. For instance, examining how societal dynamics and historical events influence extremist beliefs provides a comprehensive understanding of what drives extreme far-right movements (Saull, 2015a; Saull, 2015b). Online platforms boost and spread these sentiments, allowing individuals to connect over shared extremist views. The global context of online spaces means that economic and political events, even geographically distant, can resonate and become catalysts for extremism.

To understand far-right extremist groups beyond their fringe manifestations, it is essential to integrate various theoretical perspectives that offer a holistic view of the complex dynamics at play. This comprehensive approach, combining Social Identity Theory, Social Movement Theory, Network Theory, and Uncertainty-Identity Theory. These theories provides a multifaceted framework to analyse these groups effectively.

Social Identity Theory

Social Identity Theory is foundational in understanding the initial attraction and sustained commitment to far-right groups. It highlights the psychological appeal of these groups and how individuals define themselves through group affiliations, often based on shared racial, ethnic, or national identities. This theory explains the strong cohesion within these groups and their often hostile attitudes towards perceived out-groups (Islam, 2014, p. 1781; Magnus, 2022 Tajfel & Turner, 2004, p. 13).

Like other social collectives, far-right extremist groups are formed by individuals united by shared identity or perceived category membership. Within these groups, members (the in-group) often view themselves positively, in contrast to negatively perceived outsiders (the out-group). This separation is based on differences in norms, values, and behaviours (Islam, 2014, p. 1781; Strets & Burke, 2000, p. 225). This Social Identity Theory framework explain that in-group members see themselves as a superior group that is marginalised – and how/why they show hostility towards out-group members. These group dynamics are fluid, adapting to socio-political changes and global events. Understanding these dynamics is crucial to comprehending extremist behaviour's underlying forces and groups' flexible responses to external influences (Hogg, 2014; Wodak, 2021).

Social Movement Theory

Social Movement Theory extends this understanding by examining how these groups mobilise and structure themselves. It explores the mechanisms through which far-right movements politicise issues, rally public support, and challenge mainstream political discourse. This theory also illuminates the strategies these groups use to gain traction and how they navigate the political landscape (Tilly, 1978; Della Porta, 2008). It underlines the interconnectivity of the groups with members sharing worldviews and building shared realities. This theory reveals their ability to successfully cause fear and uncertainty by politicise issues like immigration and minority rights, which are areas that mainstream parties often neglect (Eder, 2014, pp. 37–38). By applying this lens, it is clear that these groups leverage economic and cultural grievances, particularly those arising from globalisation, to mobilise public support and propagate their narratives. This approach offers critical insights into far-right movements' strategic operations and collective dynamics (Castelli Gattinara & Pirro, 2019, p. 453).

Network Theory

Network Theory provides insights into the operational aspects of these groups. It examines the role of interpersonal relationships and online networks in spreading extremist ideologies. By understanding the network structures of these groups, it is possible to identify how radical beliefs are proliferated and reinforced within these communities (Dalgaard-Nielsen, 2010, p. 801; Sageman, 2004; Wiktorowicz, 2004). This theory also helps to understand the recruitment tactics of these groups and their ability to create close-knit, influential communities. pressures (Dalgaard-Nielsen, 2010, p. 803; Neumann, 2013). Network theory highlights that in social networks, power is based on adherence to communication protocols and inclusion criteria rather than exclusion (Castells, 2011, p. 775). This structure comprises nodes and ties, offering insights into group behaviour and influence with new media technologies, especially social networking sites. The theory helps track and assess content spread and effect across various platforms, critical for understanding far-right movements' online organisation and strategies (Borgatti & Halgin, 2011, p. 2; Liu et al., 2017, p. 10).

Uncertainty-Identity Theory

Lastly, Uncertainty-Identity Theory offers a deeper understanding of the psychological factors driving individuals towards extremism. It focuses on how uncertainty and identity crises can lead individuals to seek clarity and purpose within extremist groups. This theory is particularly relevant in explaining the allure of far-right extremist groups in times of societal upheaval, where individuals may feel disoriented and seek definitive answers and a sense of belonging (Hogg, 2000, 2021). The theory distinguishes itself with four key features: (a) it prioritises social identity and the collective self, (b) it perceives uncertainty as contextual rather than a trait, (c) it explains how social cognition translates uncertainty into group actions, and (d) its main focus is on the underlying motivations for group behaviour, even though it addresses extremism (Hogg, 2021). The Uncertainty-Identity Theory provides a nuanced perspective on online radicalisation, especially within far-right movements. The theory highlights how online spaces amplify the adoption of extremist ideologies, deepening our understanding of radicalisation in digital contexts.

Connecting the Theories

Social Identity Theory, Social Movement Theory, Network Theory, and Uncertainty-Identity Theory provide a robust framework for understanding far-right extremism beyond its marginal appearance. They offer insights into the psychological, social, and structural factors that drive individuals towards these groups and sustain their activities. Understanding these four theories provides a holistic framework to interpret the actions and strategies of far-right extremists, particularly in online spaces. The combined lens of these theories presents a dynamic lifecycle of online far-right extremism: from individual needs through networked communities to collective actions. This detailed understanding is indispensable for those aiming to comprehend and mitigate far-right extremism in digital spaces (Table 1.3).

Table 1.3 Summary of the Theoretical Foundation

Features	Characteristics
Collective Identity	All theories emphasise the crucial role of collective identity (Social Identity Theory, Social Movement Theory, Network Theory, Uncertainty-Identity Theory).
	Affiliation with groups defines identity and differentiates 'us versus them' (Social Identity Theory).
	Forms cohesive units that stereotype a common enemy.
Online Dynamics	Highlights the web as a complex network, not just individual connections (Network Theory).
	People join online groups for belonging (Social Identity Theory).
	These groups form intertwined networks (Network Theory) to spread far-right extremist ideologies and actions.
Mobilisation and Action	Online networks are dynamic, evolving with new technologies and communication methods (Network Theory).
	Transition from online campaigns to real-world protests (Social Movement Theory).
External Reactions	External changes create individual uncertainties, amplified by online platforms (Uncertainty-Identity Theory).
	Far-right narratives provide perceived clarity (Uncertainty-Identity Theory and Social Movement Theory).
Reinforcement Cycle	Emphasise how individuals seeking identity or answers join online groups (Uncertainty-Identity Theory).
	Reinforce how group identity is intensified through online echo chambers (Social Identity Theory).
	The complexity of networks intensifies by the way groups and communications spread and transforms online (Network Theory).
	Actions and responses are constantly emerging and transforming to counter status que (Social Movement Theory).

Outline of the Book

Aim and Objectives

This book delves into the troubling rise of online far-right extremism in Western societies, examining the dichotomy digital platforms face between profit-driven models and the ethical need to combat extremism. It links this phenomenon to major incidents like the US Capitol Hill attack, exploring how these movements use online strategies to disseminate extremist content and suppress dissent. The book critically examines the anti-extremism efforts of tech giants like Meta/Facebook and X/Twitter, blending criminological insights with interdisciplinary studies. It highlights the tech industry's crucial yet often inadequate role in moderating online radicalisation and scrutinises the sophisticated online tactics of modern far-right movements.

Secondary Research

The book utilises secondary research as its foundational methodology, engaging in an extensive analysis of existing literature, reports, legal documents, and scholarly works related to far-right political extremism alongside criminological perspectives. It draws upon various sources, including academic journals, observatory reports, government publications, international laws, web pages, and media reports. This approach aims to comprehensively understand far-right extremism and its manifestation in online environments. The research establishes a theoretical framework, which identifying key themes and patterns, and assesses the efficacy of actions taken by technology and social media companies.

Incorporating mass media and new media articles can enhance the secondary research methodology previously described. These articles offer timely insights into events surrounding far-right political extremism. While they provide real-time accounts and analyses, assessing their credibility and biases is essential. The reliability of the news outlet, cross-referencing with other trusted sources, and understanding any inherent viewpoint is crucial. Although newspaper articles present valuable perspectives, they come with limitations. Potential biases and the possibility of incomplete or inaccurate information must be acknowledged. As such, they should complement a diverse set of secondary sources, ensuring the findings are critically validated for accuracy and reliability (Table 1.4).

Table 1.4 Outline of the Book

Chapter	Outline
1	Analyses the far-right's impact on the Capitol Hill attack, focusing on their use of online platforms for planning and communication. It establishes a framework to understand the patterns and digital influence of far-right extremism.
2	Differentiates far-right extremism from terrorism, exploring the rise of political populism and contemporary trends in the 21st century. It clarifies the distinctions between terrorism, hate speech, and hate crimes.
3	Investigates how far-right groups use digital platforms to amplify their ideology and create echo chambers, discussing the role of falsehood, misinformation and conspiracy theories in shaping public perception.
4	Examines the role of social media and other online platforms in spreading far-right ideologies, assessing the risks in less regulated online environments.
5	Delves into extreme far-right groups' use of symbols and codes to disguise communications and foster in-group belonging. It explores their presence in far-right fashion and memes, highlighting these elements as key communication tools within extremist networks.

References

Adams, R., 2022. *From 'study guides' to trolling raids: How UK far-right groups target children online.* [Online] Available at: https://www.theguardian.com/politics /2022/aug/03/study-guides-trolling-raids-how-uk-far-right-groups-target-children -online [Accessed 11 08 2023].

Alexander, J., Kastrenakes, J. & Stephen, B., 2021. *How Facebook, Twitch, and YouTube are handling live streams of the Capitol mob attack.* [Online] Available at: https://www.theverge.com/2021/1/6/22217421/capitol-building-trump-mob -protest-live-stream-youtube-twitch-facebook [Accessed 17 08 2023].

AP, 2023. *Teen who killed 10 Black people at Buffalo supermarket given life in prison.* [Online] Available at: https://www.theguardian.com/us-news/2023/feb/15/buffalo -shooting-gunman-sentenced-life-prison [Accessed 16 08 2023].

Barry, D. F. S., 2021. *'Be there. Will be wild!': Trump all but circled the date.* [Online] Available at: https://www.nytimes.com/2021/01/06/us/politics/capitol-mob-trump -supporters.html [Accessed 17 08 2023].

BBC News, 2020. *German far-right group 'planned attacks on mosques'.* [Online] Available at: https://www.bbc.co.uk/news/world-europe-51526357 [Accessed 18 08 2022].

BBC News, 2021. *Capitol riots: Who broke into the building?.* [Online] Available at: https://www.bbc.com/news/55572805 [Accessed 17 08 2023].

BBC News, 2022. *Capitol riots timeline: What happened on 6 January 2021?. [Online]* Available at: https://www.bbc.co.uk/news/world-us-canada-56004916 [Accessed 15 08 2022].

Beckett, A., 2017. *Accelerationism: How a fringe philosophy predicted the future we live in.* [Online] Available at: https://www.theguardian.com/world/2017/may /11/accelerationism-how-a-fringe-philosophy-predicted-the-future-we-live-in [Accessed 18 08 2022].

Beckett, L., 2017. *White nationalists' latest tactic to recruit college students: Paper flyers and tape.* [Online] Available at: https://www.theguardian.com/world/2017/apr /05/white-nationalists-posters-college-student-recruitment [Accessed 19 08 2022].

Bond, S. & Allyn, B., 2021. *How the 'Stop the Steal' movement outwitted Facebook ahead of the Jan. 6 insurrection.* [Online] Available at: https://www.npr.org/2021 /10/22/1048543513/facebook-groups-jan-6-insurrection [Accessed 12 08 2023].

Borgatti, S. & Halgin, D., 2011. On network theory. *Organization Science,* 22(5), pp. 1–14.

Borger, J., 2021. *Insurrection day: When white supremacist terror came to the US Capitol.* [Online] Available at: https://www.theguardian.com/us-news/2021/jan/09/ us-capitol-insurrection-white-supremacist-terror [Accessed 07 08 2023].

Brooks, M., 2022. *US Capitol riot timeline: From Donald Trump's speech to Ashli Babbitt's death – How 2021 riots unfolded.* [Online] Available at: https://www .nationalworld.com/news/world/us-capitol-attack-timeline-from-donald-trumps -speech-to-eugene-goodmans-heroics-how-2021-riots-unfolded-3516546 [Accessed 16 08 2022].

Brown, M. et al., 2022. *Echo chambers, rabbit holes, and ideological bias: How YouTube recommends content to real users.* [Online] Available at: https://www .brookings.edu/articles/echo-chambers-rabbit-holes-and-ideological-bias-how -youtube-recommends-content-to-real-users/ [Accessed 15 08 2023].

Bruns, J., Glösel, K. & Strobl, N., 2014. *ie Identitären: Handbuch zur Jugendbewegung der Neuen Rechten in Europa.* Münster: Unrast Verlag.

Byman, D., 2022. *Spreading hate: The global rise of white supremacist terrorism.* 1st ed. Oxford: Oxford University Press.

Caiani, M. & Parenti, L., 2016. *European and Americian exterme right groups and the Internet.* London: Routledge.

Camus, J., 2021. *Génération Identitaire ban could rally supporters of the radical right in France.* [Online] Available at: https://www.opendemocracy.net/en/countering -radical-right/g%C3%A9n%C3%A9ration-identitaire-ban-could-rally-supporters -of-the-radical-right-in-france/ [Accessed 07 08 2023].

Castelli Gattinara, P. & Pirro, A., 2019. The far right as social movement. *European Societies,* 21(4), pp. 447–462.

Castells, M., 2011. A network theory of power. *International Journal of Communication,* 5, pp. 773–787.

CEP, 2022a. *Accelerationism.* [Online] Available at: https://www.counterextremism .com/content/accelerationism [Accessed 10 04 2022].

CEP, 2022b. *Great replacement theory.* [Online] Available at: https://www .counterextremism.com/content/great-replacement-theory [Accessed 19 08 2022].

CEP, 2022c. *The turner diaries' ties to extremists.* [Online] Available at: https://www .counterextremism.com/themes/custom/cep/templates/reports/turner_diaries/files/ Turner_Diaries_Ties_to_Extremists.pdf [Accessed 24 08 2022].

CoE, 2021. *Racism, intolerance, hate speech. Strassbourg: Council of Europe.*

Cohen, M., 2021. *Timeline of the coup: How Trump tried to weaponize the Justice Department to overturn the 2020 election.* [Online] Available at: https://edition.cnn.com/2021/11/05/politics/january-6-timeline-trump-coup/index.html [Accessed 16 08 2022].

Cole, S., 2021. *Archivists are preserving Capitol Hill riot livestreams before they're deleted.* [Online] Available at: https://www.vice.com/en/article/3an5e3/archivists-are-preserving-capitol-hill-riot-livestreams-before-theyre-deleted [Accessed 20 07 2023].

Committee on Homeland Security, 2020. *Assessing the threat from accelerationists and militia extremists.* [Online] Available at: https://www.congress.gov/event/116th-congress/house-event/LC65904/text?s=1&r=1 [Accessed 18 08 2022].

Culloty, E. & Suiter, J., 2021. *Disinformation and manipulation in the digital media.* Abingdon: Routledge.

Dalgaard-Nielsen, A., 2010. Violent radicalization in Europe: What we know and what we do not know. *Studies in Conflict & Terrorism,* 33(9), pp. 797–814.

Darcy, O., 2020. *Fox News hosts sow distrust in legitimacy of election.* [Online] Available at: https://edition.cnn.com/2020/11/05/media/fox-news-prime-time-election/index.html [Accessed 17 08 2023].

Della Porta, D., 2008. Research on social movements and political violence. *Qualitative Sociology,* 31, pp. 221–230.

Diab, K., 2010. *Neo-nazism is Europe's hidden terrorist menace.* [Online] Available at: https://www.theguardian.com/commentisfree/2010/jul/11/islam-white-racist-terror-attack [Accessed 18 08 2022].

Dilanian, K. & Collins, B., 2021. *There are hundreds of posts about plans to attack the Capitol. Why hasn't this evidence been used in court?.* [Online] Available at: https://www.nbcnews.com/politics/justice-department/we-found-hundreds-posts-about-plans-attack-capitol-why-aren-n1264291 [Accessed 17 08 2023].

Ebner, J., 2019. *Who are Europe's far-right identitarians?.* [Online] Available at: https://www.politico.eu/article/who-are-europe-far-right-identitarians-austria-generation-identity-martin-sellner/ [Accessed 20 04 2022].

Eder, K., 2014. Social movements in social theory. In: *The Oxford handbook of social movements.* Oxford: Oxford University Press, pp. 31–49.

Elsenhans, H., 2017. Globalisation, world capitalism and rent, and the emergence of new cultural identitarian political movements: The challenges ahead. *Indian Journal of Asian Affairs,* 30(1/2), pp. 1–14.

Erickson, J., Yan, B. & Huang, J., 2023. Bridging echo chambers? Understanding political partisanship through semantic network analysis. *Social Media + Society,* 9(3).

Eschle, C., 2004. Constructing 'the anti-globalisation movement'. *International Journal of Peace Studies,* 9(1), pp. 61–84.

European Parliament, 2021a. *Trump's disinformation 'magaphone'. Consequences, first lessons and outlook.* [Online] Available at: https://www.europarl.europa.eu/RegData/etudes/BRIE/2021/679076/EPRS_BRI(2021)679076_EN.pdf [Accessed 12 08 2023].

Europol, 2022. *European Union. Terrorist situation and trend report 2022.* Luxenbourg: Europol.

Fenton, M., 2022. *Far-Right extremists are using personal radios to plan violence.* [Online] Available at: https://slate.com/technology/2022/06/far-right-extremism -radio-jan-6.html [Accessed 27 08 2022].

Fernando, 2021. *The hidden meanings behind the far-right hate symbols on display during the US Capitol riot.* [Online] Available at: https://www.sbs.com.au/news/ article/the-hidden-meanings-behind-the-far-right-hate-symbols-on-display-during -the-us-capitol-riot/keiotibc2 [Accessed 17 08 2023].

Font, N., Graziano, P. & Tsakatika, M., 2021. Varieties of inclusionary populism? SYRIZA, podemos and the five star movement. *Government and Opposition,* 56(1), pp. 163–183.

Frenkel, S., 2021. *The storming of Capitol Hill was organized on social media.* [Online] Available at: https://www.nytimes.com/2021/01/06/us/politics/protesters-storm -capitol-hill-building.html [Accessed 16 08 2023].

Furendi, F., 2005. *Culture of fear.* 3rd ed. London: Continuum.

Garternstein-Ross, D., Hodgson, S. & Clarke, C. P., 2020. *The growing threat posed by accelerationism and accelerationist.* [Online] Available at: https://www.fpri.org /article/2020/04/the-growing-threat-posed-by-accelerationism-and-accelerationist -groups-worldwide/ [Accessed 18 08 2022].

Gattinara, P., 2022. Identitarian movements, right-wing. In: *The Wiley-Blackwell Encyclopedia of social and political movements.* Hoboken: Wiley-Blackwell.

Gaugele, E., 2019. The new obscurity in style. Alt-right faction, populist normalization, and the cultural war on fashion from the far right. *Fashion Theory,* 23(6), pp. 711–731.

González, I., Moyano, M., Lobato, R. & Trujillo, H. M., 2022. Evidence of psychological manipulation in the process of violent radicalization: An investigation of the 17-A cell. *Front Psychiatry,* 13, pp. 1-11.

Gross, T., 2021. *How a group of online sleuths are helping the FBI track down Jan. 6 rioters.* [Online] Available at: https://www.npr.org/2021/12/23/1066835433/how -a-group-of-online-sleuths-are-helping-the-fbi-track-down-jan-6-rioters [Accessed 17 08 2023].

Hardy, J., 2021. *"Siege" culture and the radical right.* [Online] Available at: https:// www.radicalrightanalysis.com/2021/03/02/siege-culture-and-the-radical-right/ [Accessed 20 08 2022].

Hogg, M., 2000. Subjective uncertainty reduction through self-categorization: A motivational theory of social identity processes. *European Review of Social Psychology,* 11(1), pp. 223–255.

Hogg, M., 2014. From uncertainty to extremism: Social categorization and identity processes. *Current Directions in Psychological Science,* 23(5), pp. 338–342.

Hogg, M., 2021. Uncertain self in a changing world: A foundation for radicalisation, populism, and autocratic leadership. *European Review of Social Psychology,* 32(2), pp. 235–268.

Horgan, J., 2009. *Walking away from terrorism: Accounts of disengagement from radical and extremist movements.* New York: Routledge.

Hughes, S. & Krill, I., 2022. *Assessing US domestic extremism in light of Capitol riot investigations.* [Online] Available at: https://www.icct.nl/publication/assessing-us -domestic-extremism-light-capitol-riot-investigations [Accessed 16 08 2023].

Hume, T., Langston, H. & Bennett, T., 2021. *The rise and fall of Europe's most influential far-right youth movement.* [Online] Available at: https://www.vice.com /en/article/5dbj98/the-rise-and-fall-of-europes-hipster-fascists [Accessed 11 04 2022].

Islam, G., 2014. Social identity theory. In: *Encyclopedia of critical psychology.* New York: Springer-Verlag, pp. 1781–1783.

Karimi, F., 2021. *Fearing more violence, online platforms are cracking down on livestreams from Washington.* [Online] Available at: https://edition.cnn.com/2021 /01/19/us/capitol-attack-livestream-companies-trnd/index.html [Accessed 17 08 2023].

Klein, E., 2020. *Why we're polarized.* London: Simon and Schuster.

Koebler, J., 2021. *Trump loyalists are livestreaming while they storm the Capitol.* [Online] Available at: https://www.vice.com/en/article/xgz4md/trump-loyalists-are -livestreaming-while-they-storm-the-capitol [Accessed 17 08 2023].

Kunzelman, M., 2021. *Capitol rioters' social media posts influencing sentencings.* [Online] Available at: https://apnews.com/article/media-prisons-social-media -capitol-siege-sentencing-0a60a821ce19635b70681faf86e6526e [Accessed 15 08 2023].

Liu, W., Sidhu, A., Beacom, A. & Valente, T., 2017. Social network theory. In: *The international encyclopedia of media effects.* London: The Wiley Blackwell-ICA.

Macfarlane, S. & Mcdonald, C., 2022. *January 6 timeline: Key moments from the attack on the Capitol.* [Online] Available at: https://www.cbsnews.com/live-updates/ january-6-capitol-riot-timeline-key-moments/ [Accessed 16 08 2022].

Magnus, K., 2022. Right- wing populism, social identity theory, and resistance to public health measures during the COVID-19 pandemic. *International Journal of Public Health,* 67, pp. 1–5.

Mak, T., 2021. *The FBI keeps using clues from volunteer sleuths to find the Jan. 6 Capitol Rioters.* [Online] Available at: https://www.npr.org/2021/08/18 /1028527768/the-fbi-keeps-using-clues-from-volunteer-sleuths-to-find-the-jan-6 -capitol-riote [Accessed 17 08 2023].

Martin, G. & Prager, F., 2019. *Terrorism. An international perspective.* London: Sage.

McEvoy, J., 2021. *Capitol attack was planned openly online for weeks—Police still weren't ready.* [Online] Available at: https://www.forbes.com/sites/jemimamcevoy /2021/01/07/capitol-attack-was-planned-openly-online-for-weeks-police-still -werent-ready/?sh=6ae929ed76e2 [Accessed 21 07 2023].

McKinley, J., Traub, A. & Closson, T., 2022. *10 people are killed and 3 are wounded in a mass shooting at a Buffalo grocery store.* [Online] Available at: https://www .nytimes.com/live/2022/05/14/nyregion/buffalo-shooting#at-least-10-people -are-killed-in-a-mass-shooting-at-a-buffalo-grocery-store-a-local-official-says [Accessed 15 08 2023].

Miller-Idriss, C., 2022. *Hate in the homeland. The new global far right.* Princeton: Princeton University Press.

Miller-Idriss, M., 2021. White supremacist extremism and the far right in the U.S. *Political Extremism and Radicalism: Far-Right Groups in America.*

Mylonas, H. & Tudor, M., 2021. Nationalism: What we know and what we still need to know. *Annual Review of Political Science,* 24, pp. 109–132.

Neumann, P., 2013. The trouble with radicalization. *International Affairs,* 89(4), pp. 873–893.

New Statesman, 2016. *What is accelerationism?. [Online] Available at: https://www .newstatesman.com/politics/2016/08/what-accelerationism [Accessed 18 08 2022].*

Nguyen, C., 2020. Echo chambers and epistemic bubbles. *Episteme,* 17(2), pp. 141–161.

Nilan, P., 2021. *Young people and the far right.* Cham: Palgrave Macmillan.

Pennycook, G. & Rand, D., 2021. *Research note: Examining false beliefs about voter fraud in the wake of the 2020 Presidential Election.* [Online] Available at: https://misinforeview.hks.harvard.edu/article/research-note-examining-false-beliefs-about-voter-fraud-in-the-wake-of-the-2020-presidential-election/ [Accessed 11 08 2023].

Sageman, M., 2004. *Understanding terror networks.* Philadelphia: University of Pennsylvania Press.

Saull, R. 2015a, Capitalism, crisis, and the far-right in the neoliberal era. *Journal of International Relations and Development,* 18, pp. 25–51.

Saull, R., 2015b. Capitalist development and the rise and 'fall' of the far-right. *Critical Sociology,* 41(4–5), pp. 619–639.

Savage, C., 2021. *Incitement to riot? What trump told supporters before mob stormed Capitol.* [Online] Available at: https://www.nytimes.com/2021/01/10/us/trump-speech-riot.html [Accessed 17 08 2023].

Schori Liang, C. & Cross, M. J., 2020. *White crusade: How to prevent right-wing ,* GCSP.

Šima, K., 2021. *National stereotyping, identity politics, European crises.* Leiden: Brill.

Simon, M. & Sidner, S., 2021. *Decoding the extremist symbols and groups at the Capitol Hill insurrection.* [Online] Available at: https://edition.cnn.com/2021/01/09/us/capitol-hill-insurrection-extremist-flags-soh/index.html [Accessed 21 08 2023].

Sommerlad, J., 2022. *What happened on 6 January 2021?. [Online]* Available at: https://www.independent.co.uk/news/world/americas/us-politics/what-happened-on-jan-6-b2131290.html?r=49806 [Accessed 16 08 2022].

SPLC, 2022. *Identity Evropa/American identity movement.* [Online] Available at: https://www.splcenter.org/fighting-hate/extremist-files/group/identity-evropaamerican-identity-movement [Accessed 19 08 2022].

Stanton, Z., 2021. *The problem isn't just one insurrection. It's mass radicalization.* [Online] Available at: https://www.politico.com/news/magazine/2021/02/11/mass-radicalization-trump-insurrection-468746 [Accessed 15 08 2023].

Stewart, B., 2020. The rise of far-right civilizationism. *Critical Sociology,* 46(7–8), pp. 1207–1220.

Strets, J. & Burke, P., 2000. Identity theory and social identity theory. *Social Psychology Quarterly,* 63(3), pp. 224–237.

Tajfel, H. & Turner, J. C., 2004. An integrative theory of intergroup conflict. In: *Organizational identity.* Oxford: Oxford University Press, pp. 56–65.

Talley, I. & Levy, R., 2021. *Extremists posted plans of Capitol attack online.* [Online] Available at: https://www.wsj.com/livecoverage/biden-trump-electoral-college-certification-congress/card/x1dwwPqnJM1XfQh5LaUj [Accessed 17 08 2023].

The Economist, 2018. How "identitarian" politics is changing Europe. [Online] Available at: https://www.economist.com/europe/2018/03/28/how-identitarian-politics-is-changing-europe [Accessed 11 04 2022].

The Guardian, 2020. *German far-right arrests reveal plot to attack multiple mosques.* [Online] Available at: https://www.theguardian.com/world/2020/feb/17/german-far-right-arrests-reveal-multiple-mosque-attacks-plot [Accessed 17 02 2022].

The Washington Post, 2021. *Identifying far-right symbols that.* [Online] Available at: https://www.washingtonpost.com/nation/interactive/2021/far-right-symbols-capitol-riot/ [Accessed 17 08 2023].

Tilly, C., 1978. *From mobilization to revolution.* Reading: Addison-Wesley.

Timberg, C., Dwoskin, E. & Albergotti, R., 2021. *Inside Facebook, Jan. 6 violence fueled anger, regret over missed warning signs.* [Online] Available at: https://www.washingtonpost.com/technology/2021/10/22/jan-6-capitol-riot-facebook/ [Accessed 15 08 2021].

Törnberg, P., Andersson, C., Lindgren, K. & Banisch, S., 2021. Modeling the emergence of affective polarization in the social media society. *Plos One,* 16(10), pp. 1–17.

Vachudova, M., 2021. Populism, democracy, and party system change in Europe. *Annual Review of Political Science,* 24, pp. 471–498.

Viala-Gaudefroy, J., 2022. *One year after the January 6 Capitol attack, the US is still dealing with the fallout from Trump's 'Big Lie'.* [Online] Available at: https://theconversation.com/one-year-after-the-january-6-capitol-attack-the-us-is-still-dealing-with-the-fallout-from-trumps-big-lie-174308 [Accessed 16 08 2022].

Wiktorowicz, Q., 2004. Introduction: Islamic activism and social movement theory. In: *Islamic activism. A social movement theory approach.* Bloomington: Indiana University Press, pp. 1–33.

Willsher, K., 2021. *France bans far-right 'paramilitary' group Génération Identitaire.* [Online] Available at: https://www.theguardian.com/world/2021/mar/03/france-bans-far-right-paramilitary-group-generation-identitaire [Accessed 07 08 2023].

Wilson, J., 2018. *Doxxing, assault, death threats: The new dangers facing US journalists covering extremism.* [Online] Available at: https://www.theguardian.com/world/2018/jun/14/doxxing-assault-death-threats-the-new-dangers-facing-us-journalists-covering-extremism [Accessed 23 08 2022].

Wilson, J., 2019. *With links to the Christchurch attacker, what is the Identitarian Movement?.* *[Online] Available at:* https://www.theguardian.com/world/2019/mar/28/with-links-to-the-christchurch-attacker-what-is-the-identitarian-movement [Accessed 19 08 2020].

Wodak, R., 2021. *The politics of fear.* 2nd ed. London: Sage.

Wong, Q., 2022. *Jan. 6 Capitol Hill riot forced social networks to look at their ugly side.* [Online] Available at: https://www.cnet.com/news/politics/jan-6-capitol-hill-riot-forced-social-networks-to-look-at-their-ugly-side/ [Accessed 15 08 2023].

Woodruff Swan, B. & Cheney, K., 2022. *Trump expressed support for hanging Pence during Capitol riot, Jan. 6 panel told.* [Online] Available at: https://www.politico.com/news/2022/05/25/trump-expressed-support-hanging-pence-capitol-riot-jan-6-00035117 [Accessed 07 08 2023].

Youngblood, M., 2020. Extremist ideology as a complex contagion: The spread of far-right radicalization in the United States between 2005 and 2017. *Humanities and Social Sciences Communications,* 7(49), pp. 1–10.

2 Hate in the Digital Age

Navigating Contemporary Far-Right Extremism and Terrorism

Populist Political Movements and Far-Right Growth

Distinct from mainstream conservatism, far-right extremism has grown online and offline, powered by diverse right-wing ideologies and growing populist parties and ideologies. Populist movements and leaders amplify nationalist and anti-establishment sentiments, bolstering far-right ideologies. This populist narrative, capitalising on societal anxieties, promotes extremist viewpoints, focusing on anti-elite, authoritarian, and nativist agendas (Miller-Idriss, 2022, p. 48; Mudde, 2007; Mudde, 2019, pp. 28–31). While connected to populist movements, the extreme far-right groups delve deeper into divisive ideologies (Magnus, 2022). Economic challenges, such as unemployment, render individuals more open to these extremist beliefs, seeking a sense of belonging and empowerment (Georgiadou et al., 2019; Bossert et al., 2023; Marino, 2023).

Socio-economic factors, especially financial hardships and job losses, often lead to blame on external groups, such as immigrants (Inglehart & Norris, 2016, p. 11; Rebechi & Rohde, 2023, pp. 3–4; Skoczylis & Andrews, 2022, pp. 150–151). For example, within the far-right extremist movements, white supremacists aim to ensure whites get more status, privileges, and rights than non-whites. That means that prowhite is on top of the hierarchy, and it is national to embrace social inequality regarding their perception of inferior people, like Jews, black people, and Muslims (Byman, 2022, p. 9). Although every group labelled as far-right is not necessarily extremist, many display exclusionary beliefs, promote conspiracy theories, and demonstrate anti-governmental sentiments. This ideology combines elements like nationalism, fascism, racism, anti-immigration sentiments, and xenophobia while opposing ideologies such as communism (Miller-Idriss, 2021; Mudde, 2019, pp. 25–31).

Globally, the ascent of populism and far-right ideologies is undeniable. Nations like Italy, Hungary, India, Brazil, Argentina, and the Netherlands have seen electoral triumphs of far-right populists who aspire to reshape political norms towards a more authoritarian direction while excluding minorities (Anievas & Saull, 2022, p. 1; BBC News, 2023; CBS News, 2023). Events like the 2016 US Presidential Election and UK's Brexit referendum, coupled with the rise of parties like Germany's Alternative für Deutschland (AfD) and Italy's Lega Nord,

DOI: 10.4324/9781003297888-2

illustrate the spread of this trend (Brown et al., 2021, p. 2; Ebner, 2019). The menace of extreme far-right factions increasingly harms the European political landscape, i.e. organisations like Identitäre Bewegung Deutschland, demonstrating the issue's severity (Jones, 2018; Castelli Gattinara & Pirro, 2019, pp. 451–452). Some, like France's Rassemblement National and AfD, have garnered significant popularity, often powered by concerns about immigration and terrorism (Conway et al., 2019, p. 2; Byman, 2022, p. 88; Koehler, 2016, p. 87; Castelli Gattinara & Pirro, 2019, p. 448).

Contemporary Trends

Far-Right Extremism in the US

In the US, far-right extremism has historical roots tracing back to President Lincoln's assassination in 1865, a violent effort against abolitionism and racial equality. The subsequent violence of the Ku Klux Klan (KKK), during the post-Civil War's Reconstruction (1865-1877), is also seen as far-right terrorism (Dafinger & Florin, 2022, p. 2; Blackmore, 2021). Founded in 1865, the KKK held diverse extremist views, including racism, anti-Semitism, and homophobia (Counter Extremist Project, 2022a). Although its influence waned, the Klan's ideology persisted, and the Klan culture had a notable resurgence of white supremacy during the Trump era (Kenes, 2021).

American far-right movements deeply entrench ultra-nationalism and white supremacism, often blending with misogyny, Christian nationalism, and governmental extremism (Miller-Idriss, 2021; DiMaggio, 2022). Over time, additional groups have developed, including Christian identity groups, white-supremacy prison gangs like the Aryan Brotherhood, and neo-Nazi factions, which are primarily inspired by international extremist movements (DiMaggio, 2022). In 2015, the US saw a significant rise in domestic extremist attacks from a mixture of these far-right groups, such as white supremacists, neo-Nazis, and anti-government militants. Victims ranged from police to LGBTQ+ activists and Black Lives Matter members. Disturbingly, some politicians and media figures seemed to endorse this violence instead of condemning it, exacerbating national polarisation and deepening societal divides (Potok, 2016).

Trump Era: Amplification of White Nationalist Sentiments

Trump's presidency further illuminated these divides. His rhetoric around Muslims, Latinos, and immigration echoed white nationalist sentiments. His perceived preference for Nordic immigrants over those from 'shithole countries' and retweets of hate messages disseminated this ideology further (Vitali et al., 2018; Kendi, 2019; Wintour et al., 2018). Additionally, this white nationalism emphasised the distaste for birthright citizenship protected by the

Fourteenth Amendment. White nationalist leaders endorsed Trump, and he responded by retweeting hate posts to a global audience. Trump's Herrenvolk Republicanism ideology implied that full membership of the US civic community was predominately reserved for white people (Perlstein, 2017; Anderson, 2019; Ehrenberg, 2022). The 2020 US Presidential Election saw the highest risk of civil unrest since 1860, intensified by unprecedented firearm sales during the COVID-19 pandemic. Belief in President Trump's victory and voter fraud concerns fuelled the US Capitol Hill insurrection (Kenes, 2021). The far-right challenges democratic values, advocating for authoritarianism and opposing freedoms like press and speech (Miller-Idriss, 2021). Such extremism continuously tests US democracy, unity, and progress.

The Growth of Far-Right Extremism in Europe

In the aftermath of World War I, Europe witnessed a rise in far-right extremism as the destruction from the war created political discontent. Many failed to accept the defeat of the central powers, creating fertile ground for far-right groups to rally followers and attack minorities (Dafinger & Florin, 2022; Griffin, 2010, p. 165). Prominent examples of this extremism include the assassinations of two German politicians, Erzberger and Rathenau, in the early 1920s by a far-right paramilitary group, the Organisation Consul (Dafinger & Florin, 2022, p. 4; Blakemore, 2018). Meanwhile, in Britain, Mosley founded the British Union of Fascists during the 1930s. This party advocated for England's total independence, an ideology that resonates in modern movements like Brexit. Though Mosley's direct influence has faded, traces of his ideas and those of other pre-WWII fascist leaders linger (Evans, 2019; BBC News, 2019b; Love, 2007).

After 1945, Euro-fascism's remnants became noticeable in periodicals echoing the ideologies of pre-war leaders, including Mosley and Evola. These publications, such as The European and Nation Europa, were nostalgic and sought to galvanise new movements with the dream of a unified fascist European Federation (Griffin, 2010, p. 166). Despite Nazi Germany's 1945 defeat, European ethno-nationalism and white supremacism thrived. This resurgence spans far-right parties, neo-Nazi factions, and apolitical protest groups. While some groups overtly promote supremacist views, others use populist arguments portraying immigrants and minorities as threats. Despite not always aligning directly with Nazi ideologies, these groups share this idea of what constitutes core threats to European identity, similar to historical fascist ideologies (Counter Extremist Project, 2022b).

Influence of the Great Replacement Theory and Its Global Impact

The contemporary rise of groups like GI has been coupled with extreme violence (Chapter 1). The 2019 Christchurch Mosque shootings in New

Zealand were executed by a shooter influenced by the Great Replacement theory. This and other attacks are dark evidence of the growing influence of far-right extremism (Evans, 2019; Counter Extremist Project, 2022). The El Paso attacker, Crusius, was similarly linked to the Great Replacement theory, espousing the belief that violent action was necessary for white survival (Counter Extremist Project, 2022). GI leaders, like Sellner, avoid openly endorsing violence, ensuring their online visibility on platforms like YouTube and X/Twitter. Sellner, who propagates the Great Replacement theory in regular posts online, shares guides like 'Media Guerrilla Warfare' to help followers boost their content. Despite numerous calls to get his online content removed, he avoided restrictions for a long time until X/Twitter banned him in July 2020 (Byman, 2022, p. 85; Ebner, 2019).

Far-Right Extremism and Its Manifestations in the 21st Century

The Lone Wolf Phenomenon

Traditionally, the term 'lone wolf' is defined as a terrorist who is not part of a group or network and has not been directed by an external person or group. However, it is not a clean-cut definition, as the person predominately commits the violent act in support of someone or something, for example, a group, movement, or ideology but is acting free of any organisational structures (Byman, 2017; Weimann, 2012, p. 77; Martin & Pranger, 2019, p. 207). Breivik's 2011 Norway attacks are prime examples; though he acted alone, he was influenced by global far-right communities online. Similarly, the Internet has been pivotal in disseminating extremist ideologies and creating echo chambers for individuals to find inspiration and likeminded people to communicate with (Ganor, 2021, p. 24; Pantucci, 2011, p. 34; Koehler, 2016, p. 88). Therefore, it is problematic to argue that lone wolf actors act solely on their own and for individual purposes.

The term 'lone wolf' is often associated with religious terrorism, and it usually involves attacks with no direct link to terrorist groups, as seen in the San Bernardino (2015), Orlando nightclub (2016), and Nice's Bastille Day (2016) attacks. However, many, like Farook and Malik in San Bernardino, had some level of contact with the extremist environment (Byman, 2017; BBC News, 2016a, 2016b; Martin & Pranger, 2019, p. 208; BBC News, 2015). High-profile cases like Breivik (Norway) and Tarrant (New Zealand) highlight the danger of self-radicalised lone wolves who, while acting independently, are influenced by online extremist communities (Smith-Spark, 2021; Byman, 2017). This pattern is evident in incidents like the 2019 attacks in Halle, Germany, and Bærum, Norway. The Internet facilitates this phenomenon, providing virtual spaces that serve as breeding grounds for extremist views and radicalisation, even aiding in attack planning (Ganor, 2021, p. 23; Byman,

2022, p. 84). In the US, the Charleston Church shooter's online radicalisation exemplifies how these communities contribute to real-world violence (Laub, 2019; Cobb, 2017).

High-Profile Incidents of Far-Right Extremism

The 21st century has witnessed countless far-right attacks, including the Norway assault, synagogue and mosque attacks in Pittsburgh, Christchurch, Halle, the El Paso mall incident, and the murder of the British Labour MP Cox. These tragedies, often labelled as domestic terrorism, targeted unsuspecting victims (Dafinger & Florin, 2022, p. 1; Miller-Idriss, 2021; Byman, 2022, p. 80). The aftermath of such events has spurred global debates on combating far-right extremism and the responsibilities of Internet and social media companies to remove the different forums and posts. Post the Capitol Hill attack, the awareness of far-right extremism is growing, demonstrating the merge of online and offline spaces, platforms and pathways. These events influenced public and private policy shifts to address the rising threat.

Oslo and Utøya Island Attacks: Merging Online Radicalisation and Violence

These attacks, often classified as domestic terrorism, have indiscriminately targeted innocent victims, igniting global discussions on countering this growing threat. Breivik's 2011 attacks in Oslo and Utøya Island, Norway, signify a disturbing blend of online radicalisation and real-world violence. Breivik's car bombing in Oslo and his shooting spree at a youth camp on Utøya Island, claiming 77 lives, were preceded by a detailed manifesto influenced by far-right ideologies. This attack highlighted the risks posed by lone-wolf extremists (Smith-Spark, 2021; BBC News, 2017 , 2022; AP, 2021; Byman, 2022, pp. 2, 78–79; Weimann, 2012, p. 77). This attack played a pivotal role in shaping the tactics of subsequent attackers, demonstrating a profound integration of online and offline realms. The online sphere notably served as an enabler in planning and conducting the attack. A key aspect was utilising social media and other digital communication channels to communicate and spread awareness of the attack. Deeply rooted in white supremacist ideology, the attack was preceded by a manifesto published online, citing far-right sources such as Stormfront and Nordisk.nu. This document has since become a source of inspiration for other extremists and most far-right attacks would today have some sort of online manual with justifications for the attack (Byman, 2022, pp. 2, 79; Mudde, 2019, p. 91; Bacigalupo & Borgeson, 2022, p. 121; Miller-Idriss, 2022, p. 32).

The Charlottesville Rally: Far-Right Extremism in the US

Other attacks have also made headlines worldwide and triggered new online responses to far-right extremist groups' online presence, such as more content moderation, change in social media terms and conditions and ban of prominent far-right personalities from mainstream platforms. The 2017 Unite the Right rally in Charlottesville, USA, marked a significant moment in American far-right extremism. This confrontation over a Confederate statue saw white nationalists opposing its removal and taking their anger to the streets in a rally (Byman, 2022, pp. 97, 128; Helmore & Beckett, 2017; Wilson, 2017; Fieldstadt, 2019). The rally, fuelled by ideologies like the Great Replacement theory, ended in the tragic death of counter-protester Heyer (Keneally, 2018; Miller-Idriss, 2022, p. 1). The event showed the polarising nature of far-right ideologies in the US and the potential for real-world violence. From his New Jersey resort, President Trump's ambiguous comments on the Charlottesville violence were seen by many as supportive of supremacist groups. His mention of 'very fine people' on both sides ignited controversy. This, coupled with rising populism and mainstream support from some key politicians, has encouraged extremist groups to deepen societal divides (Keneally, 2018; Nelson & Swanson, 2017; Helmore & Beckett, 2017; Loadenthal et al., 2022, p. 89).

Synagogue and Mosque Attacks: From Pittsburgh to Christchurch

Other attacks, driven by various motives like religion or race, have similarly contributed to the overarching ideology of the far-right. The Tree of Life synagogue shooting in Pittsburgh, USA in 2018 (Duffin, 2021; Jones, 2018; Gajanan, 2019; Laub, 2019), and the Christchurch mosque attacks in New Zealand in 2019 further exemplify the fatal consequences of far-right extremism (Ebner, 2019; Besley & Peters, 2019, p. 113; Counter Extremist Project, 2022; Macklin, 2019a). Both attackers were influenced by online hate speech and conspiracy theories, demonstrating the critical transition from online radicalisation to physical violence. The Pittsburgh attacker's online trail directly showed his hatred against the Hebrew Immigrant Aid Society (HIAS), revealing his intent just before the massacre. His account stated, "HIAS likes to bring invaders in that kill our people. I can't sit by and watch my people get slaughtered. Screw your optics. I'm going in" (Robertson et al., 2018; Chavez et al., 2018; Jones 2018; Miller-Idriss, 2022, p. 38).

The Christchurch attacker, Tarrant's manifesto, The Great Replacement, reflected white supremacist concerns about migration. Tarrant sought to provoke additional violence and societal turmoil by casting his actions as revenge. After posting his manifesto on 8Chan and lesser-known sites such as MediaFire and ZippyShare, he linked the 8Chan post to a Facebook Live stream, showcasing his assault in real-time. The harrowing feed displayed his route to Al Noor Mosque, accompanied by Serbian nationalist music, capturing the murder rampant at the first mosque. The broadcast ended before he attacked the Linwood Islamic Centre, where he took another seven lives

(Byman, 2022, p. 94; Macklin, 2019b). By disseminating his manifesto online and broadcasting the attack on Facebook Live, Tarrant amplified the nexus between online radicalisation and real-world violence.

Racially Motivated Attacks: El Paso, Buffalo, and Jacksonville

The rise of far-right extremism and its alignment with racially motivated attacks has become alarmingly evident in recent years as demonstrated by a series of tragic events. These attacks have terrorised communities and unveiled a sinister trend of racial hatred that filters through society. The El Paso Walmart (2019), the Buffalo supermarket (2022), and the Jacksonville (2023) shootings reveal the alignment of far-right extremism with racially motivated violence (BBC News, 2019a; The Buffalo News, 2023; Binley, 2023). Targeting Hispanic and African-American communities, respectively were premeditated and motivated by white supremacist ideologies and the normalisation of hate. The incident in El Paso (2019) was no impulsive act. Crusius posted a premeditated manifesto shortly before the event, which revealed numerous chilling xenophobic and white supremacist views singling out a supposed 'Hispanic invasion of Texas' (Arango et al., 2019; BBC News, 2019a; Flores, 2023).

The 2022 attack against Buffalo Tops Friendly Market demonstrated calculated planning and intent to maximise impact fuelled by a far-right conspiracy theory. Similar to other far-right extremists, the attacker Gendron posted a manifesto online and live-streamed the attack on Twitch to mirror the 2019 Christchurch Mosque shootings. The live feed was cut by Twitch shortly after it began (The Buffalo News, 2023; Cabral, 2023; AP, 2023; New York State Attorney General, 2022, p. 9). The following year, in Jacksonville, Palmeter carried out a racially motivated attack at a Dollar General store, where he directly targeted black individuals. The timing of the attack coincided with the 60th anniversary of Dr Martin Luther King Jr.'s famous speech, which demonstrated that racial hatred is still embedded in American society (Binley, 2023; Massie et al., 2023; Lunch & Caspani, 2023; Ramirez-Simon & Yang, 2023).

Addressing the Far-Right Threat

These examples collectively reveal a deep-seated issue within specific segments of society driven by far-right ideologies. The recurrence of these racially motivated attacks underscores the urgency with which this growing threat needs to be addressed. Many offline extremist acts have strong connections to online ecosystems. The digital realm provides a platform for radicalisation, recruitment, communication, and dissemination of ideologies. Whether through manifestos, live streams, or propaganda, the Internet acts as a catalyst by amplifying extremist sentiments and enabling a wider reach. This merge makes the link between online radicalisation and real-world violence indisputable (Table 2.1).

Table 2.1 Outline of Key Far-right Extremist Attacks

Attacks	Characteristics
Utøya Island and Oslo Attacks (2011)	Breivik, a far-right extremist. Conducted two attacks in Norway: Oslo car bomb (8 killed) and Utøya island shooting (69 killed). Incidents underscored the severe threat of far-right extremism Wrote a 1,500-page manifesto, '2083: A European Declaration of Independence'. Manifesto expressed xenophobic views, particularly against Islam and multiculturalism. Accused European elites of supporting Muslim immigration.
Charleston shooting (June 2015)	Roof, a far-right extremist. Conducted an attack at Charleston's Emanuel African Methodist Episcopal Church. Murdered nine African Americans, including Senator Pinckney. Aimed to incite a race war. A website associated with Roof was discovered post-attack. It contained a racist manifesto and images with white supremacist and neo-Nazi symbols.
Murder of Jo Cox (2016)	Mair, a far-right extremist. Assassinated UK Labour MP Jo Cox during Brexit referendum. Act highlighted the dangers of violent far-right ideologies and inflammatory political rhetoric. Internet search history included the BNP, white supremacy, Nazis, the KKK, and serial killers. He was fascinated with figures like Breivik and extremists.
Munich Mass Shooting (July 2016)	Sonboly, a far-right extremist. Targeted people with immigrant backgrounds in Munich mall shooting. Killed nine, then committed suicide. The incident showed the fatal impact of far-right and xenophobic ideologies. Influenced by past mass shootings, especially Breivik's 2011 Norway attack. Researched similar incidents. Active in online gaming communities, likely expressing xenophobic views.
Charlottesville Unite the Right Rally (August 2017)	Fields Jr., a white supremacist. Drove his car into counter-protesters. This resulted in one fatality and two injuries. Online activities revealed engagement with far-right and neo-Nazi content. Displayed deep-seated hatred towards Jews and African Americans.
Pittsburgh Synagogue Shooting (October 2018)	Bowers, a far-right extremist. Conducted an attack on the Tree of Life synagogue during Shabbat service. This resulted in eleven deaths and additional injuries. The incident underlined the lethal impact of anti-Semitic ideologies.

(Continued)

Table 2.1 Continued

Attacks	Characteristics
	Voiced anti-Jewish sentiments during the attack.
	Had previously expressed comparable views on Gab, popular among far-right circles.
	Hinted at his plans pre-attack, referencing a Jewish non-profit organisation.
El Paso Walmart Shooting (August 2019)	Crusius, a white supremacist.
	Launched an attack on a Walmart in El Paso, Texas, aiming at Hispanics.
	The attack caused 22 deaths and many injuries.
	The incident underscored the link between far-right ideologies, white supremacy, and domestic terrorism.
	Posted an anti-immigrant, anti-Latino manifesto on the 8chan forum.
Halle Synagogue Shooting (October 2019)	Balliet, a far-right extremist.
	Attempted to attack a synagogue in Halle, Germany, on Yom Kippur.
	Attack foiled by the synagogue's secure doors.
	Killed two bystanders and injured several others.
	Attempted to live-stream the attack on Twitch, echoing tactics of other extremists for worldwide reach.
	Manifesto uncovered post-attack revealed intense anti-Semitic and far-right ideologies.
The Chabad of Poway Synagogue, California (April 2019)	Ernest, a far-right extremist.
	Carried an AR-15-style rifle and wore a tactical vest with additional magazines.
	Fired shots in a synagogue, causing one fatality and three injuries.
	Posted a manifesto on 8chan prior to the attack.
	Manifesto blamed Jews for the alleged decline of the white race.
Christchurch Mosque Shootings (March 2019)	Tarrant, a far-right extremist.
	Launched attacks on two mosques in Christchurch, New Zealand, during Friday prayers.
	Killed 51 individuals and wounded others.
	Influenced by online white supremacist ideologies.
	Live-streamed the attack on Facebook.
	Incident underscored the influence of digital platforms in disseminating extremist content.
	Shared a manifesto on 8chan, 'The Great Replacement'.
	Manifesto outlined extreme views on immigration and Islam.
Hanau Shootings (February 2020)	Rathjen, a far-right extremist.
	Carried out shootings at two shisha bars in Hanau, Germany.
	Killed nine people, mostly immigrants.
	Later, he killed his mother and himself at home.
	Shared a manifesto and videos online, including on YouTube.
	Content revealed his radicalisation through the Internet.
	He advocated for ethnic extermination in his beliefs.

(Continued)

Table 2.1 Continued

Attacks	Characteristics
United States Capitol Hill Attack (6th January, 2021)	US Capitol attack executed by supporters of then-President Trump, highlighting the risk of far-right extremism. Driven by baseless allegations of election fraud. This led to considerable damage and loss of life. Demonstrated the tangible consequences of online conspiracy theories. Before the attack, discussions and plans circulated on platforms like Parler, TheDonald.win, and segments of Facebook and Twitter.
Buffalo Attack (May 2022)	Gendron, a far-right extremist. Attacked Tops Friendly Market. This resulted in 11 fatalities and two injuries. Influenced by online racist conspiracy theories. Distributed a manifesto on Discord. Began a Twitch livestream inspired by the 2019 Christchurch massacre. Twitch cut off the stream soon after his 22-minute journey ended in the shooting.
Jacksonville Attack (August 2023)	Palmeter, a far-right extremist. Entered a Dollar General store armed with a Glock and AR-15 rifle adorned with a Swastika. Wore a tactical vest and mask. Killed two people, wounded another, and then committed suicide. Manifestos found post-incident showed hatred for Black people. The attack seemingly timed with the fifth anniversary of a previous Jacksonville shooting.

Source: (Smith-Spark, 2021; BBC News, 2017; BBC News, 2022; AP, 2021; Byman, 2022, p. 78; GOV.UK, 2023; Bacigalupo & Borgeson, 2022, p. 121; Cobain et al., 2016; Lowe, 2016; Johnson & Parry, 2022; Sengupta, 2016; DW, 2019; Hume, 2016; Bacigalupo & Borgeson, 2022, p. 119; Fieldstadt, 2019; Helmore & Beckett, 2017; GOV.UK, 2023; Bacigalupo & Borgeson, 2022, pp. 119–120; Robertson et al., 2018; Macklin, 2019b, p. 1; Crawford et al., 2020, p. 8; GOV.UK, 2023; Crawford et al., 2020, p. 8; GOV.UK, 2023; BBC News, 2020b; Oltermann, 2020; Bacigalupo & Borgeson, 2022, p. 122; Mossburg, 2021; Medina et al., 2019; Crawford et al., 2020, p. 8; GOV.UK, 2023; Bacigalupo & Borgeson, 2022, p. 121; BBC News, 2020a; Oltermann & Connolly, 2020; Schmidt et al., 2020; Rothschild, 2021, pp. xi–xii; Sommer, 2023, p. 1; Talley & Levy, 2021; AP, 2023; The Buffalo News, 2023; New York State Attorney General, 2022, p. 9; Massie et al., 2023; Lunch & Caspani, 2023; Ramirez-Simon & Yang, 2023; Binley, 2023).

The attacks reveal a significant link to the online environment that is often overlooked. The online environment provides access to instant communication to many people. The groups and individuals constantly change their communication and use of platforms and shift between offline and online environments to avoid being locked out of the online setting. Far-right extremists migrate between platforms when they are de-platformed in one place; they quickly move to another space. An online hate ecology has emerged, where groups and individuals interact and exchange viewpoints. The attackers can flourish and promote themselves and their cause through images, text, symbols and codes, manifestos, and live streams (Chapters 4 and 5) (Miller-Idriss, 2022, p. 139; Byman, 2022, p. 101). These attacks highlight the immediate necessity for comprehensive measures to counter the spread of extremist ideologies. The incidents also emphasise the severe consequences of far-right extremism on communities, especially when vulnerable groups are targeted based on their ethnicity or religion.

Terrorism vs. Extremism: Understanding the Difference

Defining terrorism is challenging due to its subjective nature, influenced by ideology and politics. With numerous interpretations, the saying 'one man's terrorist is another man's freedom fighter' encapsulates these varied perspectives. Consequently, labelling action as terrorism or a crime depends on the party in power, making it a subjective and contentious issue (Mahan & Griset, 2013; Ganor, 2010; Cooper, 2001, p. 881; Munk, 2022). This fluidity shows the challenge of pinning down a universally accepted definition. Terrorism's definition is controversial and varies based on perspective, leading to numerous interpretations by politicians, scholars, and even terrorists (Mahan & Griset, 2013; Ganor, 2010). Terrorism sometimes blends with other violent forms like guerrilla warfare and civil wars (Laqueur, 1999; Mahan & Griset, 2013). Moreover, terrorist organisations might label themselves as 'liberators' to emphasise their goals over methods (Cooper, 2001). As the sociopolitical landscapes evolve, the face of terrorism changes. Once dominated by separatist motives, the focus has shifted from religious to political extremism in recent years (IEP, 2022, pp. 33–35).

Far-right Extremism, Terrorism, and Hate Crime

Identifying far-right extremism and hate crime is a complex challenge. The lack of clarity in defining and categorising violent acts committed by far-right extremist groups and individuals poses difficulties, with some considering these acts as terrorism while others view them as hate crimes (Koehler, 2016, p. 89). Both hate crimes and terrorist acts involve violence against individuals and property, targeting civilian populations or specific subgroups as victims (Mills et al., 2017, pp. 1193–1194; Shimamoto, 2004). Far-right extremist groups have often been overshadowed by the constant focus on religious terrorism, allowing them to operate in the shadows (Jarvis, 2022, p. 13).

Addressing far-right extremism becomes challenging when a significant portion of society sympathises with these groups, as it may be seen as criminalising a large segment of the population (Byman, 2022, p. 171). Far-right extremism, unlike organised groups like ISIS and Al Qaeda, is intricately linked to political and cultural issues in the Global North. This complexity makes it harder to develop effective responses. Far-right actors often draw on a glorified past and vision for the future, differing from terror groups whose ideologies are more alien to the general population (Byman, 2022, p. 171). The overlap between terrorism and hate crime definitions adds to the problems. Terrorism is predominantly politically, ideologically, or religiously motivated, whereas socio-political or religious biases drive hate crimes. These features complicate distinguishing between the two. For instance, the KKK in the US demonstrates both racist and terrorist motivations, highlighting the challenge of addressing far-right extremism effectively (Mills et al., 2017, p. 1194).

The Global Issue of Hate Crime

Hate crimes stand out in the spectrum of criminal offences, differentiating them from conventional crimes. While the term 'hate crime' is used globally, its definition varies across jurisdictions and lacks consensus at international levels, including bodies like the United Nations (UN), Council of Europe (CoE) and the European Union (EU). This divergence in understanding poses challenges, as states might criminalise discrimination or affiliation with extremist groups but lack a shared benchmark for defining hate beyond the bounds of free expression (Schweppe & Tong, 2021, p. 2; Perry, 2016). Hate crimes against minority and migrant groups have surged in countries like the UK and Germany. In 2021, Reuters noted a 6% rise in far-right offences in Germany, constituting over half of all politically-driven crimes - a record since 2001 (Nasr, 2021; Jarvis, 2022; Connolly, 2021). These crimes occupy a space between severe offences like terrorism and typical criminal acts. Their distinct classification is crucial, as grouping them with general crimes neglects their broader societal implications (Schweppe & Tong, 2021, p. 1).

Distinguishing between common and hate crimes is essential, with the latter covering various offences, from assault to property damage. The Organization for Security and Co-operation in Europe (OSCE) defines hate crimes as acts driven by biased motives. Their unique nature requires distinct attention, especially due to potential biases in their legal handling (Bayer & Bard, 2020; OSCE, 2009a, p. 1; 2009b, p. 1). Such tendencies can result in compromised investigations, questioning victim credibility, and overlooking evidence. Combined with underreporting, many hate crimes remain unresolved. Prejudices within law enforcement and judicial systems can lead to lenient investigations or charges harming affected communities (FRA, 2012, p. 7; Bayer & Bard, 2020, p. 101). Hence, institutions like OSCE advocate for a comprehensive, bias-aware approach to hate crimes (OSCE, 2009a, p. 21). Political leaders play a crucial role in addressing these crimes. Some, especially populists, might address the issue superficially, catering primarily to a select audience. In doing so, they overlook the complexities of hate crimes as societal issues, missing their deeper roots and resulting in inadequate responses (Bayer & Bard, 2020, p. 21) (Table 2.2).

Table 2.2 Key Definitions of Hate Crime

Institution	Definition
The UN	"[A] prejudice-motivated crime which occurs when a perpetrator targets a victim because of their membership (or perceived membership) of a certain social group or racial demographic".
The Organisation for Security and Co-operation in Europe (OSCE)	"... criminal acts committed with a bias motive. It is this motive that makes hate crimes different from other crimes. A hate crime is not one particular offence. It could be an act of intimidation, threats, property damage, assault, murder or any other criminal offence. The term "hate crime" or "bias crime", therefore, describes a type of crime, rather than a specific offence within a penal code".

Source: (United Nations, 2022; OSCE, 2009a; Department of Justice, 2020, p. 59).

Terrorism and Hate Crimes: Defining the Threats

Terrorism and hate crimes both aim to instil fear and convey potent messages. Terrorism broadly targets groups to amplify societal fear and vulnerability. In contrast, hate crimes focus on individuals due to their group identity, such as harming the individual, which sends a negative message to the broader community (Mills et al., 2017, p. 1194; FRA, 2012, p. 7). Many far-right incidents fall under hate crimes, which, like terrorism, target individuals based on group identity rather than personal actions.

Terrorism broadly targets populations to spread pervasive fear, while hate crimes target individuals based on group identity, sending a message to the larger community associated with the victim. Although both criminal acts spread fear beyond their immediate victims, they are treated differently (Koehler, 2016, p. 89; Krueger & Maleckova, 2002; The White House, 2021; UNODC, 2009).

Hate crimes are treated as severe offences within most countries' criminal codes. They require special attention and intervention by governmental authorities, reflecting their extreme nature. In contrast, terrorism is considered a more urgent and systematic threat, often addressed as a crime and a form of warfare. Externally, terrorism may prompt military responses and extensive surveillance; internally, a wide range of law enforcement tools and powers may be deployed (The White House, 2021; UNODC, 2009; Sinnar, 2022). The different frameworks for handling terrorism and hate crimes underline the layered nature of these threats and the necessity for tailored approaches in addressing them (Table 2.3).

Table 2.3 Terrorism vs. Hate Crime Conceptualisation

Key elements	Terrorism vs. hate crime
Nature and Severity of the Threat	Hate crimes are categorised under civil rights and criminal law. Terrorism is treated as a national security concern. Government responses are typically more proactive towards terrorism. This is especially evident in cases of religious extremism. Far-right hate crimes often receive a less immediate governmental response.
Motivation and Message	Both hate crimes and terrorism aim to send messages beyond their immediate victims. Hate crimes target minorities such as LGBTQ+, Jews, and Muslims to foster exclusion. Terrorism fosters an 'us vs them' dynamic, making the majority feel threatened. Hate crimes are driven by bias against specific groups. Terrorism is motivated by political or ideological objectives.
Planning and Violence	Terrorism usually entails significant planning and preparation. Hate crimes are often more impulsive in nature. Incidents like the 2021 Capitol Hill attack blur the distinction between planned and impulsive acts. Terrorism is inherently violent. Hate crimes can range in severity and destructiveness.
Claiming Responsibility	Terrorist groups often claim responsibility for their attacks. Hate crime perpetrators usually prefer anonymity. Hate crimes typically convey implicit warnings, lacking direct acknowledgement.
Law Enforcement Responses	Hate crimes are addressed reactively by law enforcement post-incident. Terrorism is managed through both proactive and reactive strategies. Hate crimes indicative of societal prejudices. Inadequate response to hate crimes may reinforce existing prejudices.

Source: (Sinnar, 2022; Byman, 2022, p. 172; Sinnar, 2022; Mills et al., 2017, p. 1195; King et al., 2017, p. 387; Mills et al., 2017, pp. 1196–1197; OSCE, 2009a, p. 21; Sinnar, 2022).

The Principles of Freedom of Expression

Freedom of expression is the right to voice opinions without fearing government or societal backlash. It is a right outlined in the Universal Declaration of Human Rights, various Human Rights Conventions and many national constitutions (UN, 1948; CoE, 2021). The UN categorises hate speech as derogatory communication targeting specific attributes like race or religion. States must debunk speech that promotes violence or violates international standards, as outlined in the International Covenant on Civil and Political

Rights (UNESCO, 2023; Lavorgna, 2020, pp. 82–83; UN, 1966; 2020, p. 8). Freedom of expression nurtures dialogue, encourages diverse opinions, and supports democracy. However, it is not an absolute right; states might impose limitations to protect national security, public order, etc. However, it must be necessary, proportionate and in accordance with law. Striking the right balance between free speech and these limitations is difficult, especially in the context of hate speech with varying definitions and enforcement powers (Yar & Steinmetz, 2019).

The Political Landscape and Hate Speech

Hate speech is a communication that demeans or degrades a person or group based on race, religion, ethnicity, gender, sexual orientation, or other protected characteristics, fostering an environment of fear and exclusion (UN, 2020, 2023). While free speech is vital for democracy, far-right extremist groups exploit this freedom to propagate their ideologies. Far-right extremist groups and individuals use free speech rights to foster fear, hostility, and exclusion among marginalised communities, potentially leading to violence, discrimination, and societal division (Yar & Steinmetz, 2019, p. 258).

In the UK, negative language has merged with the political environment, especially around immigration. Alarmist rhetoric paints migrants as invaders, often supported by divisive terms like the 'North London Elite', a veiled reference to the UK's Jewish community, invoking both xenophobia and anti-Semitism (Fowles, 2022; Cross, 2020). Such divisive language gained attention following the UK Prime Minister's speech (2020), where he criticised 'lefty human rights lawyers', leading legal experts to express concerns about the potential erosion of public trust in the legal framework (Bowcott, 2020; Mason, 2023). Politicians' repeated use of such divisive language highlights the tension between free speech and its potential misuse. It serves as a reminder of public figures' responsibility to ensure their rhetoric does not fan the flames of division and hate.

The Challenge of Regulating Hate Speech on Social Media

Far-right extremism encompasses hate speech and crimes both online and offline. Hate speech targets individuals based on attributes like ethnicity, while hate crimes are bias-motivated actions (Lavrogna, 2020). To avoid detection, far-right groups use encryption, private channels, and coded language (Centre for Analysis of the Radical Right, 2020). Combined with dis- and misinformation and provocative content, these tactics have urged calls for stricter social media regulation. Yet, concerns about curtailing freedom of expression, a cornerstone of democracy, persist. While digital platforms amplify this freedom, regulating hate speech might inadvertently suppress legitimate discourse opposition (Yar & Steinmetz, 2019, p. 259; UN, 2019; Steiner et al., 2007, p. 639).

Balancing freedom of expression speech with curbing hate speech is challenging. Ambiguous or overly restrictive laws can stop genuine debate, whereas lenient ones may enable harmful content (Warburton & Franco, 2013, p. 150; UN, 2019). Identifying hate speech is subjective, which poses risks of self-censorship or inadvertently promoting hate messengers. Differing cultural and societal norms make universal standards elusive. While some countries prosecute expressions that vilify specific groups, regardless of direct incitement to violence. Other countries, like the US, allow broader terms due to constitutional protections (Yar & Steinmetz, 2019, p. 259; Warburton & Franco, 2013, p. 151).

The Complexities of Content Moderation Online

Limiting freedom of expression risks enabling those in power to suppress dissent and marginalise minority voices. As online communication platforms grow, the debate intensifies over their role in content moderation, balancing free speech against reducing hate and disinformation. Amplified by online hate's easy spread and anonymity, digital disinformation presents distinct challenges due to its cost-effectiveness, global reach, and enduring presence (UN, 2023). The proliferation of the Internet and social media has significantly escalated the spread of hate speech and increased the incidence of hate crimes, online extremism, and terrorism. Balancing freedom of speech with the need to restrict online hate is crucial, especially since digital hate speech, once posted, is often permanent and contextless (Lavorgna, 2020; UN, 2023).

While each form of online aggression has its nuances, they often overlap. Monitoring online hate speech is vital, yet the sheer volume and technological barriers is problematic. Social media's algorithmic propagation of polarising content threatens vulnerable populations and democracies, pushing some governments to mandate content moderation and raising free speech debates (UN, 2023; Hietanen & Eddebo, 2023). Initially, platforms were not obligated to regulate hate speech. Instead they have been prioritising broad free speech values despite their harmful nature. However, early on in social media's history, some moderation was considered necessary for legal protection and user satisfaction. Based on their terms, platforms can remove users without legal intervention (Hietanen & Eddebo, 2023; Meta, 2023a, 2023b).

Free Speech Absolutism vs. Harmful Speech Amplification

Free speech absolutists argue that any limits on political speech risk abuse and lack of consensus on what should be restricted. They caution against social media platforms like X/Twitter and Meta/Facebook becoming the ultimate judges of what constitutes free speech (Brooks & Day, 2022).

Table 2.4 Summary of Online Terrorism, Online Hate Crime and Online Hate Speech
          Concepts

Online Terrorism/ Extremism	Online terrorism involves using the Internet for recruitment, radicalisation, and planning Extremist groups utilise social media and encrypted messaging for propaganda and coordination. Countering online terrorism requires sophisticated monitoring and intelligence gathering Balancing efforts with concerns for privacy and encryption presents a challenge
Hate Crime Online	Hate speech targets individuals based on their identity Rapid online spread via social media and messaging platforms Legal responses to hate speech differ across jurisdictions Freedom of expression laws complicate the balance with free speech rights
Hate Speech Online	Hate speech targets individuals by identity Rapid spread online through social media and instant messaging Legal responses to hate speech vary by jurisdiction Challenge in balancing restrictions with freedom of expression laws

Freedom of speech/ expression does not guarantee freedom to amplify harmful views. The link between online hate and real-world violence is clear. While significant platforms have policies against hate speech, they often fail to act on content like the Great Replacement theory. These platforms must either enforce their existing rules by taking down such content and banning the users who post it or update their policies to include it explicitly (ADL, 2022; ECtHR, 2023). X/Twitters' owner Musk claims to champion free speech absolutism, but his actions and the complexities of this concept suggest otherwise. The real challenge lies in determining the limits of free speech rather than advocating for absolute freedom of expression (Warburton, 2022) (Table 2.4).

Propagating Hate

The COVID-19 pandemic and events like the Hamas-Israel war have strengthened far-right groups' activities, notably amplifying racism and anti-Semitism. These groups have leveraged the crisis to heighten their public visibility, exploiting global unrest to propagate divisive ideologies. This trend underlines the growing influence of far-right extremism in the current socio-political landscape.

The Impact of COVID-19 on Xenophobia and Conspiracy Theories

COVID-19 exacerbated xenophobia, leading to the rise of racist and bigoted conspiracy theories. Far-right extremists in the US, Europe, and Oceania have used the pandemic to scapegoat non-white immigrants, spreading false narratives about the virus's origin and spread on social media platforms. They have falsely accused groups like Muslims and blamed them for high COVID-19 death rates, such as claiming the 'UK's Muslim population is responsible for a quarter of the country's Covid-19 related deaths' (Schori Liang & Cross, 2020, p. 10; Awan & Khan-Williams, 2020). Chinese and Jewish populations in the US are also targeted. The FBI warned of white supremacists intentionally spreading COVID-19 to Jewish, Muslim, and police communities through saliva (The ICSR, 2021, p. 14; Schori Liang & Cross, 2020, p. 10).

Conspiracy theories linked to COVID-19 spread online and, in some instances, led to real-world violence, such as those relating the virus to 5G technology. Attacks on 5G infrastructure and telecom workers occurred in the UK and the Netherlands, driven in part by far-right accelerationists seeking to exploit the situation for social unrest (Hern, 2020; The ICSR, 2021, p. 13; Langley, 2020). Platform governance varies, impacting the spread of misinformation. X/Twitter and Meta/Facebook have implemented measures against COVID-19 misinformation, with X/Twitter being quicker to act. Meta/Facebook's delayed response allowed conspiracy groups to grow (Theocharis et al., 2023; Jackson et al., 2021). However, the company launched plans to show messages to users who interacted with now-removed harmful coronavirus misinformation and direct them to World Health Organization (WHO) resources (Langley, 2020).

Messenger services without such content control likely saw an increase in conspiratorial content. YouTube banned videos linking COVID-19 to 5G, and X/Twitter removed health misinformation, with WhatsApp limiting message forwarding. Despite these efforts, inconsistencies remain in their implementation, highlighting the challenge of addressing extremist activity and misinformation while respecting human rights (Janin & Deverell, 2020; Theocharis et al., 2023; Marchal & Au, 2020).

Global Rise in Anti-Semitism Following the Hamas-Israel Conflict

On the 7th of October, 2023, Hamas, a designated terrorist organisation, launched a violent attack on Israel, specifically targeting civilians and causing 1,400 deaths, 210 kidnappings, and over 3,000 injuries. This attack sparked a rise in anti-Semtic incidents globally, particularly in the UK, USA, Germany, and France. Extremists are growing bolder after the deathly Hamas attack, increasing their violent rhetoric and posting hateful messages, along with calls for more aggression against Israel and its supporters (Stenzler-Koblentz et al., 2023; Hutchinson, 2023; Reals & D'Agata, 2023; ADL, 2023). On the 6th of October 2023, extremists sent 59 Telegram messages threatening violence against Jews, Israelis, and Zionists. By the first 18 hours of 7th October, this number rose to 347 messages, marking a 488% increase.

Anti-Semitic and white supremacists are expressing desires for similar violence in America, using derogatory and supremacist language. Their rhetoric includes phrases like 'day of the rope', to discuss potential attacks against Israel (Chapter 1) (ADL, 2023). White supremacists and neo-Nazis on Telegram praised Hamas's actions, blaming Jewish organisations for a potential refugee crisis in Europe, while far-right policies in some EU countries fuelled Islamophobia and racism (Benakis, 2023). Some far-right extremists, including the anti-Semitic National Justice Party led by Penovich, have expressed support for Hamas's attacks on Israel. Penovich has praised the Palestinians for challenging Israel and criticised far-right nationalists who do not support these attacks (ADL, 2023). In the US, neo-Nazis are echoing Hamas's language to incite attacks against Jews both domestically and globally. They are sharing content linked to the Qassem Brigades on Telegram and interacting with Resistance Axis groups. US and Canadian extremist groups, like the Proud Boys, are also showing violent intentions towards Jewish communities on Telegram (Dilanian et al., 2023). The spread of hate speech online poses significant challenges for automatic detection tools and human moderators, especially as many social media accounts use coded language like 'TJD' (Total Jewish Death), 'TMD' (Total Muslim Death), and 'TPD' (Total Palestinian Death) to endorse violence, making content monitoring online more difficult (ADL, 2023).

References

ADL, 2022. *Deplatform Tucker Carlson and the "great replacement" theory.* [Online] Available at: https://www.adl.org/resources/blog/deplatform-tucker-carlson-and -great-replacement-theory [Accessed 01 09 2023].

ADL, 2023. *Hamas attack draws cheers from extremists, spurs anti-semitism and conspiracies online.* [Online] Available at: https://www.adl.org/resources/blog/ hamas-attack-draws-cheers-extremists-spurs-antisemitism-and-conspiracies-online [Accessed 01 11 2023].

Anderson, T., 2019. Herrenvolk democracy: The rise of the alt-right in Trump's America. In: *Critical theory and the humanities in the age of the alt-right.* Cham: Palgrave Macmillan, pp. 81–99.

Anievas, A. & Saull, R., 2022. The far-right in world politics/world politics in the far-right. *Globalisations,* 20(1), pp. 1–17.

AP, 2021. *Norway's July 22, 2011, terror attack: A timeline.* [Online] Available at: https://apnews.com/article/europe-norway-bd6c9d2efd6ce2148c3d85cb79d73af9 [Accessed 25 08 2023].

AP, 2023. *Teen who killed 10 Black people at Buffalo supermarket given life in prison.* [Online] Available at: https://www.theguardian.com/us-news/2023/feb/15/buffalo -shooting-gunman-sentenced-life-prison [Accessed 28 08 2023].

Arango, T., Bogel-Burroughs, N. & Benner, K., 2019. *Minutes before El Paso killing, hate-filled manifesto appears online.* [Online] Available at: https://www.nytimes .com/2019/08/03/us/patrick-crusius-el-paso-shooter-manifesto.html [Accessed 28 08 2023].

Awan, I. & Khan-Williams, R., 2020. *Coronavirus, fear and how Islanophobia spreads on social media.* [Online] Available at: https://anti-muslim-hatred-working-group .home.blog/2020/04/20/ [Accessed 01 11 2023].

Bacigalupo, J. & Borgeson, K., 2022. When cyberhate turns to violence. White nationalism to the manosphere. In: *Cyberhate.* Lanham: Lexington Books, pp. 119–136.

Bayer, J. & Bard, P., 2020. *Hate speech and hate crime in the EU and the evaluation of online content regulation approaches.* Brussels: LIBE Committee.

BBC News, 2015. *San Bernardino shooting: What we know so far.* [Online] Available at: https://www.bbc.co.uk/news/world-us-canada-34993344 [Accessed 06 08 2022].

BBC News, 2016a. *Nice attack: What we know about the Bastille Day killings.* [Online] Available at: https://www.bbc.co.uk/news/world-europe-36801671 [Accessed 06 08 2022].

BBC News, 2016b. *Orlando nightclub shooting: How the attack unfolded.* [Online] Available at: https://www.bbc.co.uk/news/world-us-canada-36511778 [Accessed 06 08 2022].

BBC News, 2017. *Norway massacre: 'We could hear the gunshots getting closer'.* [Online] Available at: https://www.bbc.com/news/uk-scotland-41678010 [Accessed 25 08 2023].

BBC News, 2019a. *Texas Walmart shooting: El Paso gun attack leaves 20 dead.* [Online] Available at: https://www.bbc.com/news/world-us-canada-49221936 [Accessed 28 08 2023].

BBC News, 2019b. *Who was Sir Oswald Mosley?.* [Online] Available at: https://www .bbc.co.uk/news/stories-49405924 [Accessed 23 08 2022].

BBC News, 2020a. *Germany shooting: What we know about the Hanau attack.* [Online] Available at: https://www.bbc.com/news/world-europe-51571649 [Accessed 25 08 2023].

BBC News, 2020b. *Halle synagogue attack: Germany far-right gunman jailed for life.* [Online] Available at: https://www.bbc.com/news/world-europe-55395682 [Accessed 25 08 2023].

BBC News, 2022. *Norway mass killer Anders Breivik ordered to stay in jail.* [Online] Available at: https://www.bbc.com/news/world-europe-60219876 [Accessed 25 08 2023].

BBC News, 2023. *Dutch election: Anti-Islam populist Geert Wilders wins dramatic victory.* [Online] Available at: https://www.bbc.co.uk/news/world-europe -67504272 [Accessed 27 11 2023].

Benakis, T., 2023. *The far-right exploits the Hamas attack in Israel. Online anti-semitism and Islamophobia on the rise.* [Online] Available at: https://www.europeaninterest .eu/the-far-right-exploits-the-hamas-attack-in-israel-online-antisemitism-and -islamophobia-on-the-rise/ [Accessed 19 11 2023].

Besley, T. & Peters, M. A., 2019. Terrorism, trauma, tolerance: Bearing witness to white supremacist attack on Muslims in Christchurch, New Zealand. *Educational Philosophy and Theory,* 52(2), pp. 109–119.

Binley, A., 2023. *Jacksonville shooting: Racist gunman kills three black people in Florida store.* [Online] Available at: https://www.bbc.com/news/world-us-canada -66630263 [Accessed 28 08 2023].

Blakemore, E., 2018. *After WWI, hundreds of politicians were murdered in Germany.* [Online] Available at: https://www.history.com/news/political-assassinations -germany-weimar-republic [Accessed 24 08 2022].

Blackmore, E., 2021. *Reconstruction offered a glimpse of equality for Black Americans. Why did it fail?. [Online] Available at: https://www.nationalgeographic.com/history/article/ reconstruction-turbulent-post-civil-war-period-explained [Accessed 09 04 2022].*

Bossert, W., Clark, A. E., D'Ambrosio, C. & Lepinteur, A., 2023. Economic insecurity and political preference. *Oxford Economic Papers,* 75(3), pp. 802–825.

Bowcott, O., 2020. *Legal profession hits back at Johnson over 'lefty lawyers' speech.* [Online] Available at: https://www.theguardian.com/law/2020/oct/06/legal-profession -hits-back-at-boris-johnson-over-lefty-lawyers-speech [Accessed 25 08 2022].

Brooks, E. & Day, J., 2022. *What is free speech absolutism? Who is a free speech absolutist? Examples, pros and cons.* [Online] Available at: https://www.liberties .eu/en/stories/free-speech-absolutist/44213 [Accessed 03 09 2023].

Brown, K., Mondon, A. & Winter, A., 2021. The far right, the mainstream and mainstreaming. *Journal of Political Ideologies,* 28(2), pp. 162–179.

Byman, D., 2022. *Spreading hate: The global rise of White supremacist terrorism.* 1st ed. Oxford: Oxford University Press.

Byman, D. L., 2017. *How to hunt a lone wolf: Countering terrorists who act on their own.* [Online] Available at: https://www.brookings.edu/opinions/how-to-hunt-a -lone-wolf-countering-terrorists-who-act-on-their-own/ [Accessed 06 08 2022].

Cabral, S., 2023. *Buffalo shooting victims sue social media platforms and gun distributors.* [Online] Available at: https://www.bbc.com/news/world-us-canada -66181080 [Accessed 28 08 2023].

Castelli Gattinara, P. & Pirro, A., 2019. The far right as social movement. *European Societies,* 21(4), pp. 447–462.

CBS News, 2023. *Right-wing populist Javier Milei wins Argentina's presidency amid discontent over economy.* [Online] Available at: https://www.cbsnews.com/news /javier-milei-wins-argentina-presidential-elections-runoff/ [Accessed 27 11 2023].

Centre for Analysis of the Radical Right, 2020. *A guide to online radical-right symbols, slogans and slurs. s.l.: s.n.*

Chavez, N., Grinberg, E. & McLaughlin, E., 2018. *Pittsburgh synagogue gunman said he wanted all Jews to die, criminal complaint says.* [Online] Available at: https://edition.cnn.com/2018/10/28/us/pittsburgh-synagogue-shooting/index.html [Accessed 23 08 2023].

Cobain, I., Parveen, N. & Taylor, M., 2016. *The slow-burning hatred that led Thomas Mair to murder Jo Cox.* [Online] Available at: https://www.theguardian.com/ uk-news/2016/nov/23/thomas-mair-slow-burning-hatred-led-to-jo-cox-murder [Accessed 23 08 2023].

Cobb, J., 2017. *Inside the trial of Dylann Roof.* [Online] Available at: https://www .newyorker.com/magazine/2017/02/06/inside-the-trial-of-dylann-roof [Accessed 12 04 2022].

Connolly, K., 2021. *German society 'brutalised' as far-right crimes hit record levels.* [Online] Available at: https://www.theguardian.com/world/2021/may/04/rightwing-extremism-germany-stability-interior-minister-says [Accessed 21 08 2023].

Conway, M., Scrivens, R. & Macnair, L., 2019. *Right-wing extremists' persistent contemporary trends.* [Online] Available at: https://icct.nl/app/uploads/2019/11/Right-Wing-Extremists-Persistent-Online-Presence.pdf [Accessed 12 08 2022].

Cooper, H. H. A., 2001. Terrorism: The problem of definition revisited. *American Behavioral Scientist,* 44(6), pp. 881–893.

Council of Europepe, 2021. European Convention on Human Rights [Online] https://www.echr.coe.int/documents/convention_eng.pdf [Accessed 04 01 2023].

Counter Extremist Project, 2022a. *Great replacement theory.* [Online] Available at: https://www.counterextremism.com/content/great-replacement-theory [Accessed 19 08 2022].

Counter Extremist Project, 2022b. European Ethno-Nationalist and White Supremacy Groups. [Online] Available at: https://www.counterextremism.com/content/european-ethno-nationalist-and-white-supremacy-groups [Accsed 30 03 2024]

Counter Extremist Project, 2024. White Supremacy Groups in the United States. [Oneline] Available at: https://www.counterextremism.com/content/white-supremacy-groups-united-states [Accessed 30.03.2024]

Crawford, B., Keen, F. & Suarez de-Tangil, G., 2020. *Mimetic irony and the promotion of violence within Chan cultures. London: The Centre for Research and Evidence on Security Threats.*

Cross, M., 2020. *Johnson opens new front in war on 'lefty lawyers'.* [Online] Available at: https://www.lawgazette.co.uk/news/johnson-opens-new-front-in-war-on-lefty-lawyers/5105891.article [Accessed 24 08 2022].

Dafinger, J. & Florin, M., 2022. Right-wing terrorism in historical perspective. An introduction. In: *A transnational history of right-wing terrorism.* London: Routledge, pp. 1–16.

Department of Justice, 2020. *Learnings from approaches to hate crime in five jurisdictions. s.l.: Department of Justice.*

Dilanian, K., Ainsley, J., Winter, T. & Dienst, J., 2023. *Pro-Hamas extremists and neo-Nazis flood social media with calls for violence.* [Online] Available at: https://www.nbcnews.com/news/us-news/-hamas-extremists-neo-nazis-flood-social-media-calls-violence-rcna121043 [Accessed 01 11 2023].

DiMaggio, A. R., 2022. *Rising facism in America.* New York: Routledge.

Duffin, M., 2021. *Pittsburgh honors synagogue shooting victims and combats hate with global summit.* [Online] Available at: https://www.state.gov/dipnote-u-s-department-of-state-official-blog/pittsburgh-honors-synagogue-shooting-victims-and-combats-hate-with-global-summit/ [Accessed 23 08 2023].

DW, 2019. *'Radical right-wing' motives in Munich 2016 attack.* [Online] Available at: https://www.dw.com/en/germany-2016-munich-attack-had-radical-right-wing-motives-say-police/a-50991641 [Accessed 23 08 2023].

Ebner, J., 2019. *Who are Europe's far-right identitarians?.* [Online] Available at: https://www.politico.eu/article/who-are-europe-far-right-identitarians-austria-generation-identity-martin-sellner/ [Accessed 20 04 2022].

ECtHR, 2023. *Hate speech – Factsheet.* [Online] Available at: https://www.echr.coe.int/documents/d/echr/fs_hate_speech_eng [Accessed 19 11 2023].

Ehrenberg, J., 2022. *Whate nationalisme and the Republican party*. Abingdon: Routledge.

Evans, R., 2019. *Shitposting, inspirational terrorism, and the Christchurch Mosque Massacre*. [Online] Available at: https://www.bellingcat.com/news/rest-of-world /2019/03/15/shitposting-inspirational-terrorism-and-the-christchurch-mosque -massacre/ [Accessed 12 04 2022].

Fieldstadt, E., 2019. *James Alex Fields, driver in deadly car attack at Charlottesville rally, sentenced to life in prison*. [Online] Available at: https://www.nbcnews.com /news/us-news/james-alex-fields-driver-deadly-car-attack-charlottesville-rally -sentenced-n1024436 [Accessed 23 08 2023].

Flores, R., 2023. *Man who killed 23 people in Texas Walmart shooting targeting Latinos sentenced to 90 life terms by federal judge*. [Online] Available at: https:// edition.cnn.com/2023/07/07/us/el-paso-walmart-shooter-sentencing-friday/index .html [Accessed 23 08 2023].

Fowles, S., 2022. *Far-right conspiracy theories are now embedded in the UK mainstream*. [Online] Available at: https://www.opendemocracy.net/en/far-right -mainstream-conspiracy-theory-uk/ [Accessed 24 08 2022].

FRA, 2012. *Making hate crime visible in the European Union: Acknowledging victims' rights*. Vienna: European Union Agency for Fundamental Rights.

Gajanan, M., 2019. *'Resiliency, strength and community collaboration': How tree of life synagogue is moving forward 1 year after tragedy*. [Online] Available at: https://time.com/5710735/tree-of-life-one-year-rebuild/ [Accessed 23 08 2023].

Ganor, B., 2010. *Defining terrorism – Is one man's terrorist another man's freedom fighter*. [Online] Available at: https://www.ict.org.il/Article/1123/Defining -Terrorism-Is-One-Mans-Terrorist-Another-Mans-Freedom-Fighter#gsc.tab=0 [Accessed 18 04 2022].

Ganor, B., 2021. Understanding the motivations of "Lone Wolf" terrorists. *Perspective on Terrorism,* 15(2), pp. 23–32.

Georgiadou, V., Rori, L. & Roumanias, C., 2019. *Is the resurgence of Europe's far-right a cultural or an economic phenomenon?*. [Online] Available at: https://blogs .lse.ac.uk/europpblog/2019/10/16/is-the-resurgence-of-europes-far-right-a-cultural -or-an-economic-phenomenon/ [Accessed 15 07 2023].

GOV.UK, 2023. *The terrorism acts in 2021 – Report of the independent reviewer of terrorism legislation (accessible)*. [Online] Available at: https://www.gov.uk /government/publications/the-terrorism-acts-in-2021/the-terrorism-acts-in-2021 -report-of-the-independent-reviewer-of-terrorism-legislation-accessible [Accessed 23 08 2023].

Griffin, R., 2010. Interregnum or endgame? The radical right in the 'post-fascist' era. *Journal of Political Idologies,* 5(2), pp. 163–178.

Helmore, E. & Beckett, L., 2017. *How Charlottesville became the symbolic prize of the far right*. [Online] Available at: https://www.theguardian.com/world/2017/aug /13/charlottesville-white-supremacists-far-right-donald-trump-confederate-statue [Accessed 23 08 2023].

Hern, A., 2020. *5G conspiracy theories fuel attacks on telecom workers*. [Online] Available at: https://www.theguardian.com/business/2020/may/07/5g-conspiracy -theories-attacks-telecoms-covid [Accessed 01 11 2023].

Hietanen, M. & Eddebo, J., 2023. Towards a definition of hate speech—With a focus on online contexts. *Journal of Communication Inquiry,* 47(4), pp. 440–458.

Hume, T., 2016. *Munich gunman planned attack for a year, officials say*. [Online] Available at: https://edition.cnn.com/2016/07/24/europe/germany-munich-shooting /index.html [Accessed 25 08 2023].

Hutchinson, B., 2023. *Israel-hamas war: Timeline and key developments in month of war.* [Online] Available at: https://abcnews.go.com/International/timeline-surprise
-rocket-attack-hamas-israel/story?id=103816006#:~:text=An%20estimated%202
%2C200%20rockets%20were,to%20the%20Israel%20Defense%20Forces.&text=
Armed%20Hamas%20terrorists%2C%20many%20on,in%20kibbutzim%20an
[Accessed 19 11 2023].

IEP, 2022. *Global terrorism index 2022. Measuring the impact of terrorism.* Sydney: Institute for Economics and peace.

Inglehart, R. F. & Norris, P., 2016. Trump, Brexit, and the rise of populism: Economic have-nots and cultural backlash. *Faculty Research Working Paper Series*, 8, pp. 1–53.

Jackson, J., Heal, A. & Wall, T., 2021. Facebook *"still too slow to act on groups profiting from Covid conspiracy theories."* [Online] Available at: https://www.theguardian
.com/technology/2021/apr/11/facebook-still-too-slow-to-act-on-groups-profiting
-from-covid-conspiracy-theories [Accessed 24 11 2023].

Janin, M. & Deverell, F., 2020. *Covid-19: Far right violent extremism and tech platforms' response.* [Online] Available at: https://www.fondapol.org/en/study/
covid-19-far-right-violent-extremism-and-tech-plateforms-response/ [Accessed 01 11 2023].

Jarvis, L., 2022. Critical terrorism studies and the far-right: beyond problems and solutions?. *Critical Studies on Terrorism*, 15(1), pp. 13–37.

Johnson, B. & Parry, K., 2022. Jo Cox, public feeling and British political culture: #MoreInCommon. *European Journal of Cultural Studies*, 25(5), pp. 1504–1526.

Jones, S. G., 2018. *The rise of far-right extremism in the United States.* [Online] Available at: https://www.csis.org/analysis/rise-far-right-extremism-united-states [Accessed 1 08 2022].

Kendi, I., 2019. *The day shithole entered the presidential Lexicon.* [Online] Available at: https://www.theatlantic.com/politics/archive/2019/01/shithole-countries
/580054/ [Accessed 07 08 2023].

Keneally, M., 2018. *What to know about the violent Charlottesville protests and anniversary rallies.* [Online] Available at: https://abcnews.go.com/US/happen
-charlottesville-protest-anniversary-weekend/story?id=57107500 [Accessed 12 04 2022].

Kenes, B., 2021. *Boogaloo bois: Violent anti-Establishment extremists in festive Hawaiian shirts.* [Online] Available at: https://www.populismstudies.org/boogaloo
-bois-violent-anti-establishment-extremists-in-festive-hawaiian-shirts/ [Accessed 27 08 2022].

King, R. D., DeMarco, L. M. & VandenBerg, R. J., 2017. Similar for a distance: A comparison of terrorism and hate crime. In: *The handbook of the criminology of terrorism.* Oxford: Wiley Blackwell.

Koehler, D., 2016. Right-Wing extremism and terrorism in Europe current developments and issues for the future. *PRISM*, 6(2), pp. 85–99.

Krueger, A. B. & Maleckova, J., 2002. *Does poverty cause terrorism?. [Online] Available at: https://newrepublic.com/article/91841/does-poverty-cause-terrorism [Accessed 08 08 2022].*

Langley, H., 2020. *Rep. Adam Schiff told Google and Twitter to step up their fight against coronavirus misinformation with an unexpected message: Be more like Facebook.* [Online] Available at: https://www.businessinsider.com/adam-schiff
-tells-google-and-twitter-to-look-to-facebook-2020-4?r=US&IR=T [Accessed 25 11 2023].

Laqueur, W., 1999. *The new terrorism: Fanaticism and the arms of mass destruction.* New York: Oxford University Press.

Laub, Z., 2019. *Hate speech on social media: Global comparisons.* [Online] Available at: https://www.cfr.org/backgrounder/hate-speech-social-media-global -comparisons [Accessed 12 04 2022].

Lavrogna, A., 2020. *Cybercrimes. Critical issues in a global context.* 1st ed. London: Macmillian.

Loadenthal, M., Hausserman, S. & Thierry, M., 2022. Atomwaffen division, contemporary digital facism, and Insurrectionary accelerationism. In: *Cyberhate: The far right in the digital age.* Lanham: Lexington, pp. 87–118.

Love, G., 2007. 'What's the big idea?': Oswald Mosley, the British Union of fascists and generic fascism. *Journal of Contemporary History,* 42(3), pp. 447–468.

Lowe, D., 2016. *Jo Cox murder reminds us that terrorism comes in many forms.* [Online] Available at: https://theconversation.com/jo-cox-murder-reminds-us-that -terrorism-comes-in-many-forms-69372 [Accessed 25 08 2023].

Lunch, S. & Caspani, M., 2023. *White Florida shooter who killed three Black victims bought guns legally.* [Online] Available at: https://www.reuters.com/world/us/ sheriff-identifies-shooter-jacksonville-florida-who-killed-3-people-2023-08-27/ [Accessed 28 08 2023].

Macklin, G., 2019a. The Christchurch attacks: Livestream terror in the viral video age. *CTC Sentinel,* 12(6), pp. 18–30.

Macklin, G., 2019b. The El Paso terrorist attack: The chain reaction. *CTC-Sentinel,* 11, pp. 1–26.

Magnus, K., 2022. Right-wing populism, social identity theory, and resistance to public health measures during the COVID-19 pandemic. *International Journal of Public Health,* 67, pp. 1–5.

Mahan, S. & Griset, P. L., 2013. *Terrorism in perspective.* 3rd ed. Thousand Oaks (California): Sage.

Marchal, N. & Au, H., 2020. "Coronavirus EXPLAINED": YouTube, COVID-19, and the socio-technical mediation of expertise. *Social Media+Society,* 6(3), pp. 1–4.

Marino, F., 2023. *Economic insecurity and the rise of the radical right.* [Online] Available at: https://www.newslettereuropean.eu/economic-insecurity-and-the-rise -of-the-radical-right/ [Accessed 20 07 2023].

Martin, G. & Pranger, F., 2019. *Terrorism. An international perspective.* London: Sage.

Mason, R., 2023. 'An activist blob': Tory party attacks on lawyers – a timeline. [Online] Available at: https://www.theguardian.com/politics/2023/aug/16/tory -party-criticisms-legal-professionals-timeline [Accessed 30 11 2023].

Massie, G., Rissman, K., Rahaman Sarkar, A. & Sommerlad, J., 2023. *Ron DeSantis booed at Jacksonville vigil as police say racist Florida shooter bought weapons legally – live.* [Online] Available at: https://www.independent.co.uk/news/world /americas/crime/florida-shooting-bahama-breeze-jacksonville-b2400418.html [Accessed 28 08 2023].

Medina, J., Mele, C. & Murphy, H., 2019. *One dead in synagogue shooting near San Diego; officials call it hate crime.* [Online] Available at: https://www.nytimes.com /2019/04/27/us/poway-synagogue-shooting.html [Accessed 23 08 2023].

Meta, 2023a. *Hate speech. In Facebook community standards, transparency center.* [Online] Available at: https://transparency.fb.com/en-gb/policies/community -standards/hate-speech [Accessed 25 08 2023].

Meta, 2023b. *Terms of service.* [Online] Available at: https://www.facebook.com/legal /225652215540499 [Accessed 25 08 2023].

Miller-Idriss, C., 2022. *Hate in the homeland. The new global far right.* Princeton: Princeton University Press.

Miller-Idriss, M., 2021. White supremacist extremism and the far right in the US. *Political Extremism and Radicalism: Far-Right Groups in America.*

Mills, C. E., Freilich, J. D. & Chermmak, S. M., 2017. Extreme hatred: Revisiting the hate crime and terrorism relationship to determine wether they are "Close Cousins" or "Distant Relative". *Crime & Delinquency,* 63(10), pp. 1191–1223.

Mossburg, C., 2021. *Poway synagogue shooter sentenced to second life sentence.* [Online] Available at: https://edition.cnn.com/2021/12/28/us/poway-synagogue -shooter-sentenced/index.html [Accessed 25 08 2023].

Mudde, C., 2007. *Populist radical right parties in Europe.* New York: Cambridge University Press.

Mudde, C., 2019. *The far right today.* Cambridge: Polity Press.

Munk, T., 2022. *The rise of politically motivated cyber attacks. Actors, attacks and cybersecurity.* London: Routledge.

Nasr, 2021. *Far-right crime hits record high in Germany.* [Online] Available at: https:// www.reuters.com/world/europe/germany-arrests-suspect-over-hate-mail-using-neo -nazi-acronym-2021-05-04/#:~:text=Far%2Dright%20offences%20were%20up ,collecting%20such%20data%20in%202001 [Accessed 21 08 2023].

Nelson, L. & Swanson, K., 2017. *Full transcript: Donald Trump's press conference defending the Charlottesville rally* [Online] Available at: https://www.vox.com /2017/8/15/16154028/trump-press-conference-transcript-charlottesville [Accessed 12 04 2022].

New York State Attorney General, 2022. *Investigative report on the role of online platforms in the tragic mass shooting in Buffalo on May 14, 2022.* New York: Office of the New York State Attorney General Letitia James.

Oltermann, P., 2020. *Halle synagogue attack: Gunman sentenced to life in prison.* [Online] Available at: https://www.theguardian.com/world/2020/dec/21/halle -synagogue-attack-gunman-sentenced-life-prison-stephan-balliet [Accessed 25 08 2023].

Oltermann, P. & Connolly, K., 2020. *Germany shooting: Far-right gunman kills 10 in Hanau.* [Online] Available at: https://www.theguardian.com/world/2020/feb/19 /shooting-germany-hanau-dead-several-people-shisha-near-frankfurt [Accessed 25 08 2023].

OSCE, 2009a. *Hate crime laws. A practical guide.* Warshawa: Office for Democratic Institutions and Human Rights (ODIHR).

OSCE, 2009b. *Decision No. 9/09 combatting hate crimes.* [Online] Available at: https:// www.osce.org/files/f/documents/d/9/40695.pdf [Accessed 07 08 2023].

Pantucci, R., 2011. *A typology of lone wolves: Preliminary analysis of lone Islamist terrorists.* s.l.: s.n.

Perlstein, R., 2017. *I thought I understood the American right. Trump proved me wrong.* [Online] Available at: https://www.nytimes.com/2017/04/11/magazine/i-thought-i -understood-the-american-right-trump-proved-me-wrong.html [Accessed 07 08 2023].

Perry, J., 2016. A shared global perspective on hate crime?. *Criminal Justice Policy Review,* 27(6), pp. 610–619.

Potok, M., 2016. *The year in hate and extremism.* [Online] Available at: https://www.splcenter.org/fighting-hate/intelligence-report/2016/year-hate-and-extremism [Accessed 12 04 2022].

Ramirez-Simon, D. & Yang, M., 2023. *Florida shooting: Gunman left messages of hate before killing three Black people.* [Online] Available at: https://www.theguardian.com/us-news/2023/aug/26/dollar-general-store-shooting-jacksonville-florida [Accessed 27 08 2023].

Reals, T. & D'Agata, C., 2023. *Why did Hamas attack Israel, and why now?.* [Online] Available at: https://www.cbsnews.com/news/why-did-hamas-attack-israel-and-why-now/ [Accessed 25 10 2023].

Rebechi, A. & Rohde, N., 2023. Economic insecurity, racial anxiety, and right-wing populism. *Review of Income and Wealth,* 69(3), pp. 701–724.

Robertson, C., Mele, C. & Tavernis, S., 2018. *11 killed in synagogue Massacre; suspect charged with 29 counts.* [Online] Available at: https://www.nytimes.com/2018/10/27/us/active-shooter-pittsburgh-synagogue-shooting.html [Accessed 23 08 2023].

Rothschild, M., 2021. *The storm is upon us.* London: Monoray.

Schmidt, N., McKenzie, R., Picheta, R. & Kottasova, I., 2020. *Nine killed at two shisha bars in Germany in suspected far-right attack.* [Online] Available at: https://edition.cnn.com/2020/02/19/europe/hanau-germany-shootings-intl/index.html [Accessed 25 08 2023].

Schori Liang, C. & Cross, M. J., 2020. *White crusade: How to prevent right-Wing. s.l.:* GCSP.

Schweppe, J. & Tong, K., 2021. What is a hate crime?. *Cogent Social Sciences,* 7(1), pp. 1–15.

Sengupta, K., 2016. *The dark web is a dangerous new frontier for those who try to keep terrorists at bay.* [Online] Available at: https://www.independent.co.uk/voices/germany-munich-attack-shooting-ali-david-sonboly-a7212151.html [Accessed 25 08 2023].

Shimamoto, E., 2004. Rethinking hate crime in the age of terror. *University of Missouri-Kansas City Law Review,* 72, pp. 829–844.

Sinnar, S., 2022. Hate crimes, terrorism, and the framing of White supremacist violence. *California Law Review,* 110(2), pp. 489–565.

Skoczylis, A. & Andrews, S., 2022. Strain theory, resilience, and far-right extremism: The impact of gender, life experiences and the Internet. *Critical Studies on Terrorism,* 15(1), pp. 143–168.

Smith-Spark, L., 2021. *A far-right extremist killed 77 people in Norway. A decade on, 'the hatred is still out there' but attacker's influence is seen as low.* [Online] Available at: https://edition.cnn.com/2021/07/22/europe/anders-breivik-july-22-attacks-norway-anniversary-cmd-intl/index.html [Accessed 25 08 2023].

Sommer, W., 2023. *Trust the plan.* London: 4th Estate.

Steiner, H., Alston, P. & Goodman, R., 2007. *International human rights in context. Law, politics, moral.* Oxford: Oxford University Press.

Stenzler-Koblentz, L., Chavez, K. & Klempner, U., 2023. *Countering hate in the digital age: Analysing far-right extremist responses to the Israel-Hamas war.* [Online] Available at: https://ict.org.il/far-right-response-to-israel-hamas-war/ [Accessed 01 11 2023].

Talley, I. & Levy, R., 2021. *Extremists posted plans of Capitol attack online.* [Online] Available at: https://www.wsj.com/livecoverage/biden-trump-electoral-college-certification-congress/card/x1dwwPqnJM1XfQh5LaUj [Accessed 17 08 2023].

The Buffalo News, 2023. *Complete coverage: 10 killed, 3 wounded in mass shooting at Buffalo supermarket.* [Online] Available at: https://buffalonews.com/news/local/complete-coverage-10-killed-3-wounded-in-mass-shooting-at-buffalo-supermarket/collection_e8c7df32-d402-11ec-9ebc-e39ca6890844.html [Accessed 27 08 2023].

The ICSR, 2021. *Academic and practical research working group White paper: Extremism research horizons.* [Online] Available at: https://gifct.org/wp-content/uploads/2021/07/GIFCT-APRWG-WhitePaper.pdf [Accessed 01 11 2023].

The White House, 2021. *National strategy for countering domestic terrorism.* Washington, DC: National Security Council.

Theocharis, Y. et al., 2023. Does the platform matter? Social media and COVID-19 conspiracy theory beliefs in 17 countries. *New Media & Society,* 25(12), pp. 3412–3437.

UN, 1948. *Universal declaration of human rights.* [Online] Available at: https://www.un.org/en/about-us/universal-declaration-of-human-rights [Accessed 26 08 2023].

UN, 1966. *International covenant on civil and political rights.* [Online] Available at: https://www.ohchr.org/en/instruments-mechanisms/instruments/international-covenant-civil-and-political-rights [Accessed 26 12 2023].

UN, 2019. *Hate speech vs freedom of speech.* [Online] Available at: https://www.un.org/en/hate-speech/understanding-hate-speech/hate-speech-versus-freedom-of-speech [Accessed 11 08 2023].

UN, 2020. *United Nations strategy and plan of action on hate speech.* New York: UN.

UN, 2023. *What is hate speech?.* [Online] Available at: https://www.un.org/en/hate-speech/understanding-hate-speech/what-is-hate-speech [Accessed 27 08 2023].

Unesco, 2023. *What you need to know about hate speech.* [Online] Available at: https://www.unesco.org/en/countering-hate-speech/need-know [Accessed 27 08 2023].

United Nations, 2022. *Hate crime.* [Online] Available at: https://www.ohchr.org/en/taxonomy/term/897 [Accessed 12 08 2022].

UNODC, 2009. *Fequently asked questions on international law aspects on countering terrorism.* Vienna: United Nations.

Vitali, A., Hunt, K. & Thortp V. F., 2018. *Trump referred to Haiti and African nations as 'shithole' countries.* [Online] Available at: https://www.nbcnews.com/politics/white-house/trump-referred-haiti-african-countries-shithole-nations-n836946 [Accessed 18 08 2022].

Warburton, N., 2022. *Everyday philosophy: Elon Musk, the 'free speech absolutist'.* [Online] Available at: https://www.theneweuropean.co.uk/everyday-philosophy-elon-musk-the-free-speech-absolutist/ [Accessed 03 09 2023].

Warburton, N. & Franco, J., 2013. Should there be limits on hate speech?. *Index on Censorship,* 42(2), pp. 150–152.

Weimann, G., 2012. Lone Wolves in cyberspace. *The Centre for the Study of Terrorism and Political Violence: Journal of Terrorism Research,* 3(2), pp. 75–90.

Wilson, J., 2017. *Charlottesville: Far-right crowd with torches encircles counter-protest group.* [Online] Available at: https://www.theguardian.com/world/2017/aug/12/charlottesville-far-right-crowd-with-torches-encircles-counter-protest-group [Accessed 23 08 2023].

Wintour, P., Burke, J. & Livsey, A., 2018. *'There's no other word but racist': Trump's global rebuke for 'shithole' remark.* [Online] Available at: https://www.theguardian.com/us-news/2018/jan/12/unkind-divisive-elitist-international-outcry-over-trumps-shithole-countries-remark [Accessed 07 08 2023].

Yar, M. & Steinmetz, K. F., 2019. *Cybercrime and society.* 3rd ed. London: Sage.

3 Web of Hate

The Digital Landscape of Far-Right Extremism

Far-Right Extremism and the Online World

In the connected world, the idea of public spaces is different from traditional, in-person ones. New devices and technologies have significantly changed how these groups form and interact. Modern technology and online platforms improve involvement, communication, and the ability to unite people for various causes. They give a voice to less-heard communities and help spread their ideas (Rodríguez-Suárez et al., 2021, p. 47; Caiani, 2021; González-Bailón, 2014, p. 209; Vergeer & Hermans, 2008, p. 37). Social media opens up channels for self-expression, enabling users to connect with broader audiences and foster collaborative relationships. It creates communities of fans and enthusiasts united by common interests or causes, encouraging interaction and collective engagement around shared passions (Nacos, 2019, p. 366). Extreme far-right movements around the world are becoming more popular. They share a view that favours their ethnic group first and often claim to speak for a 'silent majority' that they believe is ignored by the elite and out-of-touch political leaders (Arzheimer, 2009; Bélanger et al., 2019, p. 910; Mudde, 2007; Backlund & Jungar, 2019).

The Impact of Online Proximity and Global Connectivity

While in-person conversations can convey urgent messages, they lack online communication's immediacy and enduring impact. The Internet's ability to preserve and repeatedly surface aggressive or hurtful content magnifies its detrimental effect on victims. Additionally, the global interconnectivity of the Internet allows perpetrators and their victims to be worlds apart, which reduces the consequences of direct, face-to-face confrontations. This aspect of online interaction amplifies the harm and adds a layer of detachment, enhancing the reach and impact of harmful content (Wallace, 2016, p. 117). Far-right networks are expanding internationally, particularly in Europe and North America, using the Internet as their primary propaganda tool. These groups use dedicated websites, social media, and various online content to promote their views publicly and secretly communicate in protected online spaces

DOI: 10.4324/9781003297888-3

(Jones, 2018). They can effortlessly swap information, exchange tactics, and draw motivation from extremist actions committed globally. For instance, Breivik's assaults in Norway inspired later attacks in New Zealand and the US. The driving force behind these attacks was detailed and broadly circulated through online manifestos and discussions in web forums (Chapters 2 and 3) (Byman, 2022, p. 6).

The Internet has been pivotal in extending the reach and sway of these groups. Its capacity to eliminate conventional geographical and temporal limits enables swift and fluid communication, which benefits far-right groups. Aggressors take refuge in the online realm, utilising it for confrontational actions such as trolling and making threats (Wallace, 2016, p. 116; Chen & Lu, 2017, p. 110). Online platforms often act like echo chambers, where users only see views that support their own and not those that challenge them. This can lead to cognitive confusion, a lack of comprehensive understanding and biases (Chen & Lu, 2017, p. 109). The anonymity afforded by the Internet permits users to indulge in more confrontational speech, aware that they might encounter fewer repercussions for their actions (Wallace, 2016, p. 117). This environment helps normalise extremist views, making them seem more acceptable to those within the echo chamber and potentially attracting new followers.

Understanding the Internet

The Internet, which includes the Surface Web, Deep Web, and Dark Web, is an extensive network of interconnected computers. It originated in 1969 as a project of the US Department of Defense and underwent a significant transformation in 1989 with Tim Berners-Lee's introduction of the World Wide Web (WWW) (Norman, 2017, p. 26; Berners-Lee et al., 1994, p. 76; Gohel, 2014, pp. 22–23; Yar & Steinmetz, 2019). Navigating the WWW is generally user-friendly, but exploring areas like the Deep and Dark Web are more challenging. These two webs have inherent barriers in their design, affecting how content is indexed and made searchable, making them less accessible than the Surface Web (Hoffman, 2022, p. 5). The Surface Web, indexed by search engines like Google, serves public purposes such as e-commerce and research (Gohel, 2014, pp. 22–23; Munk, 2022, p. 33). Where the Surface Web is accessible to everyone, there is less access to the more private areas in the Deep Web. The Deep Web contains databases often necessitating access permissions, making its content not universally accessible (Hoffman, 2022, pp. 5–6; Munk, 2022, p. 3; Yar & Steinmetz, 2019, pp. 8–10; Bin He et al., 2007).

The Migration of Extremist Groups Online

The Dark Web constitutes further issues as it is a tool for anonymous communication online. The Dark Web, a subset of the Deep Web, is accessible via specialised tools like the Onion Router (TOR) and is recognised for its encrypted content prioritising anonymity activities (Wallance, 2016, p. 9; Faizan & Khan, 2019; TOR, 2020; Hoffman, 2022, p. 6; Munk, 2022, pp. 38–40). This hidden part of the Internet is a haven for illegal activities, making it a hotspot for extremist actions and white nationalist presence. However, when individuals and groups get de-platformed on the Surface Web, they move to less visible spaces to continue their activities. After being de-platformed by Google and GoDaddy, the neo-Nazi website Daily Stormer found refuge on the Dark Web (Hoffman, 2022, p. 6). This web has emerged as a safe space for those seeking to evade the stringent measures against extremist content by mainstream tech companies. Groups often accuse platforms like Facebook of stifling free speech by banning users associated with extremism.

Consequently, there has been a notable migration to the Dark Web. Initially, NeinChan, a Dark Web forum dedicated to extreme topics, including violent events and attacker manifestos, drew these users. However, following NeinChan's closure, its users moved to Neuchan. This migration pattern continued; after Neuchan ceased operations in 2021, extremists shifted to 16chan. They eventually settled on a smaller Dark Web site, creating a new board known as /cob, a term popularised by Tarrant on 8chan (Chapter 5). This development shows that efforts to tackle extremism on mainstream platforms have unintentionally pushed some of these groups to lesser-known, unregulated spaces. On the Dark Web, they become harder to control, often shielded by encryption and operating out of sight (Crawford, 2022; Baele et al., 2021, p. 69).

Information Overload and Source Credibility

The preference for visual content in information sharing has become increasingly significant, with far-reaching implications in the political arena. During the 2016 US Presidential Election campaign, visually rich tweets from candidates Trump and Clinton notably garnered more shares than their text-only counterparts. This trend highlights the influential role of visuals in capturing attention and disseminating messages during elections (Chadwick & Vaccari, 2019, p. 2). The widespread sharing of visual content can sometimes overshadow the need for factual accuracy, making it easier to spread unverified or misleading information. News circulated through various channels becomes more challenging for users to critically assess and verify, especially when visuals are designed to be eye-catching or evoke strong emotional responses (Chapter 5).

Furthermore, the algorithmic design of many platforms tends to amplify already popular content, creating a feedback loop where posts that are frequently liked or shared gain even more visibility, regardless of their accuracy. This can lead to a skewed representation of information and understanding of key elements of the political agenda , (Sundar, 2008; Thorson, 2008; Tandoc Jr.

et al., 2018, p. 139; Wardle & Derakhshan, 2017, p. 13). The impact of this visual preference on platforms is profound, contributing significantly to the proliferation of unverified information, particularly during critical times like elections.

Online outlets now form a significant part of the democratic process, from political campaigns to holding officials accountable (Culloty & Suiter, 2021, p. 86). However, unlike traditional media, these private platforms are not subject to the same regulations. This discrepancy becomes apparent when politically motivated entities use social media to spread information and misinformation promoting a particular narrative to wow the voters (Kang et al., 2011, p. 721; Tandoc Jr. et al., 2018, p. 139). During Trump's 2016 Presidential Election campaign and tenure in the White House, neo-Nazis, white supremacists, conspiracy theorists, and other extremist factions gained notable visibility. Previously seen as marginal groups, their expansion was fuelled by far-right media outlets and the spread of online disinformation (Neiwert, 2017, pp. 2–3). Trump's rise to power was not only a result of the intense branding and use of his Twitter handle, @ RealDonaldTrump, but also by a broader online coalition and a systematic use of various online platforms and visual and non-visual communications. Aside from traditional Republicans and evangelical conservatives, a crucial part of his base included tech-savvy young men from political fringes, many of whom originated from the 4Chan message board (Chapter 4) (Singer & Brookings, 2018, p. 174).

Digital Disguise: How Far-Right Groups Mainstream Extremism in the Digital Age

Alternative far-right media like Breitbart and Infowars have been shaking up the traditional news landscape, often spreading anti-immigrant and anti-elite stories. Groups like the US National Policy Institute (NPI) use a pseudo-intellectual style to give extremist views a veneer of legitimacy. In collaboration with Radix Journal, NPI has created a platform that features podcasts and videos, all echoing extreme far-right ideologies but concealed in scholarly language (Holt et al., 2022, p. 386). This approach gives their extremist arguments a deceptive legitimacy and broadens their appeal. NPI's strategic online presence is vital to how far-right groups bring their ideologies into the mainstream and update their digital-era tactics. The impact of social media in disseminating both information and misinformation is profound. Algorithms can intensify societal splits by perpetuating a cycle of misinformation (Sundar, 2008; Thorson, 2008; Tandoc Jr. et al., 2018, p. 139; Wardle & Derakhshan, 2017, p. 13). This method of sharing specific narratives online not only strengthens group unity but also reinforces political or ideological beliefs among followers. While social media has the potential to diversify discussions, its algorithms can also entrench divisions by filtering content within echo chambers and bolstering pre-existing opinions (Chadwick & Vaccari, 2019).

Introduction to Digital Extremism

The benefits of online communication extend beyond just legitimate political movements. Terrorist organisations and individuals have migrated from traditional media to the versatility of online platforms. They use these spaces to intimidate opponents, garner support, validate violence, and project legitimacy. Online platforms aid in radicalisation, recruitment, operational planning, and fundraising (Nacos, 2019, p. 364). The rise of niche social media and a booming gaming sector has accelerated the spread of far-right extremist messages, causing more splintering within the movement. This is exacerbated by decentralised, blockchain-based platforms that resist content moderation.

Mechanisms of Online Far-Right Extremism

The digital landscape, fragmented in nature, presents varied opportunities to far-right factions. Given the diversity across platforms and groups, assuming a universal online behavioural norm would be misleading. Far-right groups use the web to further political causes, often sidestepping the label of cyberterrorism. Although these groups are commonly linked to white supremacy ideologies, they take on diverse forms (Chapter 2) (Holt et al., 2018, p. 405). Extremist groups have refined their online techniques, creating content tailored for radical audiences. They have adeptly balanced hardline stances with efforts to draw in new followers. They diversify their communication and funding sources by leveraging various platforms. While many of these activities are visible on mainstream outlets, others hide in the darker recesses of the web and encrypted channels, complicating surveillance efforts (Scholz, 2020). These groups and individuals, especially those leaning far-right ideologies, thrive on a 'leaderless resistance' model – prioritising individual actions over formal hierarchy. This decentralised nature is apt for online ecosystems, where hierarchy is problematic to uphold. This model makes it difficult to trace the group members and their communications, allowing the members to operate in the shadows (Bowman-Grieve, 2015, p. 89).

Online platforms, mainly social media, have intensified the spread of far-right ideologies, recruitment, and radicalisation. The contagious nature of online content facilitates the proliferation of extremist narratives and disinformation. Grasping online radicalisation requires understanding the strategies and platforms these extremists use. The US-based neo-Nazi group Stormfront, often seen as the pioneer in openly promoting hate online, connects white supremacists globally (Holt et al., 2022, p. 381). For instance, its UK branch identifies as a national socialist group with a significant following. In Germany, parties like the National Democratic Party of Germany (NDP) and The Third Path (III) use online platforms to rally anti-refugee, racist, anti-Semitic and anti-Muslim sentiments, often by twisting data or fabricating immigrant-related crimes, leading to organised and sometimes violent protests (Koehler, 2016, p. 95; Counter Extremism Project, 2023; BBC News, 2021).

Russia's Involvement with European Far-Right Groups

The 2022 Russian full-scale war against Ukraine, framed as 'de-Nazification', marked a significant moment in far-right extremist propaganda (Europol, 2023, p. 53). Far-right extremists supporting either Ukraine or Russia are circulating online messages on white supremacy, ethno-nationalism, and anti-Semitism, leading to a fragmented and confusing narrative. This divergence has potentially widened their audience appeal (Europol, 2023, p. 53; Cole, 2022). During the early stages of the invasion, extremist factions in France, Germany, and the UK pointed the finger at NATO and the US, simultaneously circulating pro-Russian propaganda. Far-right extremist groups in these countries predominantly favoured Russia over Ukraine, and this stance can be linked to the conspiracy theories and falsehoods narratives that were being shared across these three nations (KCL, 2022). Russia maintains links with extreme far-right groups like the Russian Imperial Movement (RIM), designated as a terrorist organisation by the US, and The Base, a neo-Nazi group operated from St. Petersburg (Wilson, 2020; Pantucci, 2023; BBC News, 2020; Pompeo, 2020). These far-right groups are involved in training and supporting extremists across Europe and in war zones like Ukraine. Additionally, Russia's connections extend to European political entities. Both Germany's AfD party and the Reichsbürger movement are suspected of receiving Moscow's support. Similarly, the UK's Britain First was investigated for financial ties, which demonstrates Russia's widespread engagement with far-right groups in Europe (Pantucci, 2023; Mulhall, 2022; Cole, 2022).

Digital Anonymity, Encryption, and Secure Communication

Digital platforms transform the political landscape, creating networks prioritising connectivity and swift information exchange. These platforms, driven by digitalisation, enable in-depth debates and enrich interactions within political communities (Munk, 2022, p. 37). A vital aspect of the online realm is the anonymity it offers. Unlike face-to-face interactions, the Internet allows individuals to selectively disclose or hide personal details like age, gender, race, or location, crafting a customised digital identity (Attrill, 2015, p. 10; Holt et al., 2022, p. 14). Online anonymity serves technical and social functions, allowing users to safeguard their identity. Often viewed as a privacy tool, it can also act as a barrier against online surveillance (Sardá et al., 2019). However, achieving complete anonymity in the digital world is complex and influenced by various factors and goals. End-to-end encryption is a crucial element in this context. This is a feature particularly valued by far-right extremist groups. This encryption ensures user anonymity by keeping messages private, even from law enforcement agencies. While encrypted apps do not inherently indicate extremist intentions, they are favoured by those seeking to evade legal repercussions for extremist language or violent schemes (Braddock et al., 2022).

Encryption turns data into a format only the intended recipient can read, ensuring confidentiality and integrity. Once exclusive to military and intelligence services, strong encryption is now widely available to the public for securing various types of communication and data storage (UN, 2015, p. 4; Koehler, 2016). Supporters of far-right extremism often connect online, using encrypted forums that offer anonymity, making them hard to track. Some form loose affiliations with global organisations like the US-based AWD (now the National Socialist Order). Additionally, US organisations like The Base and Hammerskin Nation heavily influence other groups. These networks mainly operate covertly and are inclined to act in small cells or individually, posing significant threats of violent attacks. Many members are vulnerable due to psychological or socio-economic issues, and the glorification of extremist attackers online heightens the risk of inspiring new acts of violence (Europol, 2022, pp. 53–54).

The Role of Encryption in Modern Digital Security

Numerous digital tools created to bolster privacy provide advantages unmatched by offline communication methods, particularly relevant to far-right extremism. Encryption is central in this landscape, safeguarding messages between two parties from interception. It renders communications accessible only to individuals with the appropriate key. TOR extends these capabilities, concealing a user's location and online actions via a network of servers. Although TOR is highly effective for evading political censorship, it is frequently utilised for illicit activities, a factor often exploited by far-right extremist groups (Lavorgna, 2020, p. 75; TOR Project, 2022; Holt et al., 2022, p. 14; Jardine, 2018; Sardá et al., 2019; Yar & Steinmetz, 2019, p. 98). Virtual private networks (VPNs) and proxy servers enhance online privacy for users by rerouting Internet traffic and obscuring IP addresses. This additional anonymity layer complicates tracing online activities by third parties. Yet, they do not guarantee complete security. A notable limitation is the centralisation of user data within VPNs, presenting a potential vulnerability to exploitation. This security vulnerability can impact the operations of far-right extremists online (Lavorgna, 2020, p. 75; Munk, 2018, p. 231; Sardá et al., 2019).

End-to-end encryption, essential in modern data security, implements a cryptographic technique based on a shared secret key exclusive to the sender and recipient. It encrypts messages with a public key, but only the matched private key can unlock them, creating an impenetrable two-key shield. This method effectively renders intermediaries like ISPs or servers powerless to intercept these communications. In scenarios like far-right extremism, where secrecy is paramount, this level of encryption is a game-changer. It arms extremist groups with a crucial tool, keeping their communications under lock and safe from prying eyes, thus significantly aiding in their covert planning and operations (Lutkevich & Bacon, 2021; Sardá et al., 2019). With the advent

Table 3.1 Summary of the Internet and Virtual Spaces Use

Features	Characteristics
Accessibility and Anonymity	The Internet provides straightforward access to extremist content. Anonymity on the web aids in concealing identities. Anonymity facilitates undetected recruitment and radicalisation by extremist groups.
Decentralisation	The Internet's decentralised nature allows content to cross various jurisdictions. Cross-jurisdictional spread complicates legal actions against extremism. Decentralisation enables the existence of platforms that specifically cater to extremist views.
Dark Web and Encryption	Far-right groups often communicate through encrypted channels. Utilise forums on the dark web. These practices make tracking and prosecuting these groups more challenging.
Platform Proliferation	Extremist content spreads across diverse online platforms. Shutting down one platform often leads users to migrate to another. Creates a continual cycle of platform-hopping by extremist users.
Content Moderation and Censorship	Identifying extremist content is often a contentious issue. Balancing the need for censorship with the right to free speech presents a challenge. Insufficient oversight can result in the unchecked spread of hateful content.
Online to Offline Transition	The Internet aids in disseminating ideological beliefs. Enables coordinating various activities, from organising protests to planning violent attacks.

of the digital age, encrypted messaging apps like Telegram and WhatsApp have become increasingly popular. These platforms provide a secure channel for various groups and individuals to disseminate beliefs, recruit members, and fundraise (Hamilton, 2017; Munk, 2018; Sardá et al., 2019) (Table 3.1).

Navigating the Post-Truth Society

Defining the Post-Truth Era

The post-truth era, which surfaced in the late 2010s, characterises a period where subjective beliefs and emotional perspectives overshadow objective facts in influencing public opinion, carrying significant political and cultural consequences. This movement is propelled by the surge of dis- and misinformation on social media platforms. While these platforms offer numerous advantages, they have enabled the rampant spread of unchecked information (Thacker, 2023). Post-truth can be defined by five main elements: emotion outweighing facts, the relativity of truth, politicians making contradictory claims without backlash, polarised opinions, and the nurturing of conspiracy theories (Blackburn, 2018; Lockie, 2017; Malcolm, 2021; Marwick et al., 2022).

The spread of false information and the acceptance of 'alternative truths' have become increasingly normalised, raising concerns about the regression of democratic processes and the rise of authoritarian tendencies. This trend is exemplified in the post-Brexit UK, where fabrications by politicians gained traction, leading to a growing distrust in experts and a worrying disconnect between policymakers and the public (Brown, 2016; Calcutt, 2016; Culloty & Suiter, 2021, p. 89; Poerksen, 2022, p. 27; Whitty & Wisby, 2020). Projects like ReAwaken America (2023), which disseminate unfounded claims about the 2020 US Presidential Election and COVID-19 vaccine misinformation, contribute to this trend. Creating platforms for spreading election denialism and COVID-19 vaccine myths amplifies the challenge of discerning truth in public discourse (Stone, 2023). Similarly, the Israel-Hamas war in 2023 saw the emergence of various false narratives, images, memes, and videos from both sides, which further muddled the understanding of the conflict (Center on Extremism, 2023; Dwoskin, 2023). These instances underscore the growing challenge of maintaining factual integrity in an era increasingly characterised by misinformation and 'alternative facts'.

The Impact of the COVID-19 Pandemic

The COVID-19 pandemic was a communication challenge in the post-truth era. The flood of information, mainly through social media and chat channels, blurred lines between credible and dubious sources, leading to widespread misinformation. For instance, President Trump downplayed COVID-19 risks and incorrectly promoted hydroxychloroquine as a cure. Groups like QAnon and various media platforms significantly propagated similar types of damaging misinformation, which often led to minority groups being unfairly blamed (Boccia Artieri, 2023; Parmet & Paul, 2023; Cox et al., 2021, p. v). In 2020, far-right extremist groups used COVID-19 restrictions to promote narratives linked to accelerationism and anti-immigrant sentiments. In the UK and Belgium, these communications fuelled anti-Semitic and anti-Islamic rhetoric, increasing social tensions. The COVID-19 era saw a rise in conspiracy theories and disinformation on platforms like 4Chan, Reddit, and mainstream social media - with a notable surge in user activity on channels like Telegram (Europol, 2021, p. 90; Cox et al., 2021, p. v).

Echo Chambers: A Deep Dive

An echo chamber amplifies repeated beliefs within a confined group, often encouraging members to seek only information aligning with their preconceptions, a phenomenon possibly stemming from confirmation bias. This environment can intensify polarisation and extremism by limiting exposure to counter-arguments (Erickson et al., 2023; ECPS., 2023; Garimella et al., 2018). The term 'echo chamber' is analogous to the sound echo in closed spaces and is linked to online cultural tribalism. Although the Internet offers diverse information, users often gravitate towards ideologically consistent sources. Within these chambers, repetition can make any claim seem like a fact, regardless of its truthfulness. Digital algorithms shape these experiences, tailoring content to individual preferences. This personalisation can result in 'filter bubbles', where users are shielded from diverse perspectives, often leading to increasingly polarised viewpoints (Lavorgna, 2020, p. 82).

The Psychology behind Echo Chambers

Online users often drift towards 'tribes' with shared interests and beliefs on the Internet. This virtual environment enables the discovery and formation of niche groups, but it is not always clear when someone becomes part of such a group - and users often moves in and out of different forums before they find a place of belonging. These communities' communications can have a detrimental effect by amplifying minor differences, leading to significant divisions that may disrupt democratic discourse (Bartlett, 2018, p. 49). Online echo chambers intensify beliefs and solidify group loyalty while breeding hostility against those outside the group, creating a stark 'us versus them' dynamic (Chapters 1 and 2). Agreeing even slightly with extremist views can lead to more profound radicalisation. Extremist groups tap into the existing human desire for belonging, particularly targeting individuals already distrustful of institutions like the media or government. This makes them more vulnerable to accepting misinformation that resonates with their existing biases (Benson, 2023; Miller-Idriss, 2020, p. 141).

Social media echo chambers create environments where users are exposed predominantly to opinions mirroring their own. This facilitates the dismissal of alternative viewpoints, furthering the spread of misinformation and certain beliefs. Such environments encourage conformity in thinking, heightening openness susceptibility to influence. These are significant issues in the post-truth era, where far-right groups manipulate the online users in these close fourms. This leads to harmful and deepened societal divisions, suppressing critical thinking and spreading misinformation unchecked. Such polarisations isolate individuals from more comprehensive societal viewpoints, creating a fragmented understanding of issues (Benson, 2023; Bright, 2017; Coper, 2022; Jones, 2021; Törnberg & Törnberg, 2022).

Amplifying the Echo

The influence of fake news, alternative news, and conspiracy theories is significant. However, even accurate news can be selectively presented to support a group's narrative, focusing on themes like violence, degrading values, fraud, and immigration. When such news is continuously shared within groups holding far-right extremist beliefs while omitting other perspectives, it fosters a uniform mindset among members. This selective information amplifies negative narratives, overshadowing positive stories and reinforcing group anxieties (Bartlett, 2018, pp. 56–57).

In the months preceding the 2016 US Presidential Election, fake news articles on Facebook were shared more than genuine stories from reputable sources like The New York Times (Rhodes, 2022; Silverman, 2016). These stories typically originate in political groups and are then propagated by highly engaged users and bots (Menczer, 2016; NPR, 2016; Silverman, 2016; Rhodes, 2022). Social media's algorithms push content that aligns with user preferences, keeping them engaged longer. Along with the tendency of users to associate with those who share similar opinions, echo chambers exacerbate the propagation of dis- and misinformation. This circulation tends to continue even when corrections are issued (Mims, 2017; Rhodes, 2022; Praiser, 2011; Thorson, 2016) (Table 3.2).

Table 3.2 Summary of the Post-truth Impact

Features	Characteristics
Far-Right Populism and Post-Truth	The post-truth environment contributes to the expansion of far-right movements.
	Far-right groups exploit scepticism towards institutions and media.
	They portray themselves as representing the 'real people'.
Disinformation and Propaganda	In a post-truth world, the line between fact and fiction fades.
	Far-right groups use this uncertainty, often online, to spread disinformation and advance their agendas.
Appeal to Emotion	Far-right groups employ emotional rhetoric in their communication.
	They use this approach to stoke fears about immigration.
	They also manipulate concerns regarding cultural identity.
Conspiracy Theories	Far-right groups leverage alternative news sources to undermine opponents.
	They use these platforms to foster distrust in mainstream narratives.
	These groups rally supporters through these alternative media channels.
Distrust in Media	Declining trust in mainstream media leads to the rise of alternative news sources.
	Far-right groups support these outlets, enhancing feedback loops.
	These loops reinforce followers' beliefs and isolate them from contrary opinions.

Pop Culture Meets Online Extremism

Deeply rooted in the subcultures of far-right extremism and conspiracy theories are tied to popular culture. These groups use the idea of choosing between being enlightened or staying ignorant. Far-right extremists refer to the 'red and blue pill' from the 1999 film The Matrix to suggest that only a few people choose to see the world as they do. The Internet is crucial for spreading their supposed truth and using language that strengthens unity within their group. In The Matrix, the main character, Neo, has to choose between the red pill, which shows reality – and the blue pill, which keeps him ignorant (Ellies & Dreyfuss, 2019). In contemporary online discourse, particularly within men's rights and far-right communities, to be 'red-pilled' means awakening to counter-mainstream perspectives. However, this awakening is not synonymous with factual enlightenment. The analogy reduces complex issues to a binary choice. Real-world problems and their understandings cannot always be simplified into 'truth' and 'ignorance'.

The Subcultures behind the Terminology

Various online groups, especially men's rights activists and far-right communities, have taken up the 'red pill' analogy. In these far-right circles, the red pill represents their extreme beliefs as the 'hidden truth'. They argue that common views, symbolised by the blue pill, are wrong and intentionally misleading. This 'red-pilling' suggests that people should awaken to what these groups see as the real truths about society, often based on misogynistic, racist, or other extreme ideas. Many who call themselves 'red pillers' believe they have seen beyond what they consider manipulated or false mainstream stories. Initially used in male-focused forums, this term is now also used by far-right extremists. They link it to various ideas, from opposing feminism to denying the Holocaust. Subjects like feminism and political correctness are often used to test how open someone is to extreme beliefs (Cox et al., 2021, pp. 16–17; Jones, 2021, p. 114; Bacigalupo & Borgeson, 2022, p. 124).

For instance, the online 'manosphere' community, powered by their version of the red pill theory, contends that modern society is rigged in favour of women. Adopting the red pill ideology is seen as waking up to this alleged systemic bias and actively resisting it (Tye, 2022). Red pill advocates view themselves as more enlightened than those they deem blue-pilled (Braddock et al., 2022; New America, 2023). Framing debates as a choice between 'waking up' to a singular truth or remaining ignorant discourages nuanced discussions and promotes polarisation. The red-pilling process often involves immersing oneself in alternative news sources, forums, and social media platforms that echo and reinforce the same extremist beliefs. These echo chambers can boost the reach and impact of fake news.

Table 3.3 The Matrix Blue Pill and Red Pill Division

Matrix	Far-right Adoption
Blue Pill	If Neo takes the blue pill, he will remain in the simulated reality of the Matrix and continue to live in ignorance, unaware of the larger reality around him. The blue pill symbolises comfort, denial, and the choice to remain in blissful ignorance. Maintaining one's beliefs or understanding is often seen as conventional or mainstream.
Red Pill	If he takes the red pill, he will 'wake up' and discover the harsh reality outside the Matrix. This choice symbolises the acceptance of hard truths, no matter how unsettling or challenging they may be. It is challenging mainstream narratives, with the implication of becoming enlightened or seeing the 'real truth'. This is often associated with discovering hidden truths or realities kept from the public.

Source: (Ellies & Dreyfuss, 2019).

The Dangers of the Red Pill Ideology

Labelling one's views as the red pill can be a way to position any opposing or alternate views as not just incorrect but as willfully ignorant. The Matrix provided a catchy metaphor for these ideologies, but conspiratorial thinking has deeper, older roots, with narratives like anti-Semitism predating the film by centuries. In this sense, the modern usage of the Matrix analogy is a simplified tool for conspiracy theorists to communicate complex, often twisted, worldviews (Tye, 2022). Algorithms manipulate user experiences by tailoring content based on past behaviour and mood. This results in people with extreme far-right views or conspiracy theory interests receiving more of the same content. Algorithms self-improve, keeping users engaged and deepening these informational silos (Bartlett, 2018, pp. 29–30; Miller-Idriss, 2020, pp. 148–149) (Table 3.3).

Unravelling the Web of Online Falsehoods

The online spread of different falsehoods, such as disinformation, misinformation, and malinformation, poses significant challenges involving state actors, political groups, and individual users. Various forms of false information have been documented, from outright fabrications to manipulated context and parody (Coper, 2022, pp. 84–85). The 2019 Hope not Hate report emphasises how extremists fabricate false narratives to distinguish themselves from perceived adversaries, often exaggerating differences. These groups typically cast themselves as victims, utilising these fabricated stories to justify or advocate for violence in pursuit of political objectives. Far-right extremist groups are known for oversimplifying complex issues, moulding them to fit their ideologies through generalisations and stereotypes (Cox et al., 2021, p. 18; European Commission, 2018, p. 3; Hope Not Hate, 2019). The digital landscape faces threats from AI-driven false content, which could worsen the fragile information environment (Robins-Early, 2023).

The Far-Right, Fake News and Alternative Facts

The surge of far-right extremist movements' use of digital platforms has amplified misinformation. This trend was evident during the 2016 US Presidential Election when 'fake news' became a buzzword, blending with terms like disinformation and misinformation (Tandoc Jr. et al., 2018, p. 137; Yar & Steinmetz, 2019, p. 257). Fake news is deliberately and verifiably false articles that can potentially deceive readers. It has become a versatile tool for influential groups, politicians, and dubious websites. Far-right extremists use it to challenge conventional media, cultivate scepticism, and gather support for their claims (Wardle & Derakhshan, 2017, p. 16). Despite its widespread use, its exact definition remains muddled. Groups like QAnon exploit this vagueness to spread their conspiracy theories and discredit opposing narratives (Siapera, 2018, p. 155; Wardle, 2017).

Although fake news was initially defined as intentionally false stories meant to mislead, its meaning has since been co-opted (Allcott & Gentzkow, 2017). Politicians frequently call sources they disagree with 'fake news' to undermine them while supporting those that back their plans. This weakens the meaning of fake news, turning it into a rhetorical tool. They may also call sources that match their opinions credible or reliable, whether accurate or not. As a result, fake news has lost its original meaning and is often used more for making points in arguments than as a real label for false information (Vosoughi et al., 2018, p. 1146).

The introduction of alternative facts by the US administration in January 2017 came from a false claim about an inflated number of attendees at President Trump's inauguration. This marked a concerning shift in manipulating truths for political goals (Morrissey, 2017; Hendricks & Vestergaard, 2018; Ferber, 2018). It suggests objective facts can be skewed or reinterpreted to fit specific narratives. This alternative interpretation of fact makes it difficult for people to distinguish truth from manipulation. Far-right extremist groups expertly use these methods to distort reality, misleading and potentially radicalising their audience. They consistently mix 'alternative facts' and 'fake news' into mainstream news, which undermines trust in traditional media and threatens democratic discourse. Manipulating facts may sway public opinion, but it also fosters a sceptical, polarised society, placing a significant responsibility on both communicators and the audience to be observant and challenge the information (Ferber, 2018).

The Rising Challenge of Deep Fakes

Deep fake technology, easily accessed through modern software, has introduced a new era of audience deception. This technology can produce videos by seamlessly merging faces, behaviours, and voices, facilitating the spread of visual misinformation. The convincing nature of deep fakes, extending even to voice imitations, is increasingly blurring the line between truth and falsehood, reinforcing the 'alternative facts' ideology prominent during the Trump administration. The quality of deep fakes presents a significant challenge for forensic identification, as the technique yields highly realistic-looking videos. Deep fakes can affect visuals and audio, enabling the creation of voice skins or clones to impersonate public figures (Lavorgna, 2020, p. 174; Sample, 2020). Software like deepfakes and artificial intelligence (AI) can significantly impact the political landscape and attract the attention of far-right extremists. By using deep learning, deepfakes create highly realistic visuals and sounds that can amplify the spread of false news. Conspiracy theorists and far-right extremists can weaponise this technology to advance their narratives. In the current 'seeing is believing' culture, even in a post-truth society, many may find it challenging to discredit such realistic-looking content (Helberg, 2021, pp. 136–138).

Notable figures such as President Obama, President Trump, and Meta's CEO Zuckerberg have already become subjects of these deceptive videos. Politically motivated deep fakes that harass, intimidate, demean, undermine, and destabilise are integral to the Internet's evolution and visual software use. If left unchecked, developing and distributing deep fake visuals could profoundly impact journalism, public trust, and democratic quality (Vaccari & Chadwick, 2020, p. 2). Reacting to concerns, Meta/Facebook has banned deep fake technologies on its platforms that can potentially deceive users, especially by falsely attributing statements to people. In anticipation of the 2020 US Presidential Election, this action was designed to curb the spread of deep fakes on their network (Sample, 2020; Edelman, 2020; Kelly, 2020). However, the policy primarily addresses AI- or machine learning-generated (ML) videos, sidelining other deceptive media like 'shallow fakes' or 'cheap fakes'. This selective approach faced backlash, highlighted by Facebook's decision not to remove an altered video of the previous House Speaker Pelosi that portrayed her in a misleading light (Shead, 2020; Helberg, 2021, p. 138; Kelly, 2020). For digital platforms and online businesses, ensuring the authenticity of content is paramount. The spread of deep fakes and other misinformation tactics risk eroding trust, jeopardising these platforms' perceived reliability (Vaccari & Chadwick, 2020, p. 2) (Table 3.4).

Table 3.4 Summary of the Concepts of Fake Information

Features	Characteristics
The Spectrum of Online Falsehoods	Online falsehoods vary widely in nature. They include deliberate disinformation. They also encompass unintentional misinformation and intentionally harmful malinformation.
The Role of Far-Right Groups	Far-right groups skillfully use misinformation for political objectives. They utilise online platforms to contest mainstream narratives. Their actions aim to create division and radicalise followers, undermining social cohesion and democratic values.
The Complexity of Fake News	The term's meaning has become vague and diluted over time. Political discussions often involve spreading conspiracy theories. This contributes to discrediting mainstream narratives, complicating public discourse.
Alternative Facts in Political Discourse	'Alternative facts' emerged to validate falsified information. They hinder the public's ability to distinguish between truth and falsehood. This has a broader impact, influencing societal beliefs beyond just political discourse.
Deep Fakes: The Next Frontier in Falsehoods	Deep fake technology, producing compelling videos and audio, presents a growing challenge. The proliferation of deep fakes makes discerning truth from fiction more difficult. This technology could become a potent instrument for promoting extremist ideologies.

Conspiracy Theories and Extremism: A Digital Nexus

The Rise and Impact of Conspiracy Theories

Conspiracy theories operate at the intersection of fact and fiction, crafting internally consistent narratives. These have emerged throughout history concerning significant events and are often employed by extremist groups to stoke anger or justify beliefs (Berger, 2018, p. 66; Farinelli, 2021, p. 6; Schulze et al., 2022, p. 4). This includes theories that spurred events like the US Capitol attack or the anti-vax sentiments that posit COVID-19 vaccines as governmental control tools (Tye, 2022). Within extremist circles, there is a pervasive belief that outside forces are conspiring against them, promoting secretive agendas (Berger, 2018, p. 66; Farinelli, 2021, p. 6; Europol, 2022, p. 57).

Even though many of these theories do not have solid proof, they become firmly rooted in the minds of their followers. They make complicated issues seem simple, creating a sense of being victims and overly suspicious. This unites their followers against those they see as enemies and stirs up feelings like mistrust, fear, and anger, leading to actual and sometimes violent actions. Their claims are often so complicated and unlikely that they are almost impossible to prove wrong (Lawton, 2022). Conspiracy theories propagate for various reasons, including political manoeuvring, targeting specific groups, psychological tendencies, or sometimes just for entertainment. Not all are intended to sow division or incite violence. However, once these theories are shared online, they can rapidly influence individuals prone to extreme viewpoints. While the Internet has not necessarily increased people's inclination to believe in conspiracies. However, its capability for rapid content sharing and prevalence of unverified information heightens the risk for those most susceptible to such ideas (Farinelli, 2021, p. 10).

The Intersection of Fact and Fiction

Digital platforms act as amplifiers for these ideas. They help create echo chambers where asking questions is frowned upon, and baseless beliefs are constantly supported. Mainstream media and many news outlets have also helped spread different conspiracy theories and false information. Often, extreme views are given airtime, and groups or individuals ignore or reject evidence that goes against their beliefs. When challenged, these people usually call the opposing views' fake news' or brush them off as another conspiracy (Jones, 2021, p. 234). According to Europol (2020), far-right extremism, fuelled boosted by conspiracy theories, has resulted in several attacks, such as those in Norway in 2011 and New Zealand in 2019. These conspiracy theories often describe the world simply as 'good and evil', giving their followers a greater mission, almost like a religious commitment (Farinelli, 2021, p. 10).

A particularly prominent conspiracy theory is the Great Replacement, which claims outsiders are replacing native populations. Figures in the media, such as former Fox News host Tucker Carlson, have perpetuated this idea, further normalising such views in public discourse (Fowles, 2022; ADL, 2021; Bowcott, 2020; Cross, 2020). By the end of Trump's presidency, conspiracy theories were rife. Republicans claimed the US Presidential Election was rigged, while liberals circulated tales from the 'Steele Dossiers' about Trump's alleged misdeeds (Sommer, 2023).

Conspiracy Amplification during COVID-19

During times of social isolation, such as the COVID-19 pandemic, far-right extremists flooded the Internet with racist narratives, apocalyptic views, and conspiracy theories. This created a 'perfect storm; for disinformation, particularly impacting vulnerable individuals like those struggling with mental health or social issues (Farinelli, 2021, p. 14; Europol, 2022, p. 57). During the pandemic, far-right extremists tried but failed to attract COVID-19 protestors and accused minority groups of causing the virus to spread. As the pandemic hurt the economy, they focused on struggling people and spread conspiracy theories that blamed globalisation and current political decisions for the crisis (Europol, 2022, p. 57). In a disturbing development, some US groups have urged their members who contracted COVID-19 to act as 'biological weapons', encouraging them to enter synagogues to infect Jewish communities. This malicious directive also targets Muslims, Mosques, Asians, immigrants, and people of colour (Farinelli, 2021, p. 14).

QAnon, from Fringe Conspiracy to Global Extremist Movement

QAnon called the 'Meta' conspiracy theory, has morphed into a far-right extremist movement, posing risks to democratic foundations (Fowles, 2022). QAnon emerged after the 2016 US Presidential Election as a far-right conspiracy theory, posing significant threats to democratic institutions (BBC News, 2020a; Wendling, 2020; Martin, 2020). It alleges that President Trump is battling a secret group of elite Satan-worshipping paedophiles and is waiting for the day when key people, like the 2016 US Presidential candidate Clinton, will be arrested and punished. QAnon believers think that a 'deep state' of powerful people from different areas, including government, business, and media, with well-known figures trying to thwart President Trump (BBC News, 2020a; Wendling, 2020; Martin, 2020; Fisher, 2022, pp. 222–223).

The QAnon narrative began with cryptic posts from an individual known as 'Q', building upon the baseless 2016 #Pizzagate conspiracy. This unfounded theory falsely alleged that Democratic politicians operated a child sex ring from a pizza restaurant in Washington, DC. QAnon and similar groups focus on supposed secret schemes orchestrated by the elite that one day willwill be exposed for their alleged crimes. The #Pizzagate conspiracy theory was based on a misinterpretation of emails from Clinton's campaign, and the theory even resulted in a real-life incident at the pizzeria in question (Farinelli, 2021, p. 13; Wong, 2020).

Diversification of Ideology: Expanding beyond Core Theories

Exploiting the anxieties sparked by the pandemic, QAnon emerged as a significant provider of dis- and misinformation within the US and Europe (BBC

News, 2020a; Farinelli, 2021; Wendling, 2020). Enthusiasts of the movement gravitated towards online forums, eagerly deciphering 'Q-drops' – cryptic messages believed to hold hidden truths. Much like how far-right extremist groups draw in followers by instilling a sense of purpose through divisive ideologies, QAnon is providing a framework to make sense of a bewildering world, offering solace from feelings of helplessness and insignificance (Fisher, 2022, p. 222).

Since 2017, the group has seen international growth, particularly in countries like the UK, Canada, Australia, and Germany, with numerous QAnon communities active on Telegram (Haimowitz, 2020). The pandemic has helped QAnon blend with COVID-related conspiracy theories, attracting a varied following, including European far-right extremist groups and some US Congress members. This shift towards mainstream conversation highlights its growing influence (Kovalčíková & Ramsey, 2021; Rauhala & Morris, 2020). The group transitioned rapidly from a fringe conspiracy theory to a more widespread presence, aided by the content promotion algorithms of platforms like Facebook and YouTube. Over time, QAnon's beliefs expanded beyond anti-vaccination and government distrust. Its consistent backing of Trump and advocacy for violent actions solidified its position within the far-right online community (Fisher, 2022). QAnon has evolved its approach by altering its hashtags, shifting from #QAnon to #SavetheChildren, and subtly presenting its theories to a wider audience. By employing more general tags and downplaying its extreme aspects, QAnon continues to exert influence even amidst 'Q's inactivity and Trump's Election defeat.

While Facebook has taken steps to restrict the spread of QAnon-related content, these measures have been widely criticised for their slowness and limited scope (Frenkel, 2020; Haimowitz, 2020). In 2020, Zuckerberg, the CEO of Meta/Facebook, admitted to removing some QAnon content because it could lead to violence. However, this step was seen as too little and too late. Also, Facebook's decision to remove content from the far-left group Antifa simultaneously was seen as a way to appear unbiased. This decision was further criticised for not taking more decisive action against followers of far-right extremism (Frenkel & Kang, 2021, p. 278). X/Twitter has changed its algorithm to reduce QAnon exposure, but over 93,000 accounts still mention the conspiracy (Timberg, 2020).

References

ADL, 2021. *Extremists see critical race theory as evidence of "White Genocide"*. [Online] Available at: https://www.adl.org/blog/extremists-see-critical-race-theory -as-evidence-of-white-genocide [Accessed 25 08 2022].

Allcott, H. & Gentzkow, M., 2017. Social media and fake news in the 2016 election. *Journal of Economic Perspectives,* 31(2), pp. 211–236.

Arzheimer, K., 2009. Contextual factors and the extreme right vote in Western Europe, 1980–2002. *American Journal of Political Science,* 53(2), pp. 259–275.

Attrill, A., 2015. *Cyberpsychology.* Oxford: Oxford University Press.

Bacigalupo, J. & Borgeson, K., 2022. When cyberhate turns to violence. White nationalism to the manosphere. In: *Cyberhate.* Lanham: Lexington Books, pp. 119–136.

Backlund, A. & Jungar, A., 2019. Populist radical right party-voter policy representation in Western Europe. *Journal of Representative Democracy,* 55(4), pp. 393–413.

Baele, S. J., Brace, L. & Coan, T. G., 2021. Variations on a theme? Comparing 4chan, 8kun, and other chans' far-right "/pol" boards. *Perspectives on Terrorism,* 15(1), pp. 65–80.

Bartlett, J., 2018. *The people vs. tech.* London: Penguin.

BBC News, 2020a. *Facebook removes QAnon conspiracy group with 200,000 members.* [Online] Available at: https://www.bbc.co.uk/news/technology-53692545 [Accessed 08 08 2020].

BBC News, 2020b. *Neo-Nazi Rinaldo Nazzaro running US militant group the base from Russia.* [Online] Available at: https://www.bbc.co.uk/news/world-51236915 [Accessed 01 12 2023].

BBC News, 2021. *German far-right group attempt to block migrants.* [Online] Available at: https://www.bbc.co.uk/news/world-europe-59024490 [Accessed 18 11 2023].

Bélanger, J. J. et al., 2019. Passion and moral disengagement: Different pathways to political activism. *Journal of Personality,* (87), pp. 1234–1249.

Benson, T., 2023. *The small but mighty danger of echo chamber extremism.* [Online] Available at: https://www.wired.com/story/media-echo-chamber-extremism/ [Accessed 16 08 2023].

Berger, J. M., 2018. *Extremism.* Massachusetts: The MIT Press .

Berners-Lee, T. et al., 1994. The world-wide web. *Communications of the ACM,* 27(8), pp. 76–82.

Bin He, M., Zhang, Z. & Chen-Chuan Chang, K., 2007. Accessing the deep web. *Communications of the ACM,* 50(5), pp. 94–101.

Blackburn, S., 2018. *On truth.* Oxford: Oxford University Press.

Boccia Artieri, G., 2023. Infodemic disorder: Covid-19 and post-truth. In: *Infodemic disorder.* Cham: Palgrave Macmillan, pp. 15–30.

Bowcott, O., 2020. *Legal profession hits back at Johnson over 'lefty lawyers' speech.* [Online] Available at: https://www.theguardian.com/law/2020/oct/06/legal-profession -hits-back-at-boris-johnson-over-lefty-lawyers-speech [Accessed 25 08 2022].

Bowman-Grieve, L., 2015. Cyberterrorism and moral panics. A reflection on the discourse of cyberterrorism. In: *Terrorism online. Politics, law and technology.* Abingdon: Routledge.

Braddock, K., Hughes, B. & Miller-Idriss, C., 2022. Engagement in subversive online activity predicts susceptibility to persuasion by far-right extremist propaganda. *New Media & Society.*

Bright, J., 2017. Explaining the emergence of echo chambers on social media. *SSRN Electronic Journal,* 10(3), pp. 1–19.

Brown, K. V., 2016. *Twitter has a new tool in the war against harassment, and Milo Yiannopoulos doesn't like it.* [Online] Available at: https://splinternews.com/twitter-has -a-new-tool-in-the-war-against-harassment-a-1793854026 [Accessed 10 09 2022].

Byman, D., 2022. *Spreading hate: The global rise of white supremacist terrorism*. 1st ed. Oxford: Oxford University Press.

Caiani, M., 2021. *Between real and virtual: Far-right mobilisation strategies in Eastern Europe*. [Online] Available at: https://gnet-research.org/2021/10/04/between-real-and-virtual-far-right-mobilisation-strategies-in-eastern-europe/ [Accessed 15 08 2022].

Calcutt, A., 2016. *The surprising origins of 'post-truth' – And how the liberal left spawned it*. [Online] Available at: https://theconversation.com/the-surprising-origins-of-post-truth-and-how-it-was-spawned-by-the-liberal-left-68929 [Accessed 28 08 2023].

Center on Extremism, 2023. *ADL debunk: Myths and false narratives about the Israel-Hamas War*. [Online] Available at: https://www.adl.org/resources/blog/adl-debunk-myths-and-false-narratives-about-israel-hamas-war [Accessed 12 11 2023].

Chadwick, A. & Vaccari, C., 2019. *News sharing on UK social media: Misinformation, disinformation, and correction*. Loughborough: Loughborough University.

Chen, G. M. & Lu, S., 2017. Online politcal doscourse: Exploring differences in effects of civil and uncil disagreement in news websites comments. *Journal of Broadcasting & Electronic Media,* 61(1), pp. 108–125.

Cole, B., 2022. *How Germany's far-right coup plot is linked to Russia*. [Online] Available at: https://www.newsweek.com/russia-germany-coup-plot-far-right-moscow-1765633 [Accessed 01 12 2023].

Coper, E., 2022. *Facts and other lies. Welcome to the disinformation age*. Crows Nest: A&U.

Counter Extremism Project, 2023. *National democratic party of Germany*. [Online] Available at: https://www.counterextremism.com/threat/national-democratic-party-germany [Accessed 18 11 2023].

Cox, K., Ogden, T., Jordan, V. & Paille, P., 2021. *COVID-19, disinformation and hateful extremism*. Cambridge: The Commission for Countering Extremism (CCE).

Crawford, B., 2022. *Tracing extremist platform migration on the darkweb: Lessons for deplatforming*. [Online] Available at: https://gnet-research.org/2022/01/18/tracing-extremist-platform-migration-on- [Accessed 30 08 2023].

Cross, M., 2020. *Johnson opens new front in war on 'lefty lawyers'*. [Online] Available at: https://www.lawgazette.co.uk/news/johnson-opens-new-front-in-war-on-lefty-lawyers/5105891.article [Accessed 24 08 2022].

Culloty, E. & Suiter, J., 2021. *Disinformation and manipulation in the digital media*. Abingdon: Routledge.

Dwoskin, E., 2023. *A flood of misinformation shapes views of Israel-Gaza conflict*. [Online] Available at: https://www.washingtonpost.com/technology/2023/10/14/propaganda-misinformation-israel-hamas-war-social-media/ [Accessed 14 11 2023].

ECPS., 2023. *Echo chamber*. [Online] Available at: https://www.populismstudies.org/Vocabulary/echo-chamber/ [Accessed 16 08 2023].

Edelman, G., 2020. *Facebook's deepfake ban is a solution to a distant problem*. [Online] Available at: https://www.wired.com/story/facebook-deepfake-ban-disinformation/ [Accessed 08 10 2020].

Ellies, E. & Dreyfuss, E., 2019. *The matrix's red pill or blue pill—Which is better?*. [Online] Available at: https://www.wired.com/story/matrix-red-pill-vs-blue-pill/ [Accessed 27 08 2023].

Erickson, J., Yan, B. & Huang, J., 2023. Bridging echo chambers? Understanding political partisanship through semantic network analysis. *Social Media + Society,* 9(3), pp. 1–15. https://doi.org/10.1177/20563051231186368.

European Commission, 2018. *Communication from the commission to the European Parliament, the Council, the European Economic and Social Committee and the Committee of the regions: Tackling online disinformation: A European approach.* [Online] Available at: https://eur-lex.europa.eu/legal-content/EN/TXT/?uri =CELEX:52018DC0236 [Accessed 16 08 2023].

Europol, 2021. *European Union terrorism situation and trend report 2021.* Luxembourg: Publications Office of the European Union.

Europol, 2022. *European Union. Terrorist situation and trend report 2022.* Luxenbourg: Europol.

Europol, 2023. *European Union terrorism situation and trend report 2023.* Luxembourg: Publications Office of the European Union.

Faizan, M. & Khan, R. A., 2019. Exploring and analysing the dark web: A new alchemy. *First Monday,* 24(5),.

Farinelli, F., 2021. *Conspiracy theories and right-wing extremism – Insights and recommendations for P/CVE.* Brussels: European Commission.

Ferber, D., 2018. *Fighting back against 'alternative facts': Experts share their secrets.* [Online] Available at: https://www.sciencemag.org/news/2018/02/fighting-back -against-alternative-facts-experts-share-their-secrets [Accessed 10 08 2020].

Fisher, M., 2022. *The Chaos machine.* London: Quercus.

Fowles, S., 2022. *Far-right conspiracy theories are now embedded in the UK mainstream.* [Online] Available at: https://www.opendemocracy.net/en/far-right -mainstream-conspiracy-theory-uk/ [Accessed 24 08 2022].

Frenkel, S., 2020. *Facebook removes 790 QAnon groups to fight conspiracy theory.* [Online] Available at: https://www.nytimes.com/2020/08/19/technology/facebook -qanon-groups-takedown.html [Accessed 28 08 2023].

Frenkel, S. & Kang, C., 2021. *The ugly truth. Inside Facebook's battle for domination.* London: The Bridge Street Press.

Garimella, K., De Francisci Morales, G., Gionis, A. & Mathioudakis, M., 2018. *Political discourse on social media: Echo chambers, gatekeepers, and the price of bipartisanship.* s.l.: s.n., pp. 913–922.

Gohel, H. A., 2014. Looking back at the evolution of the Internet. *CSI Communications- Knowledge Digest for IT Community,* 38(6), pp. 23–26.

González-Bailón, S., 2014. Online social networks and bottom-up politics. In: *Society and the internet: How networks of information and communication are changing our lives.* Oxford: Oxford University Press.

Haimowitz, I., 2020. *No one is immune: The spread of Q-anon through social media and the pandemic.* [Online] Available at: https://www.csis.org/blogs/strategic -technologies-blog/no-one-is-immune-spread-q-anon-through-social-media-and -pandemic [Accessed 26 08 2023].

Hamilton, A., 2017. *Interview: Telegram and terror: How data encryption shapes our lives. https://digit.fyi/whatsapp-telegram-terror/.* [Online] Available at: https://digit .fyi/whatsapp-telegram-terror/ [Accessed 28 07 2020].

Helberg, J., 2021. *The wires of war. Technology and the global struggle for power.* New York: Avid Reader Press.

Hendricks, V. F. & Vestergaard, M., 2018. Alternative facts, misinformation, and fake news. In: *Reality lost. Markets of attention, misinformation and manipulation.* Amsterdam: Springer, pp. 49–77.

Hoffman, M., 2022. Welcome to cyberspace. In: *Cyberhate. The far right in the digital age.* London: Lexington Books, pp. 3–16.

Holt, T., Bossler, A. M. & Siegfried-Spellar, K. C., 2018. *Cybercrime and digital forensics. An introduction.* 2nd ed. Abingdon: Routledge.

Holt, T. J., Bossler, A. M. & Seigfried-Spellar, K., 2022. *Cybercrime and digital forensics. An introduction.* 3rd ed. London: Sage.

Hope Not Hate, 2019. *State of hate 2019. People vs. the elite?* London: Hope Not Hate.

Jardine, E., 2018. Tor, what is it good for? Political repression and the use of online anonymity-granting technologies. *New Media & Society,* 20(2), pp. 435–452.

Jones, M., 2021. *Disinformation and you. Identify propaganda and manipulation.* Canton: Visible Ink Press.

Jones, S. G., 2018. *The rise of far-right extremism in the United States.* [Online] Available at: https://www.csis.org/analysis/rise-far-right-extremism-united-states [Accessed 1 08 2022].

Kang, H., Bae, K., Zhang, S. & Sundar, S. S., 2011. Source cues in online news: Is the proximate source more powerful than distal sources?. *Journalism & Mass Communication Quarterly,* 88(4), pp. 719–736.

KCL, 2022. *Far right groups 'using Russian invasion of Ukraine to push anti-West narratives'.* [Online] Available at: https://www.kcl.ac.uk/news/far-right-groups-using -russian-invasion-of-ukraine-to-push-anti-west-narratives [Accessed 01 12 2023].

Kelly, M., 2020. *Facebook's deepfake ban isn't winning over critics.* [Online] Available at: https://www.theverge.com/2020/1/7/21055283/facebook-deepfake-ban-political -ads-shallowfakes-rules-moderation [Accessed 10 08 2020].

Koehler, D., 2016. Right-wing extremism and terrorism in Europe current developments and issues for the future. *PRISM,* 6(2), pp. 85–99.

Kovalčíková, N. & Ramsey, C., 2021. *QAnon and anti-vax conspiracy theories pose a threat to democracy beyond national borders.* [Online] Available at: https:// securingdemocracy.gmfus.org/qanon-and-anti-vax-conspiracy-theories-pose-a -threat-to-democracy-beyond-national-borders/ [Accessed 27 08 2023].

Lavorgna, A., 2020. *Cybercrimes. Critical issues in a global context.* London: Macmillian.

Lawton, G., 2022. *Conspiracy theories.* [Online] Available at: https://www.newscientist .com/definition/conspiracy-theories/ [Accessed 25 08 2022].

Lockie, S., 2017. Post-truth politics and the social sciences. *Environmental Sociology,* 3(1), pp. 1–5.

Lutkevich, B. & Bacon, M., 2021. *End-to-end encryption (E2EE).* [Online] Available at: https://www.techtarget.com/searchsecurity/definition/end-to-end-encryption -E2EE [Accessed 31 08 2023].

Malcolm, D., 2021. Post- truth society? An Eliasian sociological analysis of knowledge in the 21st century. *Sociology,* 55(6), pp. 1063–1079.

Martin, A., 2020. *What is QAnon? The bizarre pro-Trump conspiracy theory growing ahead of the US election.* [Online] Available at: https://news.sky.com/story/what-is -qanon-the-bizarre-pro-trump-conspiracy-theory-growing-ahead-of-the-us-election -12033874 [Accessed 08 08 2020].

Marwick, A., Clancy, B. & Furl, K., 2022. *Far- right online radicalization: A review of the literature.* [Online] Available at: https://doi.org/10.21428/bfcb0bff.e9492a11 [Accessed 26 08 2023].

Menczer, F., 2016. *The spread of misinformation in social media.* s.l.: International World Wide Web Conferences Steering Committee.

Miller-Idriss, C., 2020. *Hate in the homeland. The new global far right.* Princeton: Princeton University Press.

Mims, C., 2017. *How Facebook's master algorithm powers the social network.* [Online] Available at: https://www.wsj.com/articles/how-facebooks-master-algorithm -powers-the-social-network-1508673600 [Accessed 27 08 2023].

Morrissey, L., 2017. *Alternative facts do exist: Beliefs, lies and politics.* [Online] Available at: https://theconversation.com/alternative-facts-do-exist-beliefs-lies-and -politics-84692 [Accessed 10 08 2020].

Mudde, C., 2007. *Populist radical right parties.* Cambridge: Cambridge University Press.

Mulhall, J., 2022. *Putin's British mouthpiece: Britain first leader Paul Golding's long history of pro-putin propagandising.* [Online] Available at: https://hopenothate.org .uk/2022/05/03/putins-british-mouthpiece-britain-first-leader-paul-goldings-long -history-of-pro-putin-propagandising/ [Accessed 01 12 2023].

Munk, T., 2018. Policing virtual spaces: Public and private online challenges in a legal perspective. In: *Comparative policing from a legal perspective.* Cheltenham: EE Publising, pp. 228–254.

Munk, T., 2022. *The rise of politically motivated cyber attacks. Actors, attacks and cybersecurity.* London: Routledge.

Nacos, B. L., 2019. *Terrorism and counter-terrorism.* 6th ed. Abingdon: Routledge.

Neiwert, D., 2017. *Alt-America.* London: Versobooks.

New America, 2023. *Red pill to black pill.* Retrieved 08 27, 2023, from *Misogynist Incels and Male Supremacism.* [Online] Available at: https://www.newamerica.org/ political-reform/reports/misogynist-incels-and-male-supremacism/red-pill-to-black -pill/ [Accessed 27 08 2023].

Norman, K. L., 2017. *Cyberpsychology. An introduction to human-computer interaction.* 2nd ed. Cambridge: Cambridge University Press.

NPR, 2016. *Fake news expert on how false stories spread and why people believe them.* [Online] Available at: https://www.npr.org/2016/12/14/505547295/fake-news-expert -on-how-false-stories-spread-and-why-people-believe-them [Accessed 27 08 2023].

Pantucci, R., 2023. *Russia's far-right campaign in Europe.* [Online] Available at: https://www.lawfaremedia.org/article/russias-far-right-campaign-europe [Accessed 01 12 2023].

Parmet, W. & Paul, J., 2023. Post-truth won't set us free. In: *Covid-19 and the law.* Cambridge: Cambridge University Press, pp. 58–72.

Poerksen, B., 2022. *Digital fever, taming the big businesses of disinformation.* Cham: Palgrave Macmillan.

Pompeo, M., 2020. *United States designates Russian imperial movement and leaders as global terrorists.* [Online] Available at: https://2017-2021.state.gov/united-states -designates-russian-imperial-movement-and-leaders-as-global-terrorists/index .html [Accessed 01 12 2023].

Praiser, E., 2011. *The filter bubble: How the new personalised web is changing what we read and how we think.* London: Penguin.

Rauhala, E. & Morris, L., 2020. *In the United States, QAnon is struggling. The conspiracy theory is thriving abroad.* [Online] Available at: https://www.washingtonpost.com /world/qanon-conspiracy-global-reach/2020/11/12/ca312138-13a5-11eb-a258 -614acf2b906d_story.html [Accessed 27 08 2023].

Rhodes, S., 2022. Filter bubbles, echo chambers, and fake news: How social media conditions individuals to be less critical of political misinformation. *Political Communication,* 30(1), pp. 1–22.

Robins-Early, N., 2023. *Disinformation reimagined: How AI could erode democracy in the 2024 US elections.* [Online] Available at: https://www.theguardian.com/us-news/2023/jul/19/ai-generated-disinformation-us-elections [Accessed 27 08 2023].

Rodríguez-Suárez, J., Morán-Neches, L. & Herrero-Olaizola, J., 2021. Online research, new languages and symbolism of digital activism: A systematic review. *Comunicar,* 29(69), pp. 47–58.

Sample, I., 2020. *What are deepfakes – And how can you spot them?.* [Online] Available at: https://www.theguardian.com/technology/2020/jan/13/what-are-deepfakes-and-how-can-you-spot-them [Accessed 08 10 2020].

Sardá, T., Natale, S., Sotirakopoulos, N. & Monaghan, M., 2019. Understanding online anonymity. *Media, Culture & Society,* 41(4), pp. 557–564.

Scholz, K. A., 2020. *How the Internet fosters far-right radicalisation.* [Online] Available at: https://www.dw.com/en/how-the-internet-fosters-far-right-radicalization/a-52471852 [Accessed 28 08 2022].

Schulze, H. et al., 2022. Far-right conspiracy groups on fringe platforms: A longitudinal analysis of radicalisation dynamics on Telegram. 28(4), pp. 1103–1126..

Shead, S., 2020. *Facebook to ban 'deepfakes'.* [Online] Available at: https://www.bbc.co.uk/news/technology-51018758 [Accessed 08 10 2020].

Siapera, E., 2018. *Understanding new media.* 2nd ed. London: Sage.

Silverman, C., 2016. *This analysis shows how fake election news stories outperformed real news on Facebook.* [Online] Available at: https://www.buzzfeed.com/craigsilverman/viral-fake-election-news-outperformed-real-news-on-facebook [Accessed 28 08 2023].

Singer, P. & Brookings, E., 2018. *Likewar. The weaponisation of social media.* New York: Mariner Books.

Sommer, W., 2023. *Trust the plan.* London: 4th Estate.

Stone, P., 2023. *Far-right project that pushed election lies expands mission as Trump ramps up 2024 campaign.* [Online] Available at: https://www.theguardian.com/us-news/2023/jan/30/far-right-project-disinformation-trump-2024-campaign [Accessed 01 12 2023].

Sundar, S. S., 2008. The MAIN model: A heuristic approach to understanding technology effects on credibility. In: *Digital media, youth, and credibility.* Cambridge: The MIT Press, pp. 73–100.

Tandoc Jr., E. C., Lim, Z. W. & Ling, R., 2018. Defining fake news. *Digital Journalism,* 6(2), pp. 137–153.

Thacker, J., 2023. *How a post-truth society is vulnerable to misinformation and conspiracy theories.* [Online] Available at: https://erlc.com/resource-library/articles/how-a-post-truth-society-is-vulnerable-to-misinformation-and-conspiracy-theories/ [Accessed 27 08 2023].

Thorson, E., 2008. Changing patterns of news consumption and participation. *Information, Communication and Society,* 11(4), pp. 473–489.

Thorson, E., 2016. Belief echoes: The persistent effects of corrected misinformation. *Political Communication,* 33(3), pp. 460–480.

Timberg, C., 2020. *Twitter banished worst Qanon accounts. But more then 93000 remain on the site, research shows.* [Online] Available at: https://www.washingtonpost

.com/technology/2020/10/03/twitter-banished-worst-qanon-accounts-more-than -93000-remain-site-research-shows/ [Accessed 27 08 2023].

TOR, 2020. *Browse privatly. Explore freely.* [Online] Available at: https://www .torproject.org/ [Accessed 27 07 2020].

TOR Project, 2022. *Browse privately. Explore freely.* [Online] Available at: https:// www.torproject.org/ [Accessed 17 08 2022].

Törnberg, P. & Törnberg, A., 2022. Inside a White Power echo chamber: Why fringe digital spaces are polarising politics. *New Media & Society*, pp. 1–23.

Tye, C., 2022. *The Matrix: How conspiracy theorists hijacked the 'red pill' philosophy.* [Online] Available at: https://theconversation.com/the-matrix-how-conspiracy -theorists-hijacked-the-red-pill-philosophy-174935 [Accessed 22 08 2022].

UN, 2015. *Report of the Special Rapporteur on the promotion and protection of the right to freedom of opinion and expression, David Kaye. Human Rights Council.* New York: Human Rights Council.

Vaccari, C. & Chadwick, A., 2020. Deepfakes and disinformation: Exploring the impact of synthetic political video on deception, uncertainty, and trust in news. *Social Media + Society,* 6(1).

Vergeer, M. & Hermans, L., 2008. Analysing online political discussions. Methodological considerations. *Journal of the European Institute for Communication and Culture,* 15(2), pp. 37–55.

Vosoughi, S., Roy, D. & Aral, S., 2018. The spread of true and false news online. *Science,* 359(6380), pp. 1146–1151.

Wallace, P., 2016. *The psychology of the internet.* 2nd ed. Cambridge: Cambridge University Press.

Wardle, C., 2017. *Fake news. It's complicated.* [Online] Available at: https://medium .com/1st-draft/fake-news-its-complicated-d0f773766c79 [Accessed 10 08 2020].

Wardle, C. & Derakhshan, H., 2017. *Information disorder: Towards an interdisciplinary framework for research and policy making.* Strasbourg: The Council of Europe.

Wendling, M., 2020. *QAnon: What is it and where did it come from?.* [Online] Available at: https://www.bbc.co.uk/news/53498434 [Accessed 08 08 2020].

Whitty, G. & Wisby, E., 2020. Evidence-informed policy and practice in a 'post-truth' society. In: *Handbook of education policy studies.* Singapore: Springer, pp. 399–414.

Wilson, J., 2020. *Revealed: The true identity of the leader of an American neo-Nazi terror group.* [Online] Available at: https://www.theguardian.com/world/2020/ jan/23/revealed-the-true-identity-of-the-leader-of-americas-neo-nazi-terror-group [Accessed 01 12 2023].

Wong, J., 2020. *QAnon explained: The antisemitic conspiracy theory gaining traction around the world.* [Online] Available at: https://www.theguardian.com/us-news /2020/aug/25/qanon-conspiracy-theory-explained-trump-what-is [Accessed 27 08 2023].

Yar, M. & Steinmetz, K. F., 2019. *Cybercrime and society.* 3rd ed. London: Sage.

4 Digital Dynamics of Far-Right Extremism

Platforms and Communications

Online Platforms and Communications

The digital world has become a key battleground for far-right extremist groups, magnifying their influence in unprecedented ways. These groups have adapted and thrived with the rise of Web 2.0 and social media, transforming the Internet into a powerful tool for expanding their reach and solidifying global networks. The leap from physical to digital has seen a rise in interconnected far-right communities, with extremist groups using less-regulated parts of the web to spread their views and actions (Baele et al., 2023).

Virtual platforms have diversified significantly over the years, and each platform offers unique services. Facebook and LinkedIn emphasise connections and interests, while YouTube, TikTok, and Instagram focus on media sharing; Twitch specialises in live streaming, and Reddit in in-depth discussions (Lutkevich & Wigmore, 2021). This evolution has transformed communication and information access, enabling widespread content creation and sharing, which also spills over to the political environment, influencing public opinion and participatory democratic opportunities. Social media provides a new avenue beyond traditional media for spreading far-right extremist narratives and perspectives, i.e. platforms like Reddit, X/Twitter, and Facebook (Cota et al., 2019, pp. 1–2; Lomas, 2022; Munk, 2024). Initially, these platforms were celebrated as bastions of free speech. Yet, the negative impacts of unregulated content have prompted increased moderation efforts. The challenge for these platforms lies in balancing between preserving free speech and preventing the spread of harmful ideologies. This challenge was underscored by events like the Christchurch attacks, demonstrating the urgent need for improved moderation practices to counteract the misuse of these digital spaces (Kildiş, 2020; Mudde, 2019, p. 110; Papakyriakopoulos et al., 2020; Hern & Waterson, 2019).

Navigating the Complex Landscape of Social Media: Privacy, Extremism, and Free Speech

Social Media Business Model and User Data

In the digital world, when a service is free, it often means the users are the product sold to advertisers. This is key to Meta/Facebook's strategy, where

DOI: 10.4324/9781003297888-4

buying WhatsApp and Instagram was to boost its ad reach. Meta/Facebook's primary focus is advertising, not social connections. This means that for Meta/Facebook, the advertisers are the main customers, not the users. The truth of the content on the platform is less important to them than how well their adverts reach people (McFarlane, 2022; Goel, 2023; Lanchester, 2017). This advert-supported model is standard among social media firms, with some exceptions, like X/Twitter exploring subscription services. The allure of a free platform attracts a vast user base, drawing in advertisers willing to pay a premium to engage this audience (McFarlane, 2022; Lanchester, 2017). However, this revenue model raises ethical questions. It often sacrifices user privacy, creating a quasi-surveillance state where companies exploit user data for hyper-targeted advertising (Leetaru, 2018). Consumer surveillance is becoming increasingly detailed in various sectors, from healthcare to politics (Ruckenstein & Granroth, 2020, p. 12; Zuboff, 2015; Pridmore & Lyon, 2011; Ruckenstein & Schüll, 2017).

In the digital realm, from online shopping to loyalty programs and social media engagement, consumer activities are a goldmine for data collection. Companies harness this data, enriched with sophisticated algorithms and extensive data sets, to decode complex relationships between consumer behaviours and market goals. The digital footprints left by online users become crucial commodities in the data extraction process, an aspect of what is known as surveillance capitalism. This process transforms every online action into valuable insights, turning user interactions into assets for business strategies (Zuboff, 2015; Zuboff, 2019; Donovan et al., 2022, p. 17; Laub, 2019; Ruckenstein & Granroth, 2020, p. 12).

Big Data and Algorithmic Influence

Big data is compiled from individuals' online activities, capturing everything from social media interactions to location and purchase history. Often referred to as data exhaust by technologists, this wide range of data is collected, processed, and monetised, sometimes multiple times. Framing the data as waste may make it less likely for their extraction and monetisation to be challenged (Zuboff, 2015, p. 79). Meta/Facebook and its tech counterparts wield powerful algorithms that shape user experiences and behaviours. Rooted in a data-centric, participatory advertising model, these platforms turn a profit by seizing user attention and selling this rich data trove to advertisers. Collaborations with data brokers and the relentless flow of personal information are crucial to fine-tuning their ad targeting strategies. Every click, like, and share feeds into a vast data reservoir ready for monetisation. This transforms social media algorithms into potent predictors of user behaviour, capable of serving up exceptionally personalised adverts (Bartlett, 2018, pp. 18–20; Carah, 2021, pp. 155–156). The business models for online platforms rely on prolonging user reading or viewing times. Platforms make their revenue by allowing advertisers to target specific audiences precisely, thus incentivising users to engage for extended periods (Laub, 2019).

The Debate Over Free Speech on Social Media

Hate speech and racism persist on platforms like X/Twitter and Facebook despite company policies against such content. Enforcement of these rules falls short when the companies approve provocative adverts, electoral misinformation, and conspiracy theories on the platforms (UN, 2023; Laub, 2019). The constant focus on Facebook, X/Twitter, and other social media platforms' rules, processes, and practices has led to extensive criticism. These platforms are accused of fostering hatred and spreading false information, including content related to QAnon and white supremacists (Chapters 2 and 3). The arguments from different sides vary. The political left holds them responsible for societal harm, while the political right alleges censorship (The Economist, 2020). Political and societal division can confine people within echo chambers, creating an illusion of open debate. These secluded online environments enable the propagation of disinformation designed to mislead and cause further polarisation (Lutkevich & Wigmore, 2021).

Content validation on these platforms is often twisted by user engagement metrics – likes, shares, and comments. As a result, posts that gain traction can spiral virally, constantly disseminating unverified information without critical examination (Sundar, 2008; Thorson, 2008; Tandoc Jr. et al., 2018, p. 139; Wardle & Derakhshan, 2017, p. 13). Far-right extremist groups have used social media to spread radical beliefs since the early 2000s, contributing to the growth of far-right extremism. Unlike mainstream media platforms with tighter regulations, these groups frequently employ encrypted forums like Telegram, WhatsApp, and Gab to promote radicalisation, coordinate events, and exchange informations. These forums create decentralised environments that are difficult to monitor effectively, permitting hate speech and calls for violence to flourish unchecked. Consequently, far-right extremists are becoming more dangerous as they can rapidly mobilise large supporter groups (Grelicha et al., 2021).

Mainstream Social Media's Struggle with Extremist Content

During the early spring and summer of 2020, the online conversation surrounding the upcoming US Presidential Election reached a fever pitch. Disinformation became rampant on platforms, leading major social media companies like X/Twitter, Facebook, and YouTube to impose stricter content restrictions. Consequently, far-right groups, such as the QAnon movement, migrated from mainstream platforms to alternative online spaces like Parler, Gab, and the messaging service Telegram (Grisham, 2021).

The Capitol Hill attack and some online users' subsequent bans from mainstream outlets like Meta/Facebook and X/Twitter drove far-right online users to migrate to these less-regulated spaces (Ray, 2021). This shift complicates the task of online moderation and highlights an ongoing battle to balance free speech with online safety. While mainstream platforms are taking some steps to curb disinformation and extremist content, alternative media are emerging to fill the void. The cat-and-mouse game between regulators and extremist groups continues to evolve, reflecting the broader struggle to balance freedom of speech with the need to maintain a safe and responsible online environment.

Meta/Facebook and X/Twitter, two globally recognised social media giants, grapple with persistent challenges related to far-right extremist content on their platforms. Despite their established policies and community standards, these companies have struggled to manage and remove such content effectively, allowing it to proliferate.

Meta/Facebook's Moderation Hurdles

Facebook has been discussing and updating its Community Standards and platform content rules. The new rulebook was introduced in 2019, which includes four distinct areas: authenticity, safety, privacy, and dignity (Meta, 2019, 2023). Their policy development includes bi-monthly global meetings and extensive research concerning diverse international perspectives. Updates to the standards are posted on their Community Standards website (Meta, 2019). According to Meta/Facebook, its content policy team is located in 11 offices worldwide and is tasked with creating community standards. This diverse group includes experts in hate speech, terrorism, and more, with backgrounds in law, academia, and crisis counselling. They regularly seek input from external experts to ensure their policies reflect various global perspectives on safety and expression (Meta, 2018). Meat/Facebook's policies divide unacceptable content into categories like Violence and Criminal Behavior, Safety, and Objectionable Content to address hate speech and misinformation. This approach is vital in combating far-right extremism, which often involves spreading hate and false news. By distinguishing real threats from casual statements and limiting the spread of misinformation, Meta/Facebook aims to prevent far-right extremist groups from using the platform to propagate their ideologies and incite real-world violence while still encouraging online interactions and debates (Haselton, 2018; York, 2018).

Meta/Facebook is constantly facing criticism for its moderation of content. An internal review revealed that its algorithms tend to amplify divisiveness, with a 2018 company presentation stating that they 'exploit the human brain's attraction to divisiveness' (Horwitz & Seetharaman, 2020). The review cautioned that unchecked, Facebook would continuously present users with more divisive content to retain their attention (Schori Liang & Cross, 2020; Horwitz & Seetharaman, 2020; Statt, 2020). Meta/ Facebook's algorithms, designed to maximise user engagement, inadvertently contribute to division by prioritising content that evokes strong emotional responses. Although these platforms do not deliberately aim to foster polarisation, their main objective is to boost user engagement and advertisement interaction to maximise profits, thereby satisfying stakeholder interests (Barrett et al., 2021).

Despite warnings about its impact on society, Meta/Facebook's leadership disregarded findings about its divisive role. The 2018 report suggests that reluctance to make changes stemmed from concerns that they could disproportionately affect conservative users and reduce engagement (Statt, 2020; Sonnemaker, 2020). Meta/Facebook established the Oversight Board in October 2020 to address some the concerns raised. This independent body reviews contentious content and recommends policy adjustments for Meta/ Facebook's platforms, including Facebook and Instagram. The creation of this board represents an effort to enhance content governance and address the challenges posed by vague community standards (Feiner, 2019; Kang, 2021; Salinas, 2018; Bouko et al., 2021, p. 2).

The Grey Area in Regulating Far-Right Extremism

Meta/Facebook has consistently struggled to remove far-right content, including white supremacy and neo-Nazi stores and groups. This inability to act effectively shows the company's long-term failure to enforce its Community Standards (CEP, 2019). Facebook has not only allowed these groups to communicate but has also enabled them to build up businesses selling related far-right content. Notable examples include children's t-shirts with racially charged slogans like "White baby – the future of our race" (Robins-Early, 2018). Far-right extremist groups often exist in a regulatory grey area, with tech companies reluctant to censor their content. Far-right extremists are usually treated as online activists under cybercrime laws, not terrorists under stricter counter-terrorism laws. This leads to inconsistent removal of extremist content on Meta/Facebook's platforms, highlighting the need for more transparent rules and more vigorous enforcement of moderation practices. Removing extremist content and avoiding censorship on social media is tricky. Far-right content often mixes humour and pop culture, making it hard to judge what is acceptable.

X/Twitter's Verification Controversies and Responses

X/Twitter's initial blue tick verification was meant to recognise prominent individuals and organisations, unintentionally suggesting the company's endorsement. Widening access to verification led to controversy, especially when far-right personalities were verified, appearing as though they received special treatment. Yet, this system effectively distinguished genuine accounts like @realdonaldtrump from unverified ones, such as @DonaldTrump (Wong, 2017). The decision to verify extreme far-right figures like Spencer, Kessler, and Yiannopoulos in 2016 drew substantial criticism. X/Twitter faced serious scrutiny regarding its stance on handling extremist content and the implicit endorsement these verifications could represent (Wong, 2018; Press Association, 2017; SPLC, 2022; Wong, 2017; Twitter Support, 2017). These actions suggested a potential conflict between the platform's policy on harmful content and its verification decisions, highlighting the complexities in moderating content while trying to maintain neutrality and uphold free speech

The Debate Over Twitter's Blue Tick System

After Charlottesville, X/Twitter revised its verification process and removed verification from far-right figures like Spencer, Loomer, Robinson, and Yiannopoulos. Yiannopoulos, who lost his verification in 2016 and was later banned, called for more transparency from platforms like X/Twitter (Brown, 2016; Wong, 2017; Alexander, 2016). Following an episode where Yiannopoulos led a racially abusive attack on actress Leslie Jones, X/Twitter responded without directly naming him. In their statement, they stressed that although they support a diversity of views, targeted abuse violates their policies. X/Twitter outlined their actions to tackle the problem, recognising a rise in such infractions. This includes issuing warnings and even permanent suspensions (Alexander, 2016; McCormick, 2016; Lapowsky, 2017). First Amendment attorney Randazza and others saw X/Twitter's actions as politically motivated, targeting conservative views (Brown, 2016). The social media company's commitment to free speech is balanced by its efforts to prevent harmful behaviour, particularly actions targeting or silencing marginalised groups (Twitter Help Centre, 2022). Criticism has been levelled against X/Twitter regarding its effectiveness in managing the platform and preventing misuse by far-right extremist groups. Critics argue that the platform often responds inadequately and slow, allowing these groups to continue abusing and manipulating the platform (Table 4.1).

Concerns Over Impersonation and Misuse of Verification Checkmarks

Beginning 1 April 2023, the company started phasing out its legacy Verification program. Accounts verified under the previous criteria of being active, notable, and authentic will no longer retain a blue checkmark unless they subscribe to X Premium (X, 2023). Initially, the blue tick served as a mark of authenticity and notability, confirming the identity of high-profile users. However, the distinction between verified and non-verified users

Table 4.1 Key People Associated with Far-right Extremism

People	Associations with Far-right extremism
Donald Trump	2016/ 2020 Republican Presidential candidate and the 45th US president (2017-2021). Praised by far-right groups and individuals for being an anti-establishment conservative politician or an outsider.
Milo Yiannopoulos	British far-right political commentator and social media personality. Former editor of Breitbart News. Mainly known for his outspoken critique of third-wave feminism, Islam, Social Justice and political correctness.
Steve Bannon	Executive chairman of Breitbart News. Accused of courting white supremacists within the far-right. Appointed to the position of Chief Executive in Trump's 2016 US Presidential Election campaign. Was Trump's chief strategist and senior advisor in the first part of his presidency.
Richard Spencer	American white nationalist. Founder of the think tank National Policy Institute. Describes himself as an identitarian.
Jason Kessler	One of the Unite-the-Right organisers and Proud-Boys member. A prominent white supremacist.
Laura Loomer	Islamophobe and far-right, white nationalist conspiracy theorist. Closely linked to Fuentes, a white nationalist and a supporter of former US President Trump.
Tommy Robinson	British far-right extremist Former leader of the English Defence League. Anti-Islamist influencer.
Nick Fuentes,	A white supremacist political commentator and live streamer. Organiser and podcaster/creator of a white nationalist alternative to the mainstream GOP. His 'America First' show advocates strict immigration control and opposes liberal values, attributing them to Jewish influence.

Source: (Lynskey, 2017; KnowYourMeme, 2019; BBC News, 2022; Pengelly, 2023; Walters, 2017; Silverman, 2021; ADL, 2022a; ADL, 2021; Rawlinson, 2018; Press-Reynolds, 2022).

becomes blurred with the new system, where anyone can acquire a blue tick for a monthly fee. The introduction of gold and silver ticks for brands and government figures, respectively, while helpful, does not address the issue of impersonation among other types of accounts (Kleinman, 2023; Conger, 2023; Bohannon, 2023; ADL, 2023c).

For instance, far-right extremists could exploit this system to create accounts that appear legitimate or authoritative, misleading the public. The concerns are not unfounded, as evidenced by instances where members of controversial groups, like the Taliban, managed to purchase blue verification checkmarks, although these were later revoked (Bohannon, 2023). The incident shows the risk of extremist groups exploiting the verification system. By acquiring verified accounts, these groups might amplify their propaganda, disseminate false information, or even impersonate credible entities. Thereby, they can enhance their platform presence and influence. The modifications made to X/Twitter's blue tick system, aimed at democratising verification, may unintentionally equip far-right extremists with a means to gain apparent legitimacy. This could enable them to spread their ideologies more effectively, presenting significant challenges in moderating the platform and combating the spread of public misinformation.

X/Twitter's Community Notes

The Community Notes program, launched on X/Twitter in 2022, is designed to improve global awareness by allowing users to collaboratively add context to potentially misleading posts (X, 2023). Users can contribute notes to any post; if these notes are deemed helpful by a diverse range of contributors, they are made publicly visible. Initially, Community Notes did not attract much attention but gained prominence in 2023 when Musk and X CEO Yaccarino emphasised its importance in combating misinformation, (Elliott & Gilbert, 2023; Perez, 2023). However, the system has faced criticism for its slow response to misinformation, as observed during the Israel–Hamas conflict. To address these concerns, X/Twitter introduced enhancements to Community Notes, such as faster updates and note previews for quicker verification and publication (Perez, 2023). The platform also encouraging users to update or remove content flagged by Community Notes. Additionally, media matching was enhanced to apply fact-checks to more posts with similar media content (Perez, 2023; Goggin, 2023).

Despite these improvements, concerns remain about the functionality of Community Notes. Issues include potential manipulation by external groups, lack of clarity in the note approval process, and insufficient direct oversight by the company (Elliott & Gilbert, 2023). The system's effectiveness in handling a large volume of posts, particularly those concerning terrorist attacks, is under scrutiny. Criticisms have been levelled at the program for its fact-checking procedure and for failing to attach notes to many false posts that have garnered significant viewership (Perez, 2023; Goggin, 2023). The effectiveness of Community Notes in swiftly and precisely detecting and marking deceptive content, especially those promoting extremist views, is crucial for limiting the dissemination of such information. Issues like delayed responses and the possibility of unchecked manipulation pose challenges to the program's capability to tackle far-right extremism. For instance, if misleading content spreads significantly before a Community Note is appended, this delay could undermine the program's impact (Elliott & Gilbert, 2023; Goggin, 2023).

The Rise of Alternative Social Media: Echo Chambers and Far-Right Mobilisation

The Shift to Less Regulated Platforms

Social media has boosted populism globally, allowing political messages to reach wider audiences faster than traditional media. As major social media platforms ramp up their regulations, users are shifting to alternatives like Gab and Signal, lured by the promise of fewer restrictions and enhanced privacy. While prioritising user engagement for profit, these platforms often fall short in policing misinformation and extremist threats. This oversight allows far-right groups to broadcast their recruitment messages freely, a negligence that could translate into tangible real-world impacts (Grelicha et al., 2021).

After being removed from Facebook and X/Twitter, Trump supporters and far-right groups moved to smaller platforms. Some platforms promise free speech, while others have stricter content moderation - Some welcome these new users, but others are intensifying their efforts in content moderation (Ray, 2021). Various platforms like Telegram, Reddit, Parler, Gab, and YouTube are increasingly favoured by far-right groups for spreading their ideologies and recruiting members. Each platform operates with its own set of content and privacy rules. The combination of limited regulation, minimal data sharing, and robust encryption makes these sites particularly appealing to far-right extremists, especially as they encounter stricter controls on more mainstream social media networks. These features offer them a relatively unmonitored space to operate, contributing to their growing presence on these alternative platforms (Ray, 2021; Hamilton, 2017).

Telegram: A Haven for Extremists with High-Level Secrecy Features

Telegram, launched in 2013, is favoured by far-right extremists for its public channels for open discussion and private chats for organising and radicalising (Grisham, 2021; Urman & Katz, 2022, p. 907). Telegram's advanced secrecy features have made it a refuge for extremists seeking to evade moderation on other platforms. Its private messaging services enable far-right extremist and religious extremist groups to flourish, sparking concern. However, despite its emphasis on privacy, Telegram has faced criticism for its moderation policies, especially after being associated with the 2015 terrorist attack in France (Urman & Katz, 2022, p. 907; Hamilton, 2017; Telegram, 2019; Rogers, 2020; Telegram, 2022).

Post-2020 US Capitol Hill attack, far-right users flocked to Telegram, as the company only moderated public channels, not private ones (Ray, 2021). This leniency in moderation, similar to issues on Facebook and X/Twitter, increases the risk of radicalisation (Urman & Katz, 2022; Rogers, 2020; Mudde, 2019). Prominent far-right figures banned from platforms like X/Twitter, like white nationalist Fuentes and election fraud conspiracy theorists

Wood and Frank, continue to spread their views on Telegram. Fuentes has a visible profile on Telegram, spewing the usual hostile rhetoric and his opinions about the war in Ukraine. Telegram has become a crucial part of the far-right information network, offering a space free from scrutiny where fringe groups can share misinformation and extreme views without disturbance (Bump, 2022; ADL, 2021).

Reddit: Struggles with Hate Speech and the Banning of Subreddits

With over 50 million daily users, Reddit is a popular platform for discussions and sharing content (Reddit, 2022). Reddit grapples with content management challenges and adopts a distinctive moderation strategy. Unlike significant platforms like Facebook, which outsource moderation, Reddit relies on its community-driven subreddits to self-police, entrusting users with a significant role in overseeing content (Khalili, 2021). The company addresses problematic communities through two approaches: (1) quarantining, which reduces their visibility and issues a warning upon access, and (2) banning, which eliminates the community and its content. Typically, quarantining is implemented as a preliminary measure, serving as a caution to amend behaviour before a total ban is enforced (Ribeiro et al., 2021, p. 4).

Reddits relaxed rules have allowed hate speech and violence to spread. Subreddits like r/The_Donald became centres for far-right extremist groups, leading to Reddit eventually quarantining or banning them (Gaudette et al., 2020, pp. 3494–3495; Ward, 2018; Tiffany, 2020; Singer & Brookings, 2018, p. 175). Reddit's intermittent enforcement post-Charlottesville highlights the struggle to balance free speech with preventing hate, resulting in some extremist feeds remaining active on the platform (Ward, 2018; Tiffany, 2020). Despite Reddit's ban, the subreddit r/The_Donald continued hosting extremist content, mirroring Facebook's issue of delayed action against such views. Serveing as a recruitment hub similar to the Neo-Nazi ideology of the Daily Stromer, r/The_Donald linked extreme fringe and mainstream communities (Donovan et al., 2022, p. 120; Ward, 2018).

Parler: The Free Speech Platform and Its Challenges Post-Capitol Attack

Parler, which started in 2018, is a social media platform that prides itself on allowing free speech without censorship. It is created as a mix of X/Twitter and Instagram, where users can post news, comment, and 'upvote' or 'parley' posts (Akhtar & Nguyen, 2022; Yurieff et al., 2021; Blazina & Stocking, 2022). In contrast to X/Twitter's labelling of specific posts as misleading, Parler does not mark posts as misinformation. While it aims to safeguard user data, Parler acknowledges that it cannot fully guarantee protection against data breaches or unauthorised access (Akhtar & Nguyen, 2022). Parler became popular with supporters of President Trump, especially those involved in the Capitol attack, and has verified accounts of notable conservative figures like Hannity, Levin, Loomer, Cruz, Nunes, Trump's sons, and Trump's presidential campaign (Yurieff et al., 2021).

Following the 2021 Capitol Hill insurgent, Parler faced a significant setback as it was dropped by Amazon Web Services (AWS) and removed from Apple and Google app stores, leading to a temporary shutdown (Novet, 2021). This action, prompted by Parler's inability to moderate violent content linked to the insurrection, did not stop its extreme far-right users (Fung, 2021a; Novet, 2021; Fung, 2021b). They quickly migrated to alternative platforms, underscoring the challenge of containing extremist activities. Instead of dissipating, these groups simply shifted from mainstream to smaller, less regulated sites (Fung, 2021b). In a twist, Starboard later acquired Parler, intending to repurpose it as a haven for communities feeling marginalised and censored by mainstream media (Spangler, 2023). This movement of Trump supporters to platforms like MeWe, Gab, and Rumble marked the emergence of a robust far-right online community, showcasing the resilience and adaptability of these groups in the digital landscape (Abril, 2021; Gilbert, 2020).

Gab: Increased Popularity Among Far-Right for Minimal Moderation

Gab stands out among social media platforms by offering a user experience similar to Facebook and Twitter but with minimal content moderation. This lack of moderation has attracted the far-right, resulting in an abundance of hateful and extremist content on the platform (Jasser et al., 2023). Gap, positioned as a free speech platform, became a refuge for far-right individuals after being banned from mainstream social media platforms. This shift began when well-known far-right provocateurs, such as Yiannopoulos, faced bans on Twitter, reflecting the broader efforts of social media giants to combat extremism. Paradoxically, this increased the app's popularity, particularly within the far-right community (Wong, 2018; Ray, 2021).

Gab's user numbers often rise when larger platforms like Facebook, Twitter, and Reddit tighten their rules after the Charlottesville rally in 2017 and the Capitol attack in 2021 (McSwiney et al., 2021; Gilbert, 2020). After the Capitol incident, Gab saw a significant increase in traffic, especially from Trump supporters, QAnon adherents, and followers of other far-right ideologies (Gilbert, 2020). This trend highlights the challenge mainstream social media faces in tackling extremist content. While these platforms work to control harmful ideologies, alternative sites like Gab gain users seeking less regulated spaces, showing the difficulty of balancing content moderation with free speech and the prevention of extremism.

YouTube: Difficulties in Video Content Moderation and Algorithm Changes

YouTube is a free video-sharing platform allowing users to watch – or create and upload videos (GCF Global, 2023; DU, 2023). This platform is a popular tool for connecting far-right groups worldwide, and its autoplay feature can inadvertently contribute to the spread of polarising content. After the Christchurch attacks, YouTube tagged related videos as inappropriate, yet some edited versions persisted. Modifying video content poses unique challenges, as it demands transcription and more extensive human review than text, making the process more time-consuming and complex (Chen et al., 2021; Hern & Waterson, 2019). To address this, YouTube changed its search algorithm to favour credible news over re-uploaded attack footage. Far-right extremists also use Instagram, hiding their ideologies in seemingly harmless images (Scholz, 2020; Hern & Waterson, 2019).

YouTube's open platform allows fringe opinions to compete with mainstream media. Based on viewership and watch time, its revenue model can encourage content creators to target extreme views or create controversial content (Chen et al., 2021). Online spaces connect far-right extremist groups globally, with English-language platforms often used for sharing ideas and copying actions (Scholz, 2020). Despite algorithmic changes, YouTube's autoplay feature continues to promote divisive content, potentially spreading extremist ideologies inadvertently. This feature automatically plays recommended videos based on a user's past activity, potentially shaping behaviour. The fact that the top recommendation plays immediately following the current video further increases the likelihood of users being exposed to polarising content (Chen et al., 2021; Scholz, 2020) (Table 4.2).

Table 4.2 Summary of Social Media Platform Use

Features	Characteristics
Algorithmic Amplification	Social media algorithms can lead to echo chambers. These enclosed environments amplify far-right ideologies, further radicalising users.
Recruitment and Radicalisation	Far-right groups use social media for recruitment, spreading messages, and network building. It is essential for connecting with followers or targeting supporters globally.
Content Moderation Challenges	Identifying and removing extremist content is difficult, as it is often subtle or satirical. The continuous stream of online posts and live actions complicates timely moderation.
Cross-Platform Spread	Far-right extremists frequently move between social media platforms. Constant changes and use of encryption hinder efforts to monitor and control their messages.

(Continued)

Table 4.2 Continued

Features	Characteristics
Global Reach	Social media platforms globalise the spread of far-right ideologies.
	This borderless online environment creates legal and jurisdictional challenges.
Offline Harm or Violence	Online extremist content may incite or normalise real-world violence.
	The convergence of online and offline communication via social media can lead to physical attacks.
Fake News and Misinformation	Far-right groups exploit social media to disseminate misinformation.
	Insufficient moderation and proactive measures on these platforms facilitate public opinion manipulation.
Privacy and Anonymity	Social media provides privacy, shielding extremist identities and communications.
	Allows the creation of fake profiles and use of encrypted messaging for evasion purposes.
Impact on Democracy	Social media's dissemination of far-right ideologies can impact political landscapes.
	Such spread can undermine trust in institutions and exacerbate societal polarisation.
Commercial Considerations	Need to balance user retention and the ethical responsibility to limit extremist content.
	The pursuit of engagement for business growth can conflict with the requirements of content moderation.

Understanding the Chans: Online Forums and Far-Right Ideologies

Online forums like Reddit and 4chan cater to many users and topics, including some promoting far-right ideologies. These forums appeal to far-right extremist groups because they offer relatively hidden and less regulated spaces than mainstream platforms like Facebook and X/Twitter. Far-right extremists find these alternative platforms, such as 4Chan, 8chan, and Reddit, attractive for sharing their narratives and connecting with like-minded individuals without immediate risk of being banned or de-platformed (Åkerlund, 2021, p. 1; Van der Nagel & Frith, 2015; Gaudette et al., 2020).

The Early Days of Electronic Extremism

Prior to the introduction of the Internet and platforms like 4chan, bulletin board systems played a crucial role in extremist communication. In 1984, American white supremacist Louis Beam initiated the Aryan National Liberty Net, a telephone-based network active in Idaho, Texas, and North Carolina. This network provided modem access to a range of extremist content, including hate propaganda, details about meetings, information on far-right groups, and early forms of doxing, which involved revealing the personal information of perceived enemies (Conway et al., 2019, p. 3; Fischer, 2021). Liberty Net, akin to early social media, hosted games, music, lectures, and children's activities. It enabled the offline trade of white-power music tapes, newsletters, and books (Fischer, 2021). As a hub for extremist ideology, Aryan Nations disseminated propaganda and misinformation aimed at minorities, focusing on themes like Christianity and white supremacy to draw individuals to their cause. They actively distributed controversial materials, including bomb-making guides, pirate radio instructions, and computer viruses, furthering their extremist agenda (Ray & Marsh II, 2001).

Daily, 150–400 people accessed electronic bulletin boards run by former Klansmen, neo-Nazis, and other white supremacist groups. These groups were early adopters of electronic communication, supplementing traditional media like print and radio. Leaders like Butler of the Aryan Nation movement saw the importance of technology, proclaiming, 'We must use our God-given technology in calling our race back to our Father's Organic Law' (Miller, 1985). Aryan Nation's Butler saw the significance of technology for their cause and incorporated it to promote the movement, while Metzger of White Aryan Resistance (WAR) set up the War Computer Terminal for propaganda. Metzger also used his WAR newspaper and cable-access TV show to promote this bulletin board (Conway et al., 2019, p. 3). However, the development of these communication platforms advanced further with the emergence of new online imageboards, known as the chans.

Image Boards: Anonymity and Extremist Content

The image boards are distinctive online forums that allow users to post anonymously, identified simply as 'Anonymous'. This anonymity is achieved through tripcodes instead of conventional registrations (PCMagazine, 2022; Darkowl, 2022). The minimal content regulation of these boards draws a wide range of users. Unlike platforms like Facebook that require real names, image boards like 4chan allow users to hide their identity and post under the generic username 'Anonymous' (Van der Nagel & Frith, 2015).

Prominent image boards such as 4chan, and the controversial 8chan (later 8kun.top) originated from the Japanese Futaba (2chan) imageboard (Elley, 2021, p. 2; KnowYourMeme, 2019; PCMagazine, 2022). Initially, the chans were popular spaces for sharing memes, gaming, and community experiences, but they quickly became a hub for various groups and individuals due to the anonymity they offer, such as white supremacists, far-right nationalists, and various fringe groups (BBC Trending, 2019; Gonzalez, 2019). Specific boards like Alt-chan and Wizardchan are notorious for hosting extreme content, including material related to far-right extremist ideologies and 'Incels', i.e. involuntarily celibate men with hostile attitudes towards women (Darkowl, 2022).

The problem with these chans lies in their unregulated nature, where the blend of internet humour, conspiracy theories, and political extremism can create a challenging and even dangerous environment (Bradshaw et al., 2019). The cryptic and irony-rich language of far-right extremist groups blurs the boundary between dark humour and genuine threats. Their use of coded symbols, trolling tactics, and extreme commentary creates a complex maze for law enforcement and moderators to navigate, making it challenging to discern serious dangers from mere provocative jokes (Chapter 5) (Hern, 2019). Certain image boards on the surface web implement strict guidelines regarding permissible content and comply with law enforcement requests for information, including providing logs when asked. In contrast, some image boards exclusive to the Dark Web operate under more lenient rules and moderation, allowing users to post illegal content, including violent material, pornography, and other illicit items (Chapter 3) (Darkowl, 2022).

4chan: A Hub for Internet Culture and Controversy

4chan was established in 2003, and it was initially created for discussing and sharing anime pornography but later evolved into a hub for social outsiders. It gained popularity for its Internet jokes, pranks, and tolerance for unconventional behaviour (Elley, 2021, p. 2; Colley & Moore, 2022, p. 8; Thorleifsson, 2021, p. 288). This image board operates on the bulletin board model, where users create posts with single images linked to specific topics, and replies are ranked based on controversy and the number of responses (Thorleifsson, 2021, p. 289). 4chan played a pivotal role in meme culture and birthed the hacktivist collective Anonymous (Bradshaw et al., 2019; Elley, 2021, p. 2; Munk, 2022, p. 217).

The Gamergate Controversy: A Turning Point

While far-right extremist communities have expanded beyond 4chan, the forum still holds a central position in their discussions. It is worth noting that compared to similar platforms, 4chan has introduced some moderation and is believed to be under the scrutiny of law enforcement (Darkowl, 2022). The Gamergate controversy (2014) was a defining moment for 4chan, sparking an online culture war that spread across platforms like X/Twitter and 4chan. The dispute pitted independent game developers and critics, including notable women like Wu, Day, Alexander, and Quinn. These women pushed for more inclusivity in gaming against a coalition of misogynists, anti-feminists, trolls, and those who believed a left-leaning and corrupt press was manipulating them. This clash marked a significant chapter in the digital discourse surrounding gaming and gender politics (Arthur, 2020; Dewey, 2014; Lees, 2016).

The manosphere and certain gamers bonded over a shared animosity towards women, especially visible in online spaces. They noticed women's increasing online presence, from verified X/Twitter accounts to anonymous Tumblr posts, fuelling their resentment (Donovan et al., 2022, p. 95). Traditionalists in the gaming community, resistant to changes, also aligned with this sentiment. The 2014 Gamergate controversy became pivotal igniting debates on gaming inclusivity and drawing supporters and critics (Arthur, 2020; Dewey, 2014; Lees, 2016). The aftermath of Gamergate led to 4chan banning discussions on the topic, spurring the creation of 8chan. Subsequently, in 2015, 4chan's founder, Poole, sold the site to Nishimura, known for founding and formerly owning 2chan (Arthur, 2020; Finley, 2015; Orsini, 2015). This series of events marked significant shifts in the landscape of online communities and discussions.

The Online Culture War Sparked by Gamergate

It is not only Gamergate that is linked to 4chan. 4chan also played a role in the rise of far-right movements, particularly during Trump's 2016 US Presidential Election campaign, due to its anonymity and the difficulty in distinguishing between serious calls for violence and satirical posts, known as 'shitposts' (Elley, 2021, p. 2; Thorleifsson, 2021, p. 290). Provocative postings aiming to derail conversations and expressions of transgressive fun are common, with phrases like 'I did it 4 the lulz' used to disguise racist content (Thorleifsson, 2021, p. 290). The far-right news syndicate, Breitbart, was instrumental in the Gamergate movement, a role that eventually evolved into backing the Trump campaign. They leveraged a network of far-right groups and technologically adept young men, mainly active on forums like 4chan, and harnessed their influence and reach in these digital spaces (Lees, 2016; Singer & Brookings, 2018, p. 174).

Yiannopoulos, a prominent figure in the far-right movement, mobilised his followers, known as 'truffle pigs', to support Trump. These young, online forum-active supporters, especially on /pol/, played a significant role in portraying Trump as a figurehead for online trolls, engaging in 'shitposting' and meme creation (Chapter 5). Their involvement was pivotal to both Trump's online popularity and Yiannopoulos's rise in the far-right extremists community. Similarly, Anglin of the Daily Stormer also urged his readers to support Trump fervently, highlighting the influential role of online far-right personalities (Donovan et al., 2022, pp. 120–121).

8chan: A Platform for Extremism and Its Impact

8chan, marked by its sideways '8' infinity symbol, functions through user-led moderation and topic selection, establishing itself as a platform for extremist campaigns. This includes the live streaming and posting of mass shootings, fostering a unique culture on the boards (Gonzalez, 2019; BBC Trending, 2019). Launched in 2013 by Brennan, also known as Hotwheels, 8chan gained traction after 4chan censored discussions around the Gamergate controversy. Promoted as a bastion of free speech, its rapid growth led Brennan to collaborate with Watkins in 2014 to manage its burgeoning popularity. However, the content on the platform quickly deteriorated into increasing obscenity (Darkowl, 2022).

The platform's links to extremist violence and international hate crimes, exemplified by the 2019 mass shootings in Christchurch, Poway Synagogue, and El Paso, where attackers posted racist and xenophobic manifestos on 8chan beforehand, have sparked significant concerns (Chapter 2) (Darkowl, 2022; BBC Trending, 2019; Gonzalez, 2019; Thorleifsson, 2021, pp. 286–287; Beckett & Levin, 2019). Notably, the El Paso Walmart shooter became the third person in five months to pre-announce an attack on 8chan, advocating far-right nationalist ideologies. He described his attack as a 'response to the Hispanic invasion of Texas', mirroring the language used by the New Zealand attacker, who also referred to immigrants as an 'invasion' in his manifesto (Beckett & Levin, 2019). This terminology aligns with the rhetoric used by then-US President Trump regarding migrants at the southern US border (Beckett & Levin, 2019; Beckett, 2018).

Hosting Controversies and Tech Company Responses

Cloudflare has faced criticism for hosting far-right extremist platforms, often requiring substantial public pressure to act. The tech company has been censured for enabling racist far-right extremists to connect, fundraise, and organise rallies, thereby increasing the potential for violence and hatred (Wong, 2018). Cloudflare's removal of the white supremacist site, the Daily Stormer, after the 2017 Charlottesville rally was seen as groundbreaking (Chapter 2). This action sparked discussions about the responsibilities of tech companies in moderating content. It also brought to the forefront debates about Internet governance, the limits of free speech, and the role of private companies in these areas. This debate highlighted the complex intersection of technology, ethics, and policy (Wong, 2018; Shinal, 2017; Musil, 2017). The expulsion of the Daily Stormer from mainstream web hosting pushed it into the dark web, and significantly limiting its accessibility. This move is part of a wider shift among tech companies and social media platforms, particularly following the public outcry post-Charlottesville. In response, these entities have increasingly adopted more decisive actions against users and platforms associated with hate speech and extremism, reflecting a growing commitment to combat online hate and violence (Wong, 2018).

Cloudflare's Decision to Take 8chan Offline

8chan was eventually forced offline by Cloudflare, and other providers refused to grant access to their sites. This decision came after at least three mass shooters posted their screeds on the Board (Gonzalez, 2019; BBC Trending, 2019; Townsend, 2020; Gonimah, 2019). After Cloudflare's shutdown of the Daily Stormer, users turned to encrypted messaging apps such as Telegram and Discord and social media sites like Gab and Parler, which offered new venues for their communications and activities (Paul, 2019).

Following the decline of 8chan, new image boards like 8kun, 9chan, and 16chan surfaced to fill the gap. These platforms have become closely associated with far-right groups and various digital subcultures, continuing the legacy of their predecessor in hosting such content and communities (Baele et al., 2021, pp. 65–66). These platforms are known for using coded language and memes for political purposes, creating a unique online subculture with distinct 'in-group' and 'out-group' dynamics, i.e. phrases like 'Patriots', 'Trust the Plan', 'Great Awakening', and 'WWG1WGA' (Where We Go One We Go All) (Chapter 5) (Baele et al., 2021, p. 65; Darkowl, 2022) (Table 4.3).

Table 4.3 Summary of Image Board Use

Features	Characteristics
Anonymity and Unmoderated Content	Anonymity on platforms enables unchecked extremist ideology promotion.
	Weak moderation allows far-right extremism to proliferate.
	Lack of consequences aids the spread of extremist views.
Recruitment and Radicalisation	Chans act as recruitment platforms for extremist groups.
	They facilitate the radicalisation process.
	Prejudiced beliefs are transformed into active extremist actions.
Dissemination of Hate and Violence	Mass shooters' manifestos and videos are shared and glorified on these platforms.
	This perpetuates violence and hate.
	Such content often spreads to mainstream social media.
Migration to Other Platforms	Users migrate to other platforms when chans are closed or moderated.
	Controlling extremist content becomes a continuous cat-and-mouse game.
Ambiguity and Trolling Culture	Trolling, humour, and irony on chans blur satire and extremism.
	Normalise radical views for mainstream audiences.
Links to Offline Harm and Violence	Chans linked to real-world violence, evident in pre-posted plans and manifestos for mass shootings.
	Spreading hate speech against minorities impacts them online and offline.
	Creates a hostile environment leading to real-world harm.
Legal and Ethical Challenges	Balancing free speech with controlling extremist content presents legal and ethical challenges.
	Requires nuanced approaches and effective enforcement.

Online Gaming and Video Platforms: Hotbeds for Far-Right Extremism

Online forums exhibit a clear connection due to their shared user base, language, and symbols, especially in the gaming community. These similarities make them fertile grounds for far-right extremist groups to recruit individuals. These groups typically target young people, initially engaging them with entertaining content that gradually shifts towards racist rhetoric. This strategy subtly draws individuals into extremist circles, leveraging the commonalities and dynamics of these online platforms (Fischer, 2021). Platforms like Steam, Discord, DLive, and Twitch are breeding grounds for far-right extremist recruitment, offering both public and private spaces for these communities (Bedingfield, 2021; Kamenetz, 2018). Since 2016, private, password-protected online spaces have become hubs for far-right communities. The content in these secluded forums is often more extreme than what is found on mainstream social media. Some of these spaces are associated with political movements like GI or Britain First, indicating a deeper connection between online extremist discourse and organised political activism (Davey, 2021, p. 6; Bedingfield, 2021). Far-right extremist groups like the Nordic Resistance movements, Combat 18, National Action, AWD, and Sonnenkrieg Division also have a presence on these platforms (Davey, 2021, p. 6).

Far-Right Extremism in Video Games

Far-right groups have delved into creating video games to spread their ideologies, with 'Ethnic Cleansing' and 'White Law' being prominent examples (Holt et al., 2022, p. 388; Lakhani, 2021, p. 5). Alongside these, titles like 'Feminazi: The Triggering' are embraced by some far-right extremists more as emblems of identity than for actual gameplay. These extremist-themed games are typically of low quality and may contain viruses, functioning primarily as symbols of group affiliation and ideological alignment rather than as interactive entertainment (Gallagher et al., 2021; Bedingfield, 2021; Davey, 2021, p. 9).

While bespoke games created by extremist organisations often suffer from limited resources, some online subcultures find appeal in a more amateur and crude approach, described as 'Internet Ugly'. This style may not always be about the gameplay or ideology but rather may focus on humour, 'shitposting' and transmitting fun (Chapter 5). These considerations become vital in understanding the intersection between video gaming and extremism, extending to mainstream social media platforms and more obscure sites like 4Chan and 8Kun and the meme culture (Chapter 5) (Lakhani, 2021; Douglas, 2014). This intersection of video gaming and extremism extends beyond bespoke games, encompassing mainstream social media platforms and more obscure sites like 4Chan and 8Kun, emphasising the need to understand the broader context and nuances (Lakhani, 2021; Douglas, 2014).

The Role of 'Mods' in Propagating Ideologies

'Mods' refer to modifications made to original games, introducing new elements such as characters or landscapes or allowing players to assume the role of the game's original enemy. Examples include early changes to classics like 'Wolfenstein', war adaptations like 'Quest for Bush', or newer modifications to strategy games by Paradox Interactive. Some of these mods have even catered to alternate history scenarios designed by white supremacists, showcasing a specific and concerning trend within the gaming community (Lakhani, 2021, p. 5). Far-right extremist groups are drawn to historical strategy games like 'Hearts of Iron', 'Europa Universalis', and 'Crusader Kings', where they can play out their ideological fantasies. In contrast, 'Counter-Strike: Global Offensive' is famous among these groups, not for its ideological content but rather for its widespread appeal and entertainment value, making it a preferred choice in the gaming community (Gallagher et al., 2021; Bedingfield, 2021; Davey, 2021, p. 9).

Online Games for Extremist Recruitment

There's a disturbing trend within the gaming industry, where several First-Person Shooter (FPS) games, such as 'Ethnic Cleansing', allow players to assume the roles of Klansmen or neo-Nazis, with slogans promoting white supremacy. Titles like 'Jesus Strikes Back: Judgment Day' feature controversial characters and incorporate neo-Nazi symbolism in their marketing. Additionally, modified versions of existing games, or mods, have been developed to reflect similar themes, often promoted by white nationalist figures (Lakhani, 2021; Condis, 2020, p. 147). Online games like Fortnite have been exploited for recruitment and radicalisation efforts, creating forums for discussing violence that can spill over into real-world actions (Holt et al., 2022, p. 388).

Far-right extremist groups are increasingly engaging young men on online gaming platforms, using these spaces as both communication channels and catalysts for discussions that could lead to real-world violence (Holt et al., 2022, p. 388). Players often enact role-plays of past extremist attacks, such as the 2011 Utøya Island massacre, the 2019 Christchurch mosque shootings, and the 2019 El Paso mall attack. UK-based white-nationalist Patriotic Alternative organised a 'Call of Duty Warcraft' tournament to recruit young gamers (Townsend, 2021). Additionally, provocative videos like 'The Last Battle' have become a worrying trend to agitate far-right audiences (Fischer, 2021).

Platforms like BitChute have emerged as significant outlets for far-right content, including violence, racism, and conspiracy theories, particularly after mainstream sites like Parler and Gab were de-platformed in 2020. BitChute notably hosted unedited footage of the Christchurch and Halle attacks, highlighting its role in propagating extremist content (Doward & Townsend, 2020). These developments underscore the critical intersection of online gaming, extremist ideologies, and social media platforms, underlining the urgent need for monitoring and intervention in these digital environments.

Gaming Platforms as Extremist Environments

Twitch: 'Omegle Redpilling' and Racial Abuse

Extremists play popular games like everyone else, driven by fun and community. While Steam has been identified as having the most significant issue with extremist content, such communities are on various platforms. On Twitch, a phenomenon known as 'Omegle Redpilling' occurs, where white supremacists, sometimes dressed as characters like 'Racist Super Mario' or the Joker, search through Chatroulette and Omegle to find victims to racially abuse. Clips of these streams, which sometimes remain available for over an hour before being taken down, have become popular and even made their way onto TikTok (Bedingfield, 2021; Gallagher et al., 2021)

Discord: A Virtual Home for Extremist Chats

Initially launched in 2015 as a chat app for gamers, Discord rapidly expanded, accumulating over 45 million members. However, its privacy features unintentionally attracted far-right groups, making Discord a virtual home for extremism. It enables private, invite-only chat groups, fostering far-right extremist discussions and conflicts (Roose, 2017). Initially designed for online gaming, far-right groups have widely used Discord to reach young people through gaming tournaments. Extremist groups have adopted the strategies of online influencers, established fan communities, and used memes and aggressive forms of online trolling (Bedingfield, 2021). Prominent figures like Spencer and Anglin used Discord for strategy discussions, sometimes disagreeing over alliances with groups like the KKK. Discord unintentionally evolved from a gaming hub to a far-right gathering spot (Roose, 2017).

Steam: A Hub for Far-Right Communities and Propaganda

The extent of far-right communities varies on gaming platforms. Steam hosts sizable, long-standing communities dating back to 2016. While more extreme than mainstream social media, these communities are smaller than those on platforms like Gab and Telegram. Mainly, two Steam groups are linked to violent terrorist organisations. The first group is the Nordic Resistance Movement. This group was connected to bombings in Gothenburg in 2016 and 2017. The second group is the Misanthropic Division. This Russian group is active in Ukraine, Germany, and the UK. Extremist usage of Steam varies, with some groups using it as a social media platform to spread propaganda, others forming gaming clans, or acting as a far-right extremist hub, where members can socialise, discuss ideology, and sometimes direct people on the platform to extremist organisations and other social media pages (Bedingfield, 2021; Gallagher et al., 2021).

Moderation Challenges on Gaming Platforms

Moderation efforts differ across platforms, with DLive, Discord, and Twitch exerting varying levels of control over extremist content. Discord, for instance, experienced a decrease in extremist activities following measures against groups like UK's Patriotic Alternative. This pattern shows that when platforms clamp down on far-right discussions, extremists typically relocate to less regulated spaces. Discord has faced challenges in moderating harmful content, but its activities show a notable decline when it takes action against extremist groups. Conversely, following DLive's stringent crackdown and account deletions, extremists have sought sanctuary on alternative platforms that offer fewer restrictions, allowing them to continue their activities uncensored (Bedingfield, 2021; Gallagher et al., 2021) (Table 4.4).

Table 4.4 Summary of Gaming Platform Use

Areas	Characteristics
Recruitment and Radicalisation Hub	Gaming platforms are used for far-right recruitment and radicalisation. Young individuals targeted for extremist indoctrination. The interactive nature of gaming aids in this process.
Use of Encrypted and Private Spaces	Encrypted messaging on gaming platforms protects extremist conversations. Private, password-protected areas for secure extremist content sharing. Safe havens for far-right groups to communicate and organise.
Creation, alteration and Promotion of Extremist Games:	Video games with extremist themes are created for propaganda by far-right groups. Mods alter existing games to reflect extremist ideologies. Role-playing games reenact extremist attacks used for indoctrination.
Use of Gaming Strategies by Extremists	Extremist groups use gaming strategies like memes and trolling for recruitment. Effective dissemination of ideologies within gaming communities.
Less Regulated Platforms	Changing gaming content complicates moderation against extremism. Users move to less regulated sites during crackdowns on extremist content.

References

Abril, D., 2021. *Trump supporters flock to MeWe, Gab, and Rumble after Parler goes offline.* [Online] Available at: https://fortune.com/2021/01/11/mewe-gab-rumble-growth-parler-trump-bans-social-media-violence/ [Accessed 09 08 2023].

ADL, 2021. *Nicholas J. Fuentes: Five things to know.* [Online] Available at: https://www.adl.org/resources/blog/nicholas-j-fuentes-five-things-know [Accessed 04 11 2023].

ADL, 2022. *Extremists, far right figures exploit recent changes to Twitter.* [Online] Available at: https://www.adl.org/resources/blog/extremists-far-right-figures-exploit-recent-changes-twitter [Accessed 12 10 2023].

ADL, 2023. *As war rages, X must curb the spread of misinformation and hate.* [Online] Available at: https://www.adl.org/resources/blog/war-rages-x-must-curb-spread-misinformation-and-hate [Accessed 02 11 2023].

Åkerlund, M., 2021. Influence without metrics: Analyzing the impact of far-right users in an online discussion forum. *Social Media + Society,* 7(2), pp. 1–11.

Akhtar, A. & Nguyen, B., 2022. *Everything you need to know about Parler, the right-wing social media platform Kanye West is planning to buy.* [Online] Available at: https://www.businessinsider.com/what-is-parler-app-social-media-twitter?r=US&IR=T [Accessed 31 10 2023].

Alexander, L., 2016. *Milo Yiannopoulos: Twitter banning one man won't undo his poisonous legacy.* [Online] Available at: https://www.theguardian.com/technology/2016/jul/20/milo-yiannopoulos-twitter-ban-leslie-jones-bad-idea [Accessed 23 11 2023].

Arthur, R., 2020. *The man who helped turn 4chan into the internet's racist engine.* [Online] Available at: https://www.vice.com/en/article/m7aap8/the-man-who-helped-turn-4chan-into-the-internets-racist-engine [Accessed 03 09 2022].

Baele, S. J., Brace, L. & Coan, T. G., 2021. Variations on a theme? Comparing 4chan, 8kun, and other chans' far-right "/pol" boards. *Perspectives on Terrorism,* 15(1), pp. 65–80.

Baele, S., Brace, L. & Coan, T., 2023. Uncovering the far-right online ecosystem: An analytical framework and research agenda. *Studies in Conflict & Terrorism,* 46(9), pp. 1599–1623.

Bartlett, J., 2018. *The people vs. tech.* London: Penguin.

Barrett, P., Hendrix, P. & Sims, G., 2021. *How tech platforms fuel U.S. political polarizarion and what government can do about it.* [Online] Available at: https://www.brookings.edu/articles/how-tech-platforms-fuel-u-s-political-polarization-and-what-government-can-do-about-it/ [Accessed 17 08 2023].

BBC News, 2022. *The downfall of Steve Bannon.* [Online] Available at: https://www.bbc.co.uk/news/election-us-2016-37971742 [Accessed 04 11 2023].

BBC Trending, 2019. *What is 8chan?.* *[Online] Available at:* https://www.bbc.co.uk/news/blogs-trending-49233767 [Accessed 28 07 2020].

Beckett, L., 2018. *Pittsburgh shooting: Suspect railed against Jews and Muslims on site used by 'alt-right'.* [Online] Available at: https://www.theguardian.com/us-news/2018/oct/27/pittsburgh-shooting-suspect-antisemitism [Accessed 03 09 2022].

Beckett, L. & Levin, S., 2019. *El Paso shooting: 21-year-old suspect 'posted anti-immigrant manifesto'.* *[Online] Available at:* https://www.theguardian.com/us-news/2019/aug/03/el-paso-shooting-21-year-old-suspect-in-custody-as-officials-investigate-possible-hate [Accessed 03 09 2022].

Bedingfield, W., 2021. *How the far right exploded on steam and discord.* [Online] Available at: https://www.wired.com/story/far-right-took-over-steam-discord/ [Accessed 11 08 2023].

Blazina, C. & Stocking, G., 2022. *Key facts about Parler.* [Online] Available at: https://www.pewresearch.org/short-reads/2022/10/20/fast-facts-about-parler-as-kanye-west-reportedly-plans-acquisition-of-site/ [Accessed 31 10 2023].

Bohannon, M., 2023. *Here's how Twitter's appearance has changed under Elon Musk.* [Online] Available at: https://www.forbes.com/sites/mollybohannon/2023/05/12/heres-how-twitters-appearance-has-changed-under-elon-musk/?sh=4c45c6195f68 [Accessed 13 10 2023].

Bouko, C., Van Ostaeyen, P. & Voué, P., 2021. Facebook's policies aginst extremism: ten years of struggle for more tranparency. *Firt Monday,* 26(9), pp. 1–22.

Bradshaw, T., Coulter, M. & Bond, D., 2019. *New Zealand terror attacks spark fresh criticisms of Big Tech.* [Online] Available at: https://www.ft.com/content/183e0550-474a-11e9-b168-96a37d002cd3 [Accessed 10 04 2022].

Brown, K. V., 2016. *Twitter has a new tool in the war against harassment, and Milo Yiannopoulos doesn't like it.* [Online] Available at: https://splinternews.com/twitter-has-a-new-tool-in-the-war-against-harassment-a-1793854026 [Accessed 10 09 2022].

Bump, P., 2022. *The platform where the right-wing bubble is least likely to pop.* [Online] Available at: https://www.washingtonpost.com/politics/2022/04/23/telegram-platform-right-wing/ [Accessed 01 11 2023].

Carah, N., 2021. *Media & society. Power, platforms, & participation.* London: Sage.

CEP, 2019. *The far right on Facebook. s.l.: Counter Extermism Project.*

Chen, A., Nyhan, B., Reifler, J. & Robertson, R. W. C., 2021. *Exposure to alternative & extremist content on Youtube. New York: ADL.*

Colley, M. & Moore, M., 2022. The challenges of studying 4chan and the Alt-Right: 'Come on in the water's fine'. *New Media & Society,* 24(1), pp. 5–30.

Condis, J., 2020. Hateful games why white supremacist recruiters target gamers. In: *Digital ethics: Rhtoric and responsibility in online aggression.* Abingdon: Routledge, pp. 143–159.

Conger, K., 2023. *How Elon Musk is changing the Twitter experience.* [Online] Available at: https://www.nytimes.com/2023/04/07/technology/elon-musk-twitter-changes.html [Accessed 15 10 2023].

Conway, M., Scrivens, R. & Macnair, L., 2019. *Right- wing extremists' persistent contemporary trends.* [Online] Available at: https://icct.nl/app/uploads/2019/11/Right-Wing-Extremists-Persistent-Online-Presence.pdf [Accessed 12 08 2022].

Cota, W., Ferrira, S. C., Pastor-Satorras, R. & Starnini, M., 2019. Quantifying echo chamber effects in information spreading over political communication networks. *EPJ Data Science,* 35(8), p. 1.

Darkowl, 2022. *Chan imageboards proliferate on the darknet.* [Online] Available at: https://www.darkowl.com/blog-content/chan-blog/ [Accessed 30 08 2022].

Davey, J., 2021. *Gamers who hate: An introduction to ISD's gaming and extremism series. s.l.: ISD.*

Dewey, C., 2014. *The only guide to Gamergate you will ever need to read.* [Online] Available at: https://www.washingtonpost.com/news/the-intersect/wp/2014/10/14/the-only-guide-to-gamergate-you-will-ever-need-to-read/ [Accessed 03 09 2022].

Donovan, J., Dreyfuss, E. & Friedberg, B., 2022. *Meme wars*. New York: Bloomsbury Publishing.

Douglas, N., 2014. 'It's supposed to look like shit: The Internet ugly aesthetic'. *Journal of Visual Culture,* 13(3), pp. 314–339.

Doward, J. & Townsend, M., 2020. *The UK social media platform where neo-Nazis can view terror atrocities.* [Online] Available at: https://www.theguardian.com /politics/2020/jun/28/the-uk-social-media-platform-where-neo-nazis-can-view -terror-atrocities [Accessed 28 08 2022].

DU, 2023. *What is YouTube?. [Online] Available at:* https://www.digitalunite.com/ technology-guides/tv-video/youtube/what-youtube [Accessed 21 11 2023].

Elley, B., 2021. "The rebirth of the West begins with you!"—Self-improvement as radicalisation on 4chan. *Humanities and Social Sciences Communications,* 67(8), pp. 1–10.

Elliott, V. & Gilbert, D., 2023. *Elon Musk's main tool for fighting disinformation on X is making the problem worse, insiders claim.* [Online] Available at: https://www .wired.com/story/x-community-notes-disinformation/ [Accessed 02 12 2023].

Feiner, L., 2019. *Facebook details rules for its new 'Supreme Court' that will handle controversial posts.* [Online] Available at: https://www.cnbc.com/2019/09/17/ facebook-details-plans-for-new-oversight-board.html [Accessed 14 08 2022].

Finley, K., 2015. *4chan just sold to the founder of the original 'Chan'.* [Online] Available at: https://www.wired.com/2015/09/4chan-sold/ [Accessed 03 09 2022].

Fischer, M., 2021. *From memes to race war: How extremists use popular culture to lure recruits.* [Online] Available at: https://www.washingtonpost.com/nation/2021 /04/30/extremists-recruiting-culture-community/ [Accessed 27 08 2022].

Fung, B., 2021a. *Parler has now been booted by Amazon, Apple and Google.* [Online] Available at: https://edition.cnn.com/2021/01/09/tech/parler-suspended-apple-app -store/index.html [Accessed 31 10 2023].

Fung, B., 2021b. *Parler may be gone for now. That won't stop the calls to violence online.* [Online] Available at: https://edition.cnn.com/2021/01/12/tech/parler -online-violence/index.html [Accessed 31 10 2023].

Gallagher, A. et al., 2021. *The extreme right on discord. s.l.:* ISD.

Gaudette, T., Scrivens, R. & Davies, G., 2020. Upvoting extremism: Collective identity formation and the extreme right on Reddit. *New Media & Society,* 23(12), pp. 3491–3508.

GCF Global, 2023. *What is YouTube?. [Online] Available at:* https://edu.gcfglobal.org /en/youtube/what-is-youtube/1/ [Accessed 21 11 2023].

Gilbert, D., 2020. *Parler, Gab, MeWe, and Rumble are creating a massive right-wing echo chamber.* [Online] Available at: https://www.vice.com/en/article/k7a8mz/ parler-gab-mewe-and-rumble-are-creating-a-massive-right-wing-echo-chamber [Accessed 08 08 2023].

Goel, S., 2023. *How does Facebook (Meta) make money: Business model analysis.* [Online] Available at: https://thestrategystory.com/2023/01/09/how-does-facebook -meta-make-money-business-model-analysis/ [Accessed 02 09 2023].

Goggin, B., 2023. *Inside X's community notes, fact-checks on known misinformation are delayed for days.* [Online] Available at: https://www.nbcnews.com/tech /misinformation/elon-musk-x-fact-check-israel-misinformation-rcna119658 [Accessed 02 12 2023].

Gonimah, D., 2019. *What is 8chan and why was it banned?*. [Online] Available at: https://storyful.com/resources/blog/what-is-8chan/ [Accessed 22 11 2020].

Gonzalez, O., 2019. *8chan, 8kun, 4chan, Endchan: What you need to know.* [Online] Available at: https://www.cnet.com/news/8chan-8kun-4chan-endchan-what-you-need-to-know-internet-forums/ [Accessed 28 07 2020].

Grelicha, K. et al., 2021. *Far-right extermists' use of social media platforms for communicate and spread rasdicalised beliefs.* [Online] Available at: https://www.counterterrorismgroup.com/post/far-right-extremist-use-of-social-media-platforms-to-communicate-and-spread-radicalized-beliefs [Accessed 14 10 2023].

Grisham, K., 2021. *Far-right groups move to messaging apps as tech companies crack down on extremist social media.* [Online] Available at: https://theconversation.com/far-right-groups-move-to-messaging-apps-as-tech-companies-crack-down-on-extremist-social-media-153181 [Accessed 28 08 2022].

Hamilton, A., 2017. *Interview: Telegram and terror: How data encryption shapes our lives.* [Online] Available at: https://digit.fyi/whatsapp-telegram-terror/ [Accessed 28 07 2020].

Haselton, T., 2018. *Here's Facebook's once-secret list of content that can get you banned.* [Online] Available at: https://www.cnbc.com/2018/04/24/facebook-content-that-gets-you-banned-according-to-community-standards.html [Accessed 02 12 2023].

Hern, A., 2019. *Far right groups' coded language makes threats hard to spot.* [Online] Available at: https://www.theguardian.com/world/2019/mar/17/far-right-groups-coded-language-makes-threats-hard-to-spot [Accessed 03 09 2022].

Hern, A. & Waterson, J., 2019. *Social media firms fight to delete Christchurch shooting footage.* [Online] Available at: https://www.theguardian.com/world/2019/mar/15/video-of-christchurch-attack-runs-on-social-media-and-news-sites [Accessed 03 09 2022].

Holt, T. J., Bossler, A. M. & Seigfried-Spellar, K., 2022. *Cybercrime and digital forensics. An introduction.* 3rd ed. London: Sage.

Horwitz, J. & Seetharaman, D., 2020. *Facebook executives shut down efforts to make the site less divisive.* [Online] Available at: https://www.wsj.com/articles/facebook-knows-it-encourages-division-top-executives-nixed-solutions-11590507499 [Accessed 23 11 2023].

Jasser, G., McSwiney, J., Pertwee, E. & Zannettoy, S., 2023. 'Welcome to #GabFam': Far-right virtual community on gab. *New Media & Society,* 25(7), pp. 1728–1745.

Kamenetz, A., 2018. *Right-wing hate groups are recruiting video gamers.* [Online] Available at: https://www.npr.org/2018/11/05/660642531/right-wing-hate-groups-are-recruiting-video-gamers [Accessed 27 08 2022].

Kang, C., 2021. *What is the Facebook oversight board?*. [Online] Available at: https://www.nytimes.com/2021/05/05/technology/What-Is-the-Facebook-Oversight-Board.html [Accessed 14 08 2022].

Karpova, A., Savelev, A., Vilnin, A. & Kuznetsov, S., 2022. Method for detecting far-right extremist communities on social media. *Social Science,* 11(5), pp.1–19.

Khalili, J., 2021. *How Reddit turned its millions of users into a content moderation army.* [Online] Available at: https://www.techradar.com/news/how-reddit-turned-its-millions-of-users-into-a-content-moderation-army [Accessed 23 11 2023].

Kildiş, H. P., 2020. *Post-truth and far-right politics on social media.* [Online] Available at: https://www.e-ir.info/2020/11/17/post-truth-and-far-right-politics-on-social-media/ [Accessed 29 08 2022].

Kleinman, Z., 2023. *Twitter: Five ways Elon Musk has changed the platform for users.* [Online] Available at: https://www.bbc.co.uk/news/technology-64289251 [Accessed 15 10 2023].

KnowYourMeme, 2019. *Alt-Right.* [Online] Available at: https://knowyourmeme.com/memes/cultures/alt-right [Accessed 04 11 2023].

KnowYourMeme, 2019. *Futaba channel (2chan).* [Online] Available at: https://knowyourmeme.com/memes/sites/futaba-channel-2chan [Accessed 29 08 2022].

Lakhani, S., 2021. *Extremism: An exploration of the current landscape, tends, and threats.* Luxenbourg: Publication Office of the European Union.

Lanchester, J., 2017. You are the product. *London Review of Books,* 39(16).

Lapowsky, I., 2017. *The internet gave us Milo. The internet can take him away.* [Online] Available at: https://www.wired.com/2017/02/internet-gave-us-milo-internet-can-take-away/ [Accessed 23 11 2023].

Laub, Z., 2019. *Hate speech on social media: Global comparisons.* [Online] Available at: https://www.cfr.org/backgrounder/hate-speech-social-media-global-comparisons [Accessed 14 10 2023].

Lees, M., 2016. *What Gamergate should have taught us about the 'alt-right'.* [Online] Available at: https://www.theguardian.com/technology/2016/dec/01/gamergate-alt-right-hate-trump [Accessed 03 09 2020].

Leetaru, K., 2018. *What does it mean for social media platforms to "Sell" our data?.* *[Online]* Available at: https://www.forbes.com/sites/kalevleetaru/2018/12/15/what-does-it-mean-for-social-media-platforms-to-sell-our-data/?sh=28d93a602d6c [Accessed 02 09 2023].

Lomas, N., 2022. *As EU says it'll ban Russia's 'toxic media machine', social media firms face pressure to act.* [Online] Available at: https://techcrunch.com/2022/02/28/eu-rt-sputnik-ban-social-media-pressure/ [Accessed 28 12 2022].

Lutkevich, B. & Wigmore, I., 2021. *Social media.* [Online] Available at: https://www.techtarget.com/whatis/definition/social-media [Accessed 02 09 2023].

Lynskey, D., 2017. *The rise and fall of Milo Yiannopoulos – How a shallow actor played the bad guy for money.* [Online] Available at: https://www.theguardian.com/world/2017/feb/21/milo-yiannopoulos-rise-and-fall-shallow-actor-bad-guy-hate-speech [Accessed 04 11 2023].

McCormick, R., 2016. *Twitter bans Milo Yiannopoulos, one of its worst trolls.* [Online] Available at: https://www.theverge.com/2016/7/19/12232738/twitter-bans-milo-yiannopoulos [Accessed 23 11 2023].

McFarlane, G., 2022. *How Facebook (Meta), X Corp (Twitter), social media make money from you.* [Online] Available at: https://www.investopedia.com/stock-analysis/032114/how-facebook-twitter-social-media-make-money-you-twtr-lnkd-fb-goog.aspx [Accessed 02 09 2023].

McSwiney, J., Jasser, G. & Pertwee, E., 2021. *Gab's gift to the far right.* [Online] Available at: https://www.lowyinstitute.org/the-interpreter/gab-s-gift-far-right [Accessed 01 11 2023].

Meta, 2018. *Publishing our internal enforcement guidelines and expanding our appeals process.* [Online] Available at: https://about.fb.com/news/2018/04/comprehensive-community-standards/ [Accessed 02 12 2023].

Meta, 2019. *Writing Facebook's rulebook.* [Online] Available at: https://about.fb.com/news/2019/04/insidefeed-community-standards-development-process/ [Accessed 02 12 2023].

Meta, 2023. *Facebook community standards.* [Online] Available at: https://transparency.fb.com/en-gb/policies/community-standards/?source=https%3A%2F%2Fwww.facebook.com%2Fcommunitystandards%2F [Accessed 02 12 2023].

Miller, T., 1985. *The electronic fringe.* [Online] Available at: https://www.washingtonpost.com/archive/lifestyle/magazine/1985/07/14/the-electronic-fringe/17955294-9c94-4b5d-99e4-9af799b45eae/ [Accessed 12 08 2020].

Mudde, C., 2019. *The far right today.* London: Wiley.

Munk, T., 2022. *The rise of politically motivated cyber attacks. Actors, attacks and cybersecurity.* London: Routledge.

Munk, T., 2024. *Memetic war. Online resistance in Ukraine.* Abingdon: Routledge.

Musil, S., 2017. *Daily Stormer offline again as Cloudflare pulls support.* [Online] Available at: https://www.cnet.com/news/privacy/daily-stormer-nazi-offline-cloudflare-pulls-support-racist-charlottesville/ [Accessed 03 11 2023].

Novet, J., 2021. *Parler's de-platforming shows the exceptional power of cloud providers like Amazon.* [Online] Available at: https://www.cnbc.com/2021/01/16/how-parler-deplatforming-shows-power-of-cloud-providers.html [Accessed 31 10 2023].

Orsini, L., 2015. *How The 4chan sale returns the controversial forum to its anime roots.* [Online] Available at: https://www.forbes.com/sites/laurenorsini/2015/09/21/4chan-sale-2channel-moot-christopher-poole-hiroyuki-nishimura/?sh=15cde34b53d2 [Accessed 03 09 2022].

Papakyriakopoulos, O., Serrano, J. C. M. & Hegelich, S., 2020. *The spread of COVID-19 conspiracy theories on social media and the effect of content moderation.* [Online] Available at: https://misinforeview.hks.harvard.edu/article/the-spread-of-covid-19-conspiracy-theories-on-social-media-and-the-effect-of-content-moderation/ [Accessed 29 08 2022].

Paul, K., 2019. *8chan: Ex-users of far-right site flock to new homes across internet.* [Online] Available at: https://www.theguardian.com/us-news/2019/aug/08/8chan-shutdown-users-social-media [Accessed 03 09 2022].

PCMagazine, 2022. *Image board.* [Online] Available at: https://www.pcmag.com/encyclopedia/term/image-board [Accessed 30 08 2022].

Pengelly, M., 2023. *Trump praises 'terrific' white supremacist conspiracy theorist.* [Online] Available at: https://www.theguardian.com/us-news/2023/aug/14/laura-loomer-trump-praise-white-supremacist [Accessed 04 11 2023].

Perez, S., 2023. *After delays, X updates community notes fact-checks to improve speed and distribution.* [Online] Available at: https://techcrunch.com/2023/10/12/after-delays-x-updates-community-notes-fact-checks-to-improve-speed-and-distribution/ [Accessed 02 12 2023].

Press Association, 2017. *Twitter says its system is 'broken' after far-right organiser wins blue tick.* [Online] Available at: https://www.theguardian.com/technology/2017/nov/09/twitter-system-blue-tick-verification-jason-kessler-jack-dorsey-charlottesville [Accessed 10 09 2022].

Press-Reynolds, K., 2022. *A wave of banned far-right influencers and extremists tried to rejoin Twitter after Musk announced his buyout.* [Online] Available at: https://www.insider.com/far-right-influencers-banned-twitter-elon-musk-buyout-extremism-2022-4 [Accessed 04 11 2023].

Pridmore, J. & Lyon, D., 2011. Marketing as surveillance: assembling consumers as brands. In: *Inside marketing: Practices, ideologies, devices*. New York: Oxford University Press, pp. 115–136.

Rawlinson, K., 2018. *Tommy Robinson permanently banned by Twitter*. [Online] Available at: https://www.theguardian.com/technology/2018/mar/28/tommy -robinson-permanently-banned-twitter-violating-rules-hateful-conduct [Accessed 04 11 2023].

Ray, B. & Marsh II, G. E., 2001. Recruitment by extremist groups on the internet. *Monday First*, 02.6(2).

Ray, S., 2021. *The far-right is flocking to these alternate social media apps — Not all of them are thrilled*. [Online] Available at: https://www.forbes.com/sites/siladityaray /2021/01/14/the-far-right-is-flocking-to-these-alternate-social-media-apps---not-all -of-them-are-thrilled/ [Accessed 29 08 2022].

Reddit, 2022. *How does reddit work?*. [Online] Available at: https://www.redditinc .com/ [Accessed 21 08 2022].

Ribeiro, M. et al., 2021. Do platform migrations compromise content moderation? Evidence from r/The_Donald and r/Incels. *Proceedings of the ACM on Human-Computer Interaction*, 5(316), pp. 1–24.

Robins-Early, N., 2018. *Facebook and Instagram let Neo-Nazis run clothing brands on their platforms*. [Online] Available at: https://www.huffingtonpost.co.uk/entry /facebook-nazi-clothing-extremism_n_5b5b5cb3e4b0fd5c73cf2986 [Accessed 10 09 2022].

Rogers, R., 2020. Deplatforming: Following extreme Internet celebrities to Telegram and alternative social media. *European Journal of Communcation*, 35(3), pp. 213–229.

Roose, K., 2017. *This was the alt-right's favorite Chat App. Then came Charlottesville*. [Online] Available at: https://www.nytimes.com/2017/08/15/technology/discord -chat-app-alt-right.html [Accessed 11 08 2023].

Ruckenstein, M. & Granroth, J., 2020. Algorithms, advertising and the intimacy of surveillance. *Journal of Cultural Economy*, 13(1), pp. 12–24.

Ruckenstein, M. & Schüll, N., 2017. The datafication of health. *Annual Review of Anthropology*, 46, pp. 261–278.

Salinas, S., 2018. *Mark Zuckerberg said an independent 'Supreme Court' could fix Facebook's content problems*. [Online] Available at: https://www.cnbc.com/2018 /04/02/facebook-ceo-mark-zuckerberg-on-a-supreme-court-for-content.html [Accessed 15 08 2022].

Scholz, K. A., 2020. *How the internet fosters far-right radicalisation*. [Online] Available at: https://www.dw.com/en/how-the-internet-fosters-far-right-radicalization/a -52471852 [Accessed 28 08 2022].

Schori Liang, C. & Cross, M. J., 2020. *White crusade: How to prevent right-wing. s.l.:* GCSP.

Shinal, J., 2017. *The CEO who pulled the plug on neo-Nazi site says he did it to protect his company*. [Online] Available at: https://www.cnbc.com/2017/09/24/cloudflare -ceo-matthew-prince-explains-why-he-booted-the-daily-stormer.html [Accessed 03 11 2023].

Silverman, E., 2021. *Unite the right organiser appeared to instruct followers to mislead law enforcement, court evidence suggests*. [Online] Available at: https:// www.washingtonpost.com/dc-md-va/2021/11/15/charlottesville-trial-jason-kessler -cantwell/ [Accessed 04 11 2023].

Singer, P. & Brookings, E., 2018. *Likewar. The weaponisation of social media.* New York: Mariner Books.

Sonnemaker, T., 2020. *Facebook reportedly had evidence that its algorithms were dividing people, but top executives killed or weakened proposed solutions.* [Online] Available at: https://www.businessinsider.com/facebook-knew-algorithms-divided -users-execs-killed-fixes-report-2020-5?r=US&IR=T [Accessed 23 11 2023].

Spangler, T., 2023. *Parler shut down by new owner: 'A Twitter Clone' for conservatives is not a 'viable business'.* [Online] Available at: https://variety.com/2023/digital /news/parler-shut-down-new-owner-starboard-twitter-clone-conservatives -1235583709/ [Accessed 31 10 2023].

SPLC, 2022. *Proud boys.* [Online] Available at: https://www.splcenter.org/fighting -hate/extremist-files/group/proud-boys [Accessed 10 09 2022].

Statt, N., 2020. *Facebook reportedly ignored its own research showing algorithms divided users.* [Online] Available at: https://www.theverge.com/2020/5/26 /21270659/facebook-division-news-feed-algorithms [Accessed 25 11 2023].

Sundar, S. S., 2008. The MAIN model: A heuristic approach to understanding technology effects on credibility. In: *Digital media, youth, and credibility.* Cambridge: The MIT Press, pp. 73–100.

Tandoc Jr., E. C., Lim, Z. W. & Ling, R., 2018. Defining "fake news". *Digital Journalism,* 6(2), pp. 137–153.

Telegram, 2019. *Telegram privacy policy.* [Online] Available at: https://telegram.org/ privacy [Accessed 15 08 2023].

Telegram, 2022. *FAQ.* [Online] Available at: https://telegram.org/faq [Accessed 28 08 2022].

The Economist, 2020. *How to deal with free speech on social media.* [Online] Available at: https://www.economist.com/leaders/2020/10/22/how-to-deal-with -free-speech-on-social-media?utm_medium=cpc.adword.pd&utm_source=google &ppccampaignID=18156330227&ppcadID=&utm_campaign=a.22brand_pmax &utm_content=conversion.direct-response.anonymous&gclid=CjwK [Accessed 14 10 2023].

Thorleifsson, C., 2021. From cyberfascism to terrorism: On 4chan/pol/ culture and the transnational production of memetic violence. *Nations and Nationalism,* 28(1), pp. 286–301.

Thorson, E., 2008. Changing patterns of news consumption and participation. *Information, Communication and Society,* 11(4), pp. 473–489.

Tiffany, K., 2020. *Reddit is done pretending the Donald is fine.* [Online] Available at: https://www.theatlantic.com/technology/archive/2020/06/reddit-ban-the-donald -chapo-content-policy/613639/ [Accessed 29 08 2022].

Townsend, M., 2020. *Facebook condemned for hosting neo-Nazi network with UK links.* [Online] Available at: https://www.theguardian.com/technology/2020/nov /22/facebook-condemned-for-hosting-neo-nazi-network-with-uk-links [Accessed 22 11 2020].

Townsend, M., 2021. *How far right uses video games and tech to lure and radicalise teenage recruits.* [Online] Available at: https://www.theguardian.com/world/2021/ feb/14/how-far-right-uses-video-games-tech-lure-radicalise-teenage-recruits-white -supremacists [Accessed 25 10 2023].

Twitter Help Centre, 2022. *Hateful conduct policy.* [Online] Available at: https://help .twitter.com/en/rules-and-policies/hateful-conduct-policy [Accessed 10 09 2022].

Twitter Support, 2017. *2/.* [Online] Available at: https://twitter.com/TwitterSupport/
status/930926124892168192 [Accessed 10 09 2022].

UN, 2023. *What is hate speech?.* [Online] Available at: https://www.un.org/en/hate
-speech/understanding-hate-speech/what-is-hate-speech [Accessed 27 08 2023].

Urman, A. & Katz, S., 2022. What they do in the shadows: Examining the far-
rightnetworks on Telegram. *Information, Communication & Society,* 25(7), pp.
904–923.

Van der Nagel, E. & Frith, J., 2015. Anonymity, pseudonymity, and the agency of
online identity: Explaining the social practices of r/Gonewild. *First Monday,* 20(3).

Walters, J., 2017. *Neo-Nazis, white nationalists, and internet trolls: Who's who in the
far right.* [Online] Available at: https://www.theguardian.com/world/2017/aug/17/
charlottesville-alt-right-neo-nazis-white-nationalists [Accessed 04 11 2023].

Ward, J., 2018. *Day of the trope: White nationalist memes thrive on Reddit's r/The_
Donald.* [Online] Available at: https://www.splcenter.org/hatewatch/2018/04/19
/day-trope-white-nationalist-memes-thrive-reddits-rthedonald [Accessed 29 08
2022].

Wardle, C. & Derakhshan, H., 2017. *Information disorder: Towards an interdisciplinary
framework for research and policy making.* Strasbourg: The Council of Europe.

Wong, C. J., 2017. *Richard Spencer and others lose Twitter verified status under new
guidelines.* [Online] Available at: https://www.theguardian.com/technology/2017/
nov/15/twitter-verified-blue-checkmarks-richard-spencer [Accessed 10 09 2022].

Wong, J. C., 2018. *A year after Charlottesville, why can't big tech delete white
supremacists?.* [Online] Available at: https://www.theguardian.com/world/2018/
jul/25/charlottesville-white-supremacists-big-tech-failure-remove [Accessed 10 09
2022].

X, 2023. *About community notes on X. [Online]* Available at: https://help.twitter.com
/en/using-x/community-notes#:~:text=Community%20Notes%20aim%20to%2
0create,publicly%20shown%20on%20a%20post. [Accessed 02 12 2023].

X, 2023. *How to get the blue checkmark on X. [Online]* Available at: https://help
.twitter.com/en/managing-your-account/about-x-verified-accounts#:~:text
=Starting%20April%201%2C%202023%20we,are%20subscribed%20to%20X
%20Premium. [Accessed 02 12 2023].

York, J., 2018. *Facebook releases first-ever community standards enforcement report.*
[Online] Available at: https://www.eff.org/deeplinks/2018/05/facebook-releases
-first-ever-community-standards-enforcement-report [Accessed 02 12 2023].

Yurieff, K., Fung, B. & O'Sullivan, D., 2021. *Parler: Everything you need to know
about the banned conservative social media platform.* [Online] Available at: https://
edition.cnn.com/2021/01/10/tech/what-is-parler/index.html [Accessed 20 10 2023].

Zuboff, S., 2015. Big other: Surveillance capitalism and the prospects of an information
civilisation. *Journal of Information Technology,* 30(1), pp. 75–89.

Zuboff, S., 2019. *The age of surveillance capitalism. The fight for a human future at the
new frontier of power.* London: Profile Books.

5 Merging the Online and Offline Environments

Codes and Symbols

Communication, Codes, and Memes

Political groups use everyday, recognisable pop culture images to emphasise their political power. These symbols and icons are designed to articulate specific ideological worldviews, shaping others' perspectives and understandings within a common framework (Bogerts & Fielitz, 2019, p. 139). Some symbols and codes, infiltrating mainstream culture and media, gain broader cultural significance. This broad recognition of the meaning of symbols can serve as a recruiting tool, drawing in individuals who might be curious or sympathetic to the symbol's underlying ideology.

Far-right extremist groups are increasingly using humour to spread racist ideologies and incite violence subtly. This approach, often driven by the far-right, blends playful tones with harmful messages, targeting minorities and potentially fuelling violent actions. This strategy allows these groups to disseminate hateful narratives while evading direct responsibility (Chapters 2 and 3) (EU Commission, 2021; Fielitz & Ahmed, 2021). Users are driven by the communal joy of lulz, which is the amusement derived from others' distress. They often view emotions as a trap, using trolling to exploit emotions in others and ignore them in themselves. This leads to the production of transgressive content, which is instrumental in progressing racist and offensive themes (Thorleifsson, 2021; Philips, 2015, pp. 27, 29). Some messages are concealed in symbols and codes, understandable only to those in the know. The term 'dog-whistling' means using seemingly ordinary language with a secret meaning for specific groups. This method subtly conveys contentious or unpopular ideas in a way that lets the speaker avoid direct blame or controversy. It is a common political strategy for indirectly discussing delicate topics without explicitly mentioning them (Bhat & Klein, 2020; Albertson, 2015; Mendelberg, 2001).

Many groups, including those with anti-government conspiracy theories, have created virtual communities based on their common stance. These communities use popular culture to entertain and recruit young members, engaging them with catchy memes, games, edgy humour, and merchandise. All these activities and communications are enforced and promoted on multiple levels to keep the members closely together, from live streams to coffee mugs

DOI: 10.4324/9781003297888-5

(Munk, 2024, p. 63; Fischer, 2021). In-group jokes and memes are valuable tools to glue the members together, and together as a unit, they propagate hate against the out-groups, such as minorities and the mainstream. This makes the group appealing to those who feel disconnected from mainstream culture (Chapters 3 and 4) (Fielitz & Ahmed, 2021, p. 9; Marwick & Lewis, 2017).

Understanding Far-Right Symbols

The distinct symbols employed by these groups make them easily recognisable, reinforcing a sense of unity and solidarity within online communities where members feel free to express themselves. This online environment often fosters an acceptance of viewpoints that may not be encountered offline, thereby accelerating the dissemination of knowledge about symbols and codes beyond the internal group members (Caiani & Parenti, 2016). Some symbols, such as the Eureka Flag in Australia, are shared with non-extremist groups, which adds to the issues about decoding the symbols. It is important to note that most symbols associated with white nationalist and far-right extremists are primarily linked to events or codes developed in Europe, the Americas, and Oceania, despite ultra-nationalist movements existing in other parts of the world like India, Israel, Japan, and Turkey (Colborne, 2023).

Complexity of Identifying Symbols

Symbols can carry inherent meanings but may also hold significance through online users' associations, revealing more profound or hidden connotations. Their impact often stems from social interactions and the values assigned to them rather than language alone (Athique, 2015, p. 97). De Saussure (1966) observed that a symbol is never entirely arbitrary or devoid of meaning; instead, it possesses a fundamental connection between the signifier and the signified. For example, the sign of justice, represented by a pair of scales, cannot be arbitrarily replaced by another symbol like a chariot (De Saussure, 2017 [1966], p. 120; Miller-Idriss, 2019b, p. 124). White supremacists' use of coded language has evolved with Web 2.0. Tools like Google's Perspective, which detects online toxicity, have pushed these groups to subtly use symbols and keywords online, exemplified by 4chan's Operation Google, which is aimed at bypassing AI detection (Bhat & Klein, 2020; Sanchez, 2018).

The far-right extremist groups and individuals are using codes and terms for particular groups of people, which keeps them under the radar for AI detection and online platform moderators. An example is using specific phrases like 'Skypes' for Jews, 'Googles' for black people, 'Skittles' for Muslims, 'Butterflies' for LBGTQ+ and particular nationals, i.e. 'Bing' is used for Chinese people, 'Yahoo' for Mexicans, etc. These codes are spread in conjunction with visual symbols that resonate with those in the know (Bouko et al., 2021; Magu & Luo, 2018; Bhat & Klein, 2020). Symbols create a sense of belonging among those who understand them, and distinguishing between cloaked and benign content remains challenging online and offline. Extremists use creative techniques to convey their messages subtly and navigate legal grey areas by being overtly vague but covertly clear in their extremist intent (Miller-Idriss, 2017; Bouko et al., 2021).

Another example is how far-right groups use triple parentheses ((())) to signal their beliefs about a global Jewish cabal – or if used around a name, it symbolises that the person is Jewish (Schori Liang & Cross, 2020, p. 16; ADL, 2023d; Williams, 2016; Bhat & Klein, 2020). Automated flagging of such nuances is complex, and using human moderators is too resource-intensive. Facebook updated its Violence and Incitement policy to ban 'boogaloo' and related terms linked with violence promotion. Despite this, the Boogaloo Bois quickly adapted, using similar sounding terms like #BigLuau, #BlueIgloo, or #Boojahideen, rendering Facebook's efforts ineffective (Schori Liang & Cross, 2020, p. 16; Peters, 2020; Meta, 2020).

The once benign OK hand gesture now carries connotations of white supremacy. While often harmless, it has been co-opted by far-right extremist groups as a symbol of white power, notably used by the Christchurch mosque attacker in New Zealand (Weale, 2022). Forming a 'W' and 'P' with the hand signals 'White Power' and is prevalent in online far-right circles. The Three Percenters militia and members of the Arizona Proud Boys during the Capitol insurrection have used this sign, linking it to support for former President Trump and the Save America/ Stop the Steal event. This gesture, typically a universal sign of affirmation, now holds divisive meanings, sparking public debate and confusion about its intent (Neiwert, 2018; The Washington Post, 2021; BBC News, 2019; Weale, 2022).

Introduction to Far-Right Symbols

American and European far-right extremist groups use propaganda to reso-nate with current members and attract outsiders. This includes the dissemi-nation of documents, photos, and propaganda materials utilising Fascist and Nazi symbols like burning crosses or Swastikas, as well as animals like wolves, eagles, and lions, or Celtic images like runes and crosses (Caiani & Parenti, 2016).

Historical and Cultural Significance

Far-right extremist groups often change or update their symbols to evade detection by authorities and anti-extremist groups, keeping their messaging covert and influential. Symbols might have precise meanings that a wider audience can decode, but far-right groups also use coded symbols understood only within their circles. These codes help them operate within legal lim-its while spreading extremist views. As these symbols evolve, they provide new ways to communicate political extremism to those in the know, creating a hierarchy within the group based on understanding these codes (CARR, 2020, p. 5). Among the most well-known symbols of far-right extremism is the Swastika. This symbol, infamously adopted by the Nazis, remains a common emblem among neo-Nazis, anti-Semites, and white supremacists. It is closely associated with the Schutzstaffel (SS), the elite paramilitary branch of the Nazi Party, and continues to be used by modern neo-Nazis and Holocaust deniers (Weale, 2022).

Far-right extremists often use number codes like 14 or 14W, referencing the neo-Nazi slogan "We must secure the existence of our people and a future for white children" (Richardson, 2020, p. 38; Bhat & Klein, 2020), which is a citation from Hitler's Mein Kampf. Another code, 88, stands for 'Heil Hitler'. The code '1488' combines this slogan with 'Heil Hitler', illustrating how these symbols and numbers encapsulate the deeply rooted ideologies and beliefs of far-right extremist groups (Colborne, 2023; Richardson, 2020, p. 39; Bhat & Klein, 2020). Used as tools for communication, they convey their agenda and cultivate a sense of solidarity among their members, reinforcing their collective identity and purpose (Weale, 2022).

Colours and Their Connotations

The phrase 'colours of tradition' implies that the use of black, white, and red holds particular significance. These colours not only correspond to the old Imperial German flag but also to the flag of Nazi Germany. Hitler himself emphasised in Mein Kampf why the Nazis should adopt these colours. Neo-Nazis in Germany, Austria, and other regions have historically used these colours as a veiled reference to these flags, allowing them to circumvent prohibitions on Swastikas and other overtly Nazi symbols (Colborne, 2023). The US Confederate flag, emblematic of slavery, racism, and white supremacy, is frequently displayed alongside other symbols like the Swastika and the Celtic Cross, each carrying its own historical and ideological connotations (CARR, 2020, p. 16; Richardson, 2020, pp. 14–16; Weale, 2022). Originally a traditional Christian symbol, the Celtic cross has been co-opted by neo-Nazis, racist skinheads, KKK members, and other white supremacist groups. Organisations like Stormfront have integrated it into their flag, combining it with colours reminiscent of old Nazism and shaping it into a sun cross (ADL, 2023; CARR, 2020, pp. 14–15).

Neo-Pagan and Norse Symbols

Neo-pagan or Norse symbols like the vegvísir (compass) and mjölnir (Thor's hammer) and runes are often seen in clothing, jewellery, and tattoos (Colborne, 2023; Richardson, 2020, p. 25). Ancient runes, particularly from the Elder Futhark system, have been misappropriated by extremist groups, including their incorporation into Nazi Germany's iconography. Initially representing diverse concepts in early Germanic culture, these symbols were repurposed and assigned new meanings within Nazi ideology and symbolism, leading to complex contemporary associations (CARR, 2020, pp. 24–27). Different types of pagan symbols, such as the Black Sun, are taken out of their original context. The Nazis repurposed these ancient symbols to fabricate a mythical Aryan/Norse heritage (CARR, 2020, p. 12; ADL, 2023; Wilson, 2020).

Neo-Nazi and far-right extremist symbols, while associated with such ideologies, are also used in contexts unrelated to far-right beliefs. For instance, bikers, religious groups, and heavy metal fans often employ these symbols. They have deep connections to Viking and Norse culture and are integral to Scandinavian heritage. Consequently, while these symbols may hint at far-right affiliations, they are not conclusive indicators on their own. Accurate interpretation requires considering the broader context in which they are used (Richardson, 2020, p. 25; Colborne, 2023) (Table 5.1 and Table 5.2).

Table 5.1 Outline of Far-right Codes and Symbols – Clothes

Clothing:	Characteristics
Uniforms	Far-right extremist groups often wear uniforms inspired by paramilitary groups during rallies and gatherings.
	Traditional nationalist dress elements are commonly incorporated.
	Uniforms create a distinct visual identity and group cohesion.
	The uniform appearance can be used to intimidate others.
Insignia for National Socialist Army Divisions	Symbols like SS bolts, swastikas, eagles, skulls, and runes, reflecting Nazi ideology.
	Varied colour schemes indicated different ranks and divisions.
	Unique insignia linked to division-specific symbols, such as the Waffen-SS (Skulls and Totenkopf).
Casual Brands	Far-right extremist groups may adopt specific brands as part of their identity.
	These brands become symbols within the far-right extremist groups without the brand's consent.
	Regular consumers may be unaware of these associations, leading to confusion.
Hats and Masks	'Make America Great Again' hats emerged as symbols of far-right support during Trump's Presidency.
	Face masks and balaclavas often conceal identities during rallies or violent acts.
	Such items have become more than just apparel, representing political statements.

Source: (Simon & Sidner, 2021; Fernando, 2021; The Washington Post, 2021; McNeil-Willson, 2020; Caiani & Parenti, 2016).

Table 5.2 Outline of Far-right Groups Codes and Symbols - Accessories

Symbols & Insignias:	
Flags	Emblematic of white supremacy and Southern rebellion.
	Frequently used by white supremacists.
	Both symbols carry significant historical implications.
	Their usage and meaning vary between the US and Europe.
Numbers	88 represents 'Heil Hitler,' with 'H' being the 8th letter of the alphabet.
	14 and the Fourteen Words symbolises a white supremacist mantra.
	Particular numbers carry specific meanings within extremist circles.
Tattoos	Iron Cross Tattoos indicate alignment with certain far-right ideologies.
	The number 28 (VRWX) for 'Blood and Soil' illustrates a connection to nationalist, far-right beliefs.
	Tattoos serve as permanent markers of allegiance to specific groups or ideologies.
Runes and Norse Symbols	Norse symbols, like Valknut/ Black Sun, have been appropriated by white supremacists/ far-right groups.
	These symbols do not inherently have supremacist connotations.
	Misuse of historical and cultural symbols for extremist ideologies.
	These symbols maintain their cultural significance while being co-opted by extremists.

Source: (Colborne, 2023; Hodge & Hallgrimsdottir, 2020; CARR, 2020; Thorleifsson, 2021; Richardson, 2020; The Washington Post, 2021; Noor, 2019; McNeil-Willson, 2020).

Symbols Displayed on the 6th of January 2021

In the USA, the QAnon conspiracy theory had a role in the unprecedented attack on Capitol Hill, which shook the foundations of American democracy. Conspiracy theories often flourish in times of crisis, providing straightforward answers to complex issues and pinpointing enemies. The recent economic trouble, migration issues, and the COVID-19 pandemic have been a breeding ground for the quick spread of far-right extremist conspiracy theories (Chapter 3) (Thorleifsson, 2021). The crowd used and displayed various symbols and codes during the Capitol Hill insurrection. These symbols gained wider attention through social media, photos, and live streams from the event. These symbols, originating from marginal far-right extremist groups, quickly became well-known due to their constant exposure. They show the impact of online culture on real-world actions. The riot highlighted a deep divide in American society and displayed many symbols typically linked to far-right extremism, reflecting some participants' underlying ideologies and beliefs (Fernando, 2021; The Washington Post, 2021; Simon & Sidner, 2021).

Several symbols used on the 6th of January came from online forums (chans) and gaming communities (Chapter 4). They help people with similar views recognise each other while avoiding attention from the law and online moderators. The Internet is a key place where people become more radical. The lack of opposing views on chan platforms amplifies the echo chamber effect, reinforcing ideologies within a closed network, which spills over to actions in the real world (Chapter 3) (Thorleifsson, 2021; Bowman-Grieve, 2013, p. 2; Griffin, 2013). On the /pol/ forum, extreme white supremacists criticise less extreme far-right groups for not taking enough action. They do not believe in using democratic ways to get power and instead want to speed up society's collapse to create a future dominated by white people (Thorleifsson, 2021) (Table 5.3).

Table 5.3 Symbols Used During the 6th of January Attack on Capitol Hill

Symbols	Meaning
Noose and Gallows:	Evokes America's history of lynching, particularly in the Southern states
	Symbolises punitive intent towards perceived traitors.
Confederate Flag	Emblematic of the Civil War and later segregation.
	Its presence in the Capitol marked a historical first.
	Demonstrates its adoption by white supremacist groups worldwide.
Gadsden Flag	Originates from the American Revolution.
	Recently adopted as a symbol of anti-government sentiments.
Three Percenters Flag	Symbolises a revisionist view of history.
	Associated with the Three Percenters group (III%ers, 3%ers, or Threepers).
	Named after a mistaken belief that only 3% of the American population fought in the Revolution to overthrow the government.
Stop The Steal Flag	Linked to modern political conspiracy theories.
	Symbolises the false claim about election fraud.
America First Flag	Criticised for its anti-Semitic connotations linked to World War II.
	Represents far-right commentator Fuentes and the 'Groyper army'.
	Symbolises their vision of a white, Christian America.
VDARE Flag	Linked to the ethnonationalist website VDARE.
	Named after Virginia Dare.
	Considered to be the first white child born in the New World.

(Continued)

Table 5.3 Continued

Symbols	Meaning
Kek Flag	Inspired by an Egyptian deity.
	Symbolises a fictional country.
	Has been displayed at various far-right events.
Pepe the Frog	Originated as a meme.
	Adopted by far-right groups.
	Utilised at offline events alongside extremist symbols.
QAnon Symbols	Symbolises conspiracy theories.
	Used widely as a protest against election fraud.
	Represents opposition to mask-wearing and vaccines.
Release the Kraken Flag	Symbolising supposed election fraud evidence.
	It is rooted in Scandinavian folklore.
	Popular in QAnon circles online, i.e. #ReleaseTheKraken.
OK Hand Gesture	Once harmless, it is now linked to white supremacy.
	Used by groups like the Three Percenters militia and the Proud Boys.
	Symbolise support of Trump.

Source: (Fernando, 2021; Simon & Sidner, 2021; The Washington Post, 2021; Simon & Sidner, 2021; Fernando, 2021; The Washington Post, 2021; Richardson, 2020, pp. 16–17; Walker, 2016; Bruski, 2021; The Washington Post, 2021; Simon & Sidner, 2021; Fernando, 2021; SPLC, 2023; Simon & Sidner, 2021; Fernando, 2021; Simon & Sidner, 2021; The Washington Post, 2021; The Washington Post, 2021; Fernando, 2021; CARR, 2020, p. 17; The Washington Post, 2021; CARR, 2020, pp. 20–24; BBC News, 2016; The Washington Post, 2021; Fernando, 2021; The Washington Post, 2021; Simon & Sidner, 2021; BBC News, 2020; The Washington Post, 2021; Neiwert, 2018; Simon & Sidner, 2021).

Fashion as a Far-Right Tool

Originally from the UK, the skinhead style was adopted by racist groups in the 1980s and 1990s, becoming their predominant style for about 25 years. This look involved shaved heads, steel-toe boots, and other distinctive clothing (Conti, 2018; Gaugele, 2019; Benton & Peterka-Benton, 2020, p. 8). For decades, clothing has been a key identity marker for far-right extremist groups, serving various functions like protection, appearance enhancement, and making statements. Clothing and brands carry symbolic meanings, often indicating membership in subcultural movements (Benton & Peterka-Benton, 2020, p. 8; Dodd & Kinnally, 2020, p. 4). Yet, the actual style of the groups has changed from a hardcore militaristic style to more subtle fashion statements. This enables new members to engage with the far-right extremist movement without altering their appearance radically. Far-right consumers can select from a wide array of products, either from the group's brand or an established brand adopted by these groups (Spitznagel, 2022).

Extremist Ideologies through Fashion

Nationalistic streetwear and brands bear covert or overt symbols beyond being mere clothing. This allows like-minded individuals to identify each other (Miller-Idriss, 2019b, p. 69; Darwish et al., 2019). The streetwear provides the group members with a sense of purpose and identity, all while masking racist and xenophobic sentiments. These seemingly ordinary T-shirts are, in fact, powerful tools within a broader youth subculture, reinforcing racist and nationalist identities and fuelling extremist actions and violence (Darwish et al., 2019). Some coding is only decipherable to the in-group members, offering plausible deniability to authorities. For instance, a purple T-shirt with the text 'MY FAVORITE COLOR IS WHITE' can be seen as either a white supremacist message or humour linked to the T-shirt colour. Less obvious links are also used in the group member's fashion statements. Alphanumeric codes replace racist or nationalist phrases, such as '2YT4U' for 'too white for you' (Darwish et al., 2019; Miller-Idriss, 2017).

Influence and Mobilisation

Fashion has become a potent tool for far-right movements, allowing them to express and advance their extremist ideologies by carrying symbol that reinforces a sense of distinctiveness and belonging to a group (Benton & Peterka-Benton, 2020; Dodd & Kinnally, 2020). Many far-right extremists blend into society, eschewing noticeable appearances to infiltrate mainstream politics and evade detection by authorities such as law enforcement and educators (Jones, 2018; Spitznagel, 2022; Miller-Idriss, 2019a; Benton & Peterka-Benton, 2020, pp. 8–9). They express their group identity and political beliefs through their style, which is crucial given their predominant online interactions and limited face-to-face connections. This is often reflected in their choice of clothing and accessories (Colborne, 2019). Intriguingly, certain fashion brands have unintentionally mirrored symbols associated with far-right extremist groups, inadvertently making these ideologies more attractive to a broader, younger audience (Spitznagel, 2022).

Online Marketplaces for Far-Right Fashion

Fashion is a significant statement of belonging and a tool for extremist movements to influence and mobilise followers who resonate with their messages. Simultaneously, subcultures such as football hooligans and fans of far-right extremist rock music have played a significant role in shaping the far-right as a cultural sphere (Colborne, 2019; Gaugele, 2019; Benton & Peterka-Benton, 2020; Dodd & Kinnally, 2020). Numerous e-stores specialising in far-right merchandise have emerged, offering various products from conventional to the extreme far-right. For instance, LegioGloria has a broad selection and promotes European aesthetics and views. Purchasing its clothing is considered a commitment to self-determination. Their range includes casual wear, gym apparel, polos, shirts, and accessories like amulets and wristwraps (Baele et al., 2020).

Fashion profiling has been significant in far-right extremist movements, with fashion choices often indicating traits of potential followers. This concept was utilised by Cambridge Analytica in its research, influencing the development of the far-right and the 2016 US Presidential Election. Fra-right extremist fashion is about selling identity and helping people navigate questions about their place in society, balancing individuality with group norms (Gaugele, 2019; Kansara, 2018). The far-right extremists self-identifie as a distinct group by emphasising differences in gender and skin colour from the liberal mainstream, which they view as feminised and repugnant (Miller-Idriss, 2017; Patrick, 2011). The far-right extremist identity often sharpens in the face of liberal criticism, fuelled by disputes over language and subtle social distinctions. This reactionary stance becomes more pronounced amid debates and opposition from progressive circles (Miller-Idriss, 2017).

E-stores and Merchandise

Fashion products can support extremist groups and, in some cases, rely on services from well-known businesses that have policies against promoting hate groups. Several far-right and neo-Nazi online stores openly use services from significant payment processors, commercial content management systems, and web domain registrars (Postma, 2022). Globally, references to Nazi history, seen in phrases like 'White Fist', 'Hate Club', and others, are commonplace in far-right extremist fashion (Darwish et al., 2019; Miller-Idriss, 2017).

This dynamic strengthens the bond within the in-group, simultaneously alienating outsiders. Clothing adorned with violent imagery and revolutionary slogans plays a role in radicalisation, paralleling influences from music, online forums, and charged political rhetoric. This blend of visual and verbal cues reinforces ideological solidarity and exclusionary practices (Darwish et al., 2019). Major platforms like Amazon, Google, and Wish have taken steps to remove such material, forcing some groups to sell their brands online despite lacking proper infrastructure. They have resorted to platforms like Telegram, even though they are not optimised for trade but for communication (Postma, 2022; Miller-Idriss, 2020).

Consumer Power in Extremism

Several brands in Europe and North America are selling high-quality clothing with hidden extremist symbols and messages. These are subtly incorporated into T-shirts and sweatshirts, aimed at promoting white supremacy and inciting violence against immigrants, Muslims, and Jews (Miller-Idriss, 2020, pp. 78–79; Darwish, et al., 2019). These brands also encourage opposition to liberal values. Their websites often have translations and currency options to appeal to international buyers. Some even modify clothing from well-known brands like J Crew or Abercrombie and Fitch to spread these far-right symbols. These companies may not be part of the extreme far-right movement, but they become part of the far-right consumer market (Conti, 2018). When a brand's identity or products are co-opted by a group not in their intended audience, often contrary to the brand's values. This is known as 'brand hijacking' or, in this context, hatejacking, where a brand experiences a negative brand association, which can have a detrimental effect on the brand image or target audience. This phenomenon can be an expensive challenge as the brands need to change the negative and unintended associations to protect their reputation (Benton & Peterka-Benton, 2020; Wipperfürth, 2006).

Global Spread of Far-Right Fashion

Europe's Extremist Fashion Scene

Online shops often target specific far-right subcultures. For instance, in France, Alabastro promotes Gallic and European identities with Pagan-themed T-shirt designs, similar to LegioGloria's Nordic and Medieval symbols. Reichsversand in Germany sells Nazi memorabilia, and Lokis Truhe features runic symbolism (Baele et al., 2020). In recent years, far-right fashion brands like Ansgar Aryan, Patriotic Ink, and Consdaple have gained popularity in Europe, promoting neo-Nazi ideology through street-style fashion. Schröder of Germany's National Democratic Party introduced Ansgar Aryan and Patriotic Ink, while Glasauer started Consdaple, incorporating the NSDAP acronym from Hitler's Nationalsozialistische Deutsche Arbeiterpartei in the name (Colborne, 2019; Gaugele, 2019). Thor Steinar, now based in Dubai but popular in Germany, sells clothing with Nordic themes and slogans like 'Save the White Continent', using two banned Nazi-era symbols like the T-rune and Wolfsangel in its logo (Colborne, 2019; Gaugele, 2019; Conti, 2018).

In 2011, French Bloc Identitaire member Vardon highlighted the role of fashion designers in far-right extremist activism, stressing the influence of pop-culture symbols, film, and music in creating an extreme-right counterculture. This led to the European Identitarian Movement using modified brand images in xenophobic and racist campaigns (Gaugele, 2019). After European far-right extremist youth movements united in 2012, Sellner of the Austrian GI Movement designed the Phalanx Europa clothing line. This collection, featuring racist, Islamophobic, and white supremacist messages, aimed to normalise extremist ideologies within the movement (Gaugele, 2019). These clothes, sold on the Phalanx Europa online platform, demonstrate the online environment's role in spreading far-right extremist ideology (Phalanx Europa, 2023).

The American Market

Several American brands, like Grunt Style, cater to a far-right niche market, targeting veterans and the pro-gun community. They link patriotism to violence and use symbols such as '1776' and 'Infidel' (Miller-Idriss, 2020, p. 81; Grunt Style, 2023). More prominent players like Jones' Infowar and Breitbart have developed a market for extremist products, including T-shirts with slogans like 'I Stand with Trump' and anti-antifa messages. These websites also feature anti-immigration slogans and conspiracy theories, like stickers stating '9/11 was an insider job' and baseball caps with the OK symbol with a marketing message to sell the product, stating: 'The new "It's OK to be OK" Politically Incorrect Designer Snapback Hat is now available!' (Miller-Idriss, 2020). In 2018, Infowars owner Jones was banned from platforms like Facebook, Twitter, and YouTube for false claims about the Sandy Hook shooting. Infowars later filed for bankruptcy following related legal judgments (Darcy, 2022; Hals & Stempel, 2022; Weber & Collins, 2022; Squire & Hayden, 2023). Today, their website offers less controversial items, such as 'Trump 2024' t-shirts and items with Texan symbols, suggesting secession from the Federation (Infowars Store, 2023).

Boycott Movements and Platform Policies

Breitbart sells products with messages like 'Fight for Freedom', 'Border Wall Construction Co', and 'Deplorable University' on their website, which are still available in 2023 (Miller-Idriss, 2020; Pearson, 2017; Breitbart Store, 2023). This is a controversial area where there were calls for boycotting Breitbart's fashion line due to the racist undertones. In 2017, the e-commerce service Shopify, used by Breitbart to sell products like 'Border Wall Construction Co' T-shirts, faced a boycott movement on Twitter with the hashtag #DeleteShopify (Alba, 2017; Pearson, 2017). Like X/Twitter and Meta/Facebook, Shopify has faced scrutiny for selling far-right goods. Despite guidelines allowing the removal of objectionable content, Shopify maintains its neutrality, stating that hosting a store does not equal endorsement (Alba, 2017; Pearson, 2017). In the current political climate, companies are increasingly scrutinised for their connections to controversial content as public activism grows stronger and information is circulated to a large online audience. This new form of counterattacks on the far-right extremist movements and singling out negative associations with groups impacts brand and company decisions (Alba, 2017).

Co-opting Fashion: How Far-Right Groups Adopt Mainstream Brands

During the Charlotteville Rally in 2017, it was notable that the far-right extremist fashion code had changed to white polo shirts with khakis. This has since been replaced with other clothing and brands containing codes and symbols associated with far-right extremism (Miller-Idriss, 2020, p. 78). Some clothing and fashion brands have been unwillingly co-opted by these groups, contributing to the transition from traditional skinhead attire.

In 2020, the British fashion company Fred Perry announced they would cease selling their gold and black laurel polo shirts in the US and Canada. The brand's design has become synonymous with the Proud Boys. Fred Perry's laurel wreath logo bears similarities to the yellow wreath found in some Nazi flags (Spitznagel, 2022; Benton & Peterka-Benton, 2020, p. 13; Iqbal, 2020; Woolf, 2017). Before the insurrection, the Proud Boys swapped their usual black-and-gold outfits for all-black with orange hats. However, some still wore gear with the Proud Boys logo (The Washington Post, 2021).

Neo-Nazi Co-option of Brand Imagery

Other brands, like New Balance sneakers, have also been linked to white supremacist groups due to associations with symbolism like the letter 'N' representing Nazis, nationalists, or National Socialists (Benton & Peterka-Benton, 2020, p. 15; Miller-Idriss, 2017; Iqbal, 2020). In the 2016 US Presidential Election, the CEO of New Balance made a pro-Trump statement, leading the neo-Nazi website, the Daily Stormer, to label them as "the official shoe of white people" (Notopoulos & Broderick, 2017). Similar to the Consdaple, the sports brand Lonsdale's brand name can be used to signal an extremist belonging. The sports brand 'Lonsdale' has been hijacked by neo-Nazi groups, with the jacket's half-zipped state revealing the initials 'NSDA', resembling the acronym for Hitler's party – a symbol prohibited in Europe (Benton & Peterka-Benton, 2020, p. 14; Conti, 2018).

The Boogaloo Bois' Hawaiian Shirts

Another example is the American Boogaloo Bois, who have adopted Hawaiian shirts as their signature attire. Group members are often seen armed and dressed in Hawaiian-style floral shirts reminiscent of the US TV show 'Magnum PI' (1980-1988, 2018-2022), and they embody key characteristics of an anti-establishment far-right extremist group with strong ties to accelerationism (IMDb, 2022a, 2022b; Gallagher, 2020; Pemberton, 2020; Byman, 2022, p. 103). Members are frequently observed on the fringes of gatherings in states like Texas, Georgia, and Pennsylvania, signalling their desire for a second American War, or 'boogaloo', to overthrow a perceived corrupt system (Gallagher, 2020; Kenes, 2021) (Table 5.4).

Table 5.4 Summary Codes and Symbols Use

Difficulty in Monitoring and Regulation	Covert symbols and codes complicate the monitoring and regulation of extremist content. Dual meanings make it challenging to determine whether they are used for extremism or innocence.
Algorithmic Amplification	Social media algorithms can inadvertently promote extremism. Recommend related content based on user behaviour and symbols.
Intellectual Property Misuse	Far-right extremist groups exploiting well-known symbols or logos for propaganda The brand-hijacking harms brand reputations. This misuse also raises issues concerning intellectual property rights.
Understanding the Nuance of Symbolism	Public and law enforcement education on the nuances of symbols is crucial. Lack of expertise can lead to misunderstandings and ineffective responses.
Threats to Free Speech and Expression	Balancing the fight against far-right extremism with free speech rights is challenging. Far-right extremists often use codes and symbols to evade social media moderation.

Humour as a Tool

The blending of insults and abrasive humour on image-based forums has become a hallmark of digital subcultures and a vital tool for far-right extremist recruitment. This approach, full of ambiguities, mischief, and edginess, fosters a community-building dynamic and has shifted from hierarchical extremist groups to more fluid 'swarms'. Discerning organised and organic online behaviour is often challenging, but this ambiguity is not a weakness. Instead, it reflects a strategic aim to engage individuals with extremist ideas through jokes, pranks, and parodies, leveraging the unique nature of the online environment (Fielitz & Ahmed, 2021, p. 8).

In the far-right online community, forums and apps often use humour and irony as tools to normalise and trivialise extremist views and violence. Continuous exposure to playful images with underlying hateful undertones can lead to the normalisation of these beliefs within these communities. This effect is further reinforced by repeated exposure and a lack of resistance to such micro-aggressions (Marwick & Lewis, 2017; Fielitz & Ahmed, 2021). Mainstreaming techniques include covert strategies where extremists use coded language to bypass bans and present their content as benign. This often makes extremist content seem humorous and entertaining, thereby normalising it.

Unravelling the Kek Phenomenon

'Kek' originated in the online gaming community, particularly from World of Warcraft, as a variant of 'lol', representing laughter (Yar & Steinmetz, 2019, p. 259). However, its usage evolved significantly within the white nationalist movement. They developed a semi-ironic religion around Kek, a deity symbolised by a frog's head and associated with chaos and darkness (CARR, 2020, p. 17; Richardson, 2020, pp. 17–18). Kek has come to represent the far-right extremist's notion of 'meme magic', which they credit for their influence and Trump's political success. This figure captures the essence of the far-right, intertwining juvenile humour and racism with a pseudo-intellectual allure, thus appealing to young ideologues. Kek stands at the intersection of satire and serious ideology, serving as both a tool to mock liberals and a representation of the extreme far-right's self-perceived role as agents of societal chaos (Neiwert, 2017).

Kek is linked to Egyptian mythology, where Kek is depicted with frog or cat features. This god has been adopted by the far-right extremists as a symbol of chaos and darkness (Neiwert, 2017). Online subcultures have interpreted the hieroglyph for Kek as meme magic, showing a person at a computer (Palau & Roozenbek, 2017; Richardson, 2020, p. 18). Anti-feminist blogger Benjamin, known as 'Sargon of Akkad', has played a role in popularising this concept through memes (CARR, 2020, p. 17; Richardson, 2020, pp. 17–18). This concept of Kek has merged with the Pepe the Frog meme on platforms like 4chan, symbolising far-right extremism and widely used in President Trump's presidential campaigns. This fusion of ancient and digital culture led to the 'Cult of Kek' within these groups, aiming to disrupt the status quo (Neiwert, 2017).

Kekistan: Imaginary Realm, Real Impact

Central to this belief is Kekistan, an imaginary country established for worshipping Kek. This concept is mainly used to amuse and challenge liberals and conservatives (CARR, 2020, p. 17; Richardson, 2020, pp. 17–18; Neiwert, 2017). The Kekistani flag from the far-right mimics the Nazi flag but changes its meaning when it becomes a meme code in a new historical context. This exemplifies how extremists play with symbols and narratives on social platforms to fit their narrative (Bouko et al., 2021; Tuters, 2019). The Kekistan flag is a provocative adaptation of the infamous German Reichskriegsflagge, which was the Nazi war flag. In this edition, the anonymous message board 4chan logo replaces the Iron Cross, and the Kek symbol is used instead of the Swastika.

Additionally, the flag's primary colour has shifted from red to green. This emblem is purposefully designed to troll individuals familiar with its symbolism, targeting primarily liberals and certain conservatives (CARR, 2020, p. 17; Richardson, 2020, pp. 17–18; Tuters, 2019). The similarity with the

Nazi flag is an intentional form of provocation from the far-right extremist intending to trigger opponents into accusing them of being Nazis (Tuters, 2019). Deliberate provocations to trigger overreactions often involve creating ambiguous or exaggerated statements that seem controversial yet have plausible deniability, often under the pretext of humour or satire. When the target reacts strongly, the provocateur can dismiss their response as an overreaction or misinterpretation, portraying them as overly sensitive or humourless. This tactic aims to undermine the credibility of the responder.

Pepe the Frog: From Innocent Comic to Extremist Icon

The subforum '/pol/' on 4chan is a hub for diverse extremist ideologies, from anarchists to white supremacists. 4chan, central to Internet subculture, offers varied sub-forums on topics like video games, anime, and politics (Chapter 4). It is known for promoting a communication culture rich in memes, catchy texts, and images, often incorporating pop culture references and characters used in various contexts. The German far-right activists known as Generation D declared in 2007 that 'people respond to images in a stronger way than to text. By using images, we can engage in effective memetic warfare and articulate our narratives to the people' (Bogerts & Fielitz, 2019, p. 137).

Pepe the Frog, originally from the comic series Boy's Club by Matt Furie, became famous online beyond niche message boards. The series, featuring characters like Pepe, Brett, Andy, and Landwolf, depicted a laid-back lifestyle centred around pizza and video games (Know Your Meme, 2020; Klee, 2016; Richardson, 2020, p. 20; Vice, 2021). Pepe first appeared in 2008 and became famous for the 'Feels Good Man' reaction image. This image gained traction on 4chan's /b/ board, especially after Hendren (@fart) posted it. Soon, variants like 'Feels Bad Man' emerged. By 2014, Pepe content had spread to platforms like Tumblr, Instagram, Reddit, and Facebook, creating dedicated spaces for sharing these memes (Know Your Meme, 2020; Taveria & Balfour, 2016; Richardson, 2020, p. 21).

The Political Co-option of Pepe the Frog

Interestingly, Pepe was employed to bolster Trump's presidential campaign with a rendition of Pepe donning a 'Make America Great Again' cap resonating with Trump's base (Palau & Roozenbek, 2017; Richardson, 2020, p. 22). Platforms like Reddit and the notably aggressive 4chan became radicalisation hotspots targeting primarily young white males. These platforms echo far-right ideologies, including nationalism, anti-feminism, anti-Semitism, anti-multiculturalism, and white supremacy. Notably, these far-right factions championed Trump, aiming to co-opt 4chan's meme culture. Emblematic of this shift, Pepe the Frog evolved into a symbol for white supremacist groups, where the cartoon was combinded with Nazi propaganda (Taveria & Balfour,

2016). Pepe the Frog illustrates the dual nature of some symbols, appearing as a humorous cartoon to some yet profoundly embedded in far-right online communications to others (Miller-Idriss, 2019b; BBC News, 2016)

Memes like Pepe the Frog have evolved from their innocent origins to become tools for spreading extreme ideologies. This led to media outlets and organisations like the Anti-Defamation League categorising Pepe alongside other hate symbols such as the Swastika and KKK's Blood Drop Cross (BBC News, 2016; Vice, 2021). The meme has been associated with gun rights advocates and white supremacists, often hinting at a potential race war or second civil war through the term 'boogaloo'. The Boogaloo movement, known for its satirical approach, has also adopted armed versions of Pepe (Farinelli, 2021, p. 12). In 2015, a 4chan post by Maldraw showing Trump as Pepe the Frog gained traction, especially after Trump's retweets of the image and various Trump-Pepe renditions (BBC News, 2016). Despite legal actions by Pepe's creator, Furie, against its use in far-right contexts, Pepe, along with variants like Groyper, remains associated with extreme far-right extremist symbolism (Richardson, 2020, p. 22; Swinyard, 2019; Gault, 2017).

The 2016 Meme War: The Clash of Memes and Political Narratives

A crucial moment in the development of far-right extremism occurred during the 2016 US presidential campaign. The meme trolls flooded the Internet with pro-Trump content, pivotal in reshaping public perception to favour Trump (ISD, 2023). During the 2016 US Presidential Election, Pepe the Frog became a point of contention when the Clinton campaign associated the meme with some Trump supporters. This led to an online meme war between the supporters of both candidates (Know Your Meme, 2020). Clinton's comment about Trump's supporters being a 'basket of deplorables' went viral, sparking numerous Photoshop creations, including parodies featuring Trump-themed Pepe the Frog (Klee, 2016; BBC News, 2016; Donovan et al., 2022, pp. 142–144).

On Clinton's official blog in 2016, Pepe the Frog was labelled as 'more sinister than you might realise' (BBC News, 2016; Know Your Meme, 2020) and a 'symbol associated with white supremacy' (Know Your Meme, 2020; BBC News, 2016). This portrayal sparked debates on various Reddit forums, where users argued that Clinton and the media misunderstood Pepe's original, non-political nature. For example, the Daily Dot published an article defending Pepe, stating he was not inherently political or a Nazi symbol (Know Your Meme, 2020; Klee, 2016)

Memes and Codes: Offensive Memetic Warfare

The term 'meme' was coined by biologist Dawkins in his 1976 book, The Selfish Gene. Dawkins introduced memes as cultural units of transmission, similar to genes, that spread through copying or imitation (Munk, 2023, p. 63; Shifman, 2013, p. 363; Singer & Brookings, 2018, p. 190). Memes encompass various elements like melodies, catchphrases, and beliefs, just as genes do in biology. Memes go through processes of variation, competition, selection, and retention. Numerous memes compete for attention, but only those well-suited to their cultural context thrive, while others fade away (ISD, 2023; Munk, 2024, pp. 115–117; Shifman, 2013, p. 363). Online chats and memes are clever ways to focus on certain topics and get people involved in online activism. This is part of memetic warfare, where people express political views and participate in conflicts online. It lets Internet users quickly react to current political events by adding comments and continuing the conversation (Denisova, 2020, p. 34; Ross & Rivers, 2017, p. 3; Munk, 2024, p. 63).

Memes are adeptly used to turn complex ideas into simple, shareable memes, to quickly reaching vast audiences on platforms like 4chan and gaming communities (ISD, 2023; Hodge & Hallgrimsdottir, 2020). Often humorous or symbolic by nature, memes spread quickly online and impact societal and political views. The way meme groups and individuals use humour, irony, and sarcasm makes extreme ideas appear more acceptable, mainly targeting young people online who respond to spontaneous, visual content (Munk, 2024, p. 64; Dynel & Messerli, 2020; Barnes et al., 2021, p. 2; Fielitz & Ahmed, 2021, p. 7; Miller-Idriss, 2020). Far-right extremist groups use memes to spread their ideologies, creating a sharp in-group versus out-group mentality reinforcing unity within while viewing outsiders as threats (Bogerts & Fielitz, 2019, p. 139). The memes are powerful in conveying ideologies, justifying judgments, and excluding those deemed as outsiders, especially by using covert and overt symbols to support far-right ideologies (Hogg, 2016, p. 6; Munk, 2024, pp. 62, 76; Peters & Allan, 2022, p. 218; Crawford et al., 2020).

Russian Propaganda and Memetic Strategies

Between 2016 and 2018, many far-right memes were traced back to coordinated efforts by external actors, particularly Russian intelligence and Russia-backed hackers, rather than just Internet trolls (Hodge & Hallgrimsdottir, 2020; Hatmaker, 2018; Ohlin, 2017; Shane, 2017). These groups used social media platforms like X/Twitter and Facebook to spread disinformation and influence American political opinions through bots and targeted adverts (Hodge & Hallgrimsdottir, 2020, p. 571; Timberg, 2017). This tactic, part of Russia's broader propaganda/ information disorder strategy, was also evident in their actions during the Crimea annexation in 2014 and intensified with the invasion of Ukraine in 2022. Far-right extremist groups increasingly adopt such strategies (Munk, 2023, p. 6). Memes are also instrumental in Russia's 2022 full-scale war against Ukraine to spread falsehoods, where both Russian and Ukrainian authorities and online trolls engage in memetic warfare (Munk, 2024).

Trump's Online Meme Army

The meme generation hub for the Trump online trolling army, MAGA3X, described itself as 'freedom's secret weapon' (Singer & Brookings, 2018, p. 192). Before the 2016 US Presidential Election, online groups pushed pro-Trump messages via memes, Twitter bots, and YouTube, influencing mainstream media. This led to more focus on Clinton conspiracy theories than Trump's controversies in major outlets like *The Washington Post* and *The New York Times* (Marwick & Lewis, 2017). In memes popular among extremist Trump supporters, a blend of hatred, patriotism, and religion emerges, with imagery of American flags, Christian crosses, and depictions of Trump as a superhero or emperor. Common symbols include the Confederate flag, former Chilean dictator Pinochet, and Pepe the Frog. These memes evoke strong emotional reactions in the MAGA World, painting a picture of a nation in dire need of salvation from various crises. While focusing on the actions of MAGA extremists is common, it risks missing the broader picture of radicalism and the underlying aggression. This extremism is often orchestrated and fuelled in obscure online realms, rich with coded language that remains elusive to those outside these circles (D'Antonio & Cohen, 2021).

Far-right extremist groups deftly navigate legal boundaries through coded language, a strategy that is ever-evolving in response to social and legal shifts. This cryptic communication paves the way for a nuanced expression of political extremism. Those in the know, can decode the messages and find novel meanings to perpetuate their ideologies. To the uninitiated, words, memes, icons, and signs might appear innocuous, yet they serve as complex tools for conveying and reinforcing extremist views. This coded language distinguishes insiders from outsiders and establishes a hierarchy within the group based on knowledge and adherence to group discourse, creating new layers of inclusion and exclusion (Chapters 1 and 2) (CARR, 2020, p. 5).

Memes as a Weapon

Using memes as a strategic decision to troll people or political opponents aggressively is the tactic of memetic warfare. Memetic warfare is a form of information warfare conducted online through memes and other tactics to achieve political, strategic, or ideological objectives. It involves the offensive or defensive circulation of content to influence public opinion, disrupt discourse, and advance the interests of those engaged in the campaign (Munk, 2024).

The Evolution of Meme Creation

Creating memes is an ever-evolving process closely tied to current events and issues. Memes serve as a unique form of communication, utilising images and text to highlight specific narratives. They play a crucial role in shaping and reinforcing group dynamics by employing stereotypes and imagery in various contexts. While /pol/ features older fascist themes, it also incorporates new symbols and signifiers from digital, far-right, gaming culture, and popular aesthetics. The memes contain a mixture of visuals and non-visuals in a combination of images, videos and text, which constantly changes to disseminate viewpoints (Knobel & Lankshear, 2007; Thorleifsson, 2021; Munk, 2024, p. 63).

Far-right groups have adeptly used memes to simplify and spread extremist ideologies online, and this format makes them more appealing, especially to younger audiences (ISD, 2023). Such exposure can desensitise people to violent and hateful ideas. Shocking and violent memes in these online communities erode barriers (ISD, 2023; Hodge & Hallgrimsdottir, 2020). Many memes on the /pol/ forum are racist and dehumanising, promoting racial stereotypes and fears of cultural differences. Users with fascist views see minorities, including those of different races, religions, and sexual orientations, as threats to a 'pure' white nation. Liberals, feminists, and leftists are labelled as traitors for supporting ideas like multiculturalism and antiracism. Transnational bodies like the EU and progressive politicians are accused of weakening white nations by endorsing diversity and feminist values (Thorleifsson, 2021).

Memes in Far-Right Ideology

Rapidly evolving emojis serve as signals for in-group members and provocations for out-groups. For instance, far-right extremist X/Twitter users used a big red X on their handles to indicate they believed they were shadowbanned. Far-right online trolls make seemingly bizarre and harmless choices in their symbolism, like adopting the milk emoji to claim the superiority of white people due to their ability to drink milk (while many other ethical racial groups are less tolerant) (Miller-Idriss, 2020, p. 152; Noor, 2019). Key white supremacist figures, like Spencer, adopted milk bottle emojis on their Twitter profiles. They used the hashtag #Milk or #MilkTwitter to promote traditional gender roles and white patriarchy, often mocking multiculturalism and feminism (Bhat & Klein, 2020). This transformation of everyday symbols into objects of fear is part of a larger strategy to signal political belonging and outsmart those they believe are deceiving (Miller-Idriss, 2020, p. 152; Noor, 2019).

These cultural symbols employ provocative imagery but twist their meanings to signal a rejection of mainstream conventions. For example, on the 8chan board /pol/, it is easy to get across Holocaust images used for humour or as part of discussions defending white culture or white nations from perceived threats (Hodge & Hallgrimsdottir, 2020). Specific terms or phrases within gaming communities, initially harmless or related solely to gameplay, might be co-opted and twisted. The word NPC, borrowed from 'non-playable character' in gaming lingo, has been used to mock people perceived as thinking mainstream thoughts without critical analysis (Roose, 2018; Sommerlad,

2018; Gallagher & Topinka, 2023). Terms like 'snowflake', 'SJW' (social justice warrior), or 'cuck' (Cuckold) are used sarcastically to belittle and dismiss anyone arguing against extremist views or standing up for social justice issues (Porter, 2017; Caffier, 2017; Petrow, 2017; Bhat & Klein, 2020).

Various themes are included in the memes, from indirect references to the far right to more explicitly and aggressive memes used for trolling particular groups. Instagram's image-centric nature facilitates the 'shitposting' style popular among Internet-savvy, far-right extremist youth by sharing images that convey specific ideological messages. Some accounts, like @the_typical_liberal and @gen_z_ (the account has been removed), adopt a visual style centred around memes, a significant element in certain extreme far-right subcultures (Baele et al., 2020). Some groups turn to Instagram, using accounts like Europa Invicta to glorify a perceived European Golden Age and its future. Their posts are a collage of idyllic natural landscapes, historical architecture, and images of robust white individuals. The far-right undertones are woven into captions like 'For the Love of Europe', 'The West Is the Best', and 'Fight for European Children'. Additionally, certain Instagram accounts are devoted to portraying what they regard as Aryan women, echoing the themes of similar Facebook pages and websites. These platforms become digital showcases for their idealised visions of race and heritage (Baele et al., 2020).

White Masculinity

The far-right extremist groups frequently circulates memes online that blend pro-Nazi and anti-Semitic imagery with texts that express hatred or incite violence. These memes skilfully employ humour and familiar images, altered to convey sarcasm straightforwardly. At first glance, they might appear harmless, amusing or clever (Holt et al., 2022, p. 384). However, not all far-right memes are overtly violent or racist; their extremist meanings often become apparent only in the context of far-right culture. A notable example is the meme character 'Chad' or the 'Nordic Gamer', created in 2016. This character, depicting an idealised 'Aryan' male, is widely used by the far-right to associate whiteness with positive attributes like attractiveness and intelligence. Affinity for this character can indicate ties to conservative extremism due to its promotion of toxic masculinity, misogyny, and far-right extremist ideologies, including anti-Semitism (Molas, 2023).

Chad-memes

The 'Chad' meme varies in form, with its far-right nuances often only recognisable to those familiar with its hidden messages. For example, the 'Yes Chad' meme seems harmless to many and is widely used in general social media. Yet, on platforms like 4chan, it becomes a symbol of /pol/ culture, often used to mock left-wing politics or endorse racist views through its simple 'yes' response (ISD, 2023; Thorleifsson, 2021). Sometimes, Chad memes are used to depict violence and aggression. The 'Chad Saint Brenton' meme, exemplifies this trend by glorifying violence as a form of 'sanctified' masculinity (ISD, 2023). These memes establish a visual link between the violent Incel culture, an offshoot of the Manosphere and the violent extreme far-right culture. They frame violent acts as a way for young white men to reclaim perceived lost masculinity, blending gender issues with extremist ideologies (Mattheis, 2019; Thorleifsson, 2021).

Chad memes in Incel culture glorify attackers from incidents like those in Christchurch, New Zealand, Poway, US, and Bærum Norway, portraying them as heroes. These memes present the New Zealand attacker as a 'Saint', suggesting attacks are seen as rites of passage to manhood in this culture (Mattheis, 2019; Thorleifsson, 2021). They have been key in radicalising individuals and recruiting for far-right extremist groups, as seen with the Proud Boys (ISD, 2023). The New Zealand mosque attacker's manifesto, filled with insider memes, was posted on 8chan's '/pol/' board, fostering solidarity and leading to a wave of violent memes post-attack (ISD, 2023; Vice, 2021). Similar trends followed other right-wing extremist attacks in 2019. These events underline the powerful role of memes in these communities. The challenge lies in controlling online hate, which normalises violence and can escalate from online rhetoric to real-world terrorism Christchurch - and so far the tech and social media companies have not been able manage the online hate incorporated in the memes (Fielitz & Ahmed, 2021, p. 9; ISD, 2023).

The Reichsbürger

In December 2022, Germany faced an attempted coup by the Reichsbürger, a group embodying a range of extremist beliefs, including anti-vax, anti-Semitism, and QAnon support. They sought to establish an unconstitutional monarchy or absolutist state, blending extremism with monarchist aspirations. Online, this group and others use memes not just for humour but to spread their ideology. These include extreme far-right and Incel themes, promoting anti-feminist views, such as depicting Queen Victoria as an anti-feminist 'Chad'. The use of labels like 'Chads' and 'Virgins' reflects an alarming mix of manosphere ideologies, increasingly prevalent online (Molas, 2023). The pandemic further fuelled the rise of far-right groups in Europe, with activists gaining followers on platforms like Telegram, attracting those wary of government actions and offering conspiracy theory-laden explanations (Smith & Brockling, 2022).

Race and Religion

ANTI-SEMITISM

Racist content on /pol/ takes various forms and often combines conspiracy theories. A dominant theory claims that Jews are orchestrating the use of Muslims and migrants as tools to weaken the white race for global control.

This blends age-old anti-Semitic themes with Islamophobia. The Eurabia concept, alleging covert Muslim colonisation endorsed by some European politicians, is also prevalent. This narrative falsely depicts Christian nations as besieged by forceful Islamisation, portraying Muslims as a formidable enemy. This is a notion that is especially prominent in Western Europe. These theories fuse various forms of bigotry, amplifying followers' fear and mistrust (Thorleifsson, 2021; Esposito & Kalin, 2011).

Online communities rapidly share memes, especially on networks like /pol/ and Gab, where hateful and racist content proliferates. These often include various anti-Semitic and pro-Nazi memes, like the 'Happy Merchant', portraying stereotypical images of the Greedy Jew (De Cristofaro, 2018; Byman, 2022, p. 105). Memes using derogatory phrases such as 'The Goyim Know/Shut it Down' to mock Jews by suggesting they conceal conspiracies. The phrase 'Oy Vey', a Yiddish expression, is twisted in memes to parody Jewish reactions, while 'Good Goy' is used to mockingly imply someone is either defending Jews or entangled in Jewish conspiracies (KnowYourMeme, 2020b). These memes, which also combine Jewish imagery with the COVID-19 virus, promote anti-Semitic stereotypes and foster group cohesion through their editable and co-creative nature (Khan-Ruf, 2021, p. 33).

MUSLIM MEMES

Just as Jewish-focused memes are widespread, numerous memes targeting Muslims have also emerged. A common theme in these memes is associating Muslims with terrorism. An example is the 'Ordinary Muslim Man' meme, which features a man in a Muslim taqiyah hat and captions that start with seemingly anti-American statements before ending with benign phrases. However, some captions subtly embed negative stereotypes, like an early Reddit post with "I am da bomb / at making falafels", cleverly avoiding removal (KnowYourMeme, 2013). In a similar vein, campaigns like "It's OK to be White" from 4chan in 2017 and "Islam is Right About Women", which spread online and through physical posters, linking the Muslim faith with controversial topics like feminism, to stir debate and controversy (KnowYourMeme, 2020a; KnowYourMeme, 2018).

Memes related to the 2023 conflict between Hamas and Israel have been circulating online. These memes support both sides, with several depicting Pepe the Frog as either a Hamas fighter or a Palestine supporter (Know Your Meme, 2023; Hansted,, 2023). Post has emerged about Happy Merchant stereotypes, but other memes are blaming Israel for various societal issues (Know Your Meme, 2023). White supremacist leaders have openly supported Hamas' attacks on Israel, using violent imagery against Israelis and calling for increased violence against Jews globally (ADL, 2023a). Additionally, racist and anti-Semitic groups on Telegram and 4chan are creating propaganda using Generative Artificial Intelligence (GAI) tools. These efforts are part of memetic warfare, aiming to create and share images that glorify one side, demonise the other, and spread misleading narratives about the war (ADL, 2023b).

RACIAL MEMES

Racial themes have been prominently featured in far-right extremist ideologies, especially following the emergence of the Black Lives Matter movement and a sense of marginalisation among some white far-right extremist supporters. A notable instance is the term 'White Boy Summer' (WBS), coined in a 2020 Instagram video by actor and rapper Hanks. Although Hanks intended no racial prejudice, far-right extremists have appropriated the term on platforms like Telegram, Discord, 4Chan, and Twitter (Evans, 2021; ADL, 2021; KnowYourMeme, 2021b). They use it to subtly inject racist beliefs into mainstream dialogues, disguised as irony or humour (ADL, 2021). The WBS memes, blending Nazi imagery with conservative symbols, might influence moderate far-right extremists towards extremist ideologies. As the memes echo the type of communication found on 8chan, the content has become more visible after the Capitol insurrection, aiding neo-Nazis in recruiting and radicalising followers through coded messaging (Evans, 2021).

Memes often depict black men negatively, with some showing a black man looting and a white officer kneeling, ridiculing the Black Lives Matter supporters. They dehumanise by exaggerating features and contrast this with depictions of white individuals as strong or suppressed by political correctness. Such memes not only stereotype black men as criminals but also trivialise protests. The deaths of George Floyd and Ahmaud Arbery were also mocked in memes, indicating a lack of regard for Black lives and highlighting prevalent online racism. The term 'jogger' was used as a covert racial slur in the context of Arbery's murder (Crawford et al., 2020; KnowYourMeme, 2021a). Similarly, terms like 'BBQ Becky' and 'Permit Patty' in memes refer to instances where white individuals unnecessarily called the police on black people, often for minor reasons. These everyday examples of white supremacy are frequently overlooked in mainstream discussions but continue to perpetuate white dominance (Williams, 2020; Vera & Ly, 2020; Lee, 2018). The BBQ Becky memes, combining alliteration, humour, and satire, showcase a white woman calling the police on a black family for simply having a picnic, illustrating a form of white supremacist vigilantism (Williams, 2020; Lee, 2018; KnowYourMeme, 2023) (Table 5.5).

Table 5.5 Summary of Memetic Use

Features	Characteristics
Memetic Warfare	Memes in strategic trolling and political conflicts (offensive).
	Memetic warfare in influencing opinions and disrupting discourse.
The Dynamic Nature of Meme Creation	Memes evolving with current events.
	Role in group dynamics and reinforcing ideologies.
	Everyday symbols are political tools in far-right culture.
Far-Right Ideology in Memes	Simplifying extremist views for wider appeal.
	Potential desensitisation to violence and hate.
	Influencing moderate individuals towards extremism.
Racial and Religious Stereotyping	Racist and dehumanising content in far-right forums.
	Targeting minorities and promoting conspiracy theories.
	Co-opting terms to subtly promote racist beliefs.
	Combining conspiracy theories against Jews and Muslims.
The Spread and Impact of Racially Charged Memes	Rapid sharing of hateful and racist content.
	Stereotyping and promoting false narratives about minorities.

References

ADL, 2021. *"White boy summer:" From meme to mobilization.* [Online] Available at: https://www.adl.org/resources/blog/white-boy-summer-meme-mobilization [Accessed 27 11 2023].

ADL, 2023a. *White supremacist leaders applaud Hamas and violence against Israelis.* [Online] Available at: https://www.adl.org/resources/blog/white-supremacist -leaders-applaud-hamas-and-violence-against-israelis [Accessed 27 11 2023].

ADL, 2023b. *Generative Artificial Intelligence (GAI) and the Israel-Hamas war.* [Online] Available at: https://www.adl.org/resources/blog/generative-artificial -intelligence-gai-and-israel-hamas-war [Accessed 27 11 2023].

ADL, 2023c. *Celtic cross.* [Online] Available at: https://www.adl.org/resources/hate -symbol/celtic-cross [Accessed 28 11 2023].

ADL, 2023d. *Echo.* [Online] Available at: https://www.adl.org/resources/hate-symbol/ echo [Accessed 26 11 2023].

ADL, 2023e. *Sonnenrad.* [Online] Available at: https://www.adl.org/resources/hate -symbol/sonnenrad [Accessed 28 11 2023].

Alba, D., 2017. *Shopify's Breitbart fight proves it: These days, tech has to take a side.* [Online] Available at: https://www.wired.com/2017/02/shopifys-breitbart-fight -proves-days-tech-take-side/ [Accessed 06 11 2023].

Albertson, B. L., 2015. Dog-whistle politics: Multifocal communication and religious appeals. *Political Behavior,* 37(1), pp. 3–26.

Athique, A., 2015. *Digital media and society. An introduction.* 2nd ed. Cambridge: Polity Press.

Baele, S., Brace, L. & Coan, T., 2020. Uncovering the far-right online ecosystem: An analytical framework and research agenda. 46(9), pp. 1599–1623.

Barnes, K., Riesenmy, T., Trinh, M. D. & Lleshi, E., 2021. Dank or not? Analysing and predicting. *Applied Network Science,* 6(21), pp. 1–24.

BBC News, 2016. *Pepe the Frog meme branded a 'hate symbol'.* [Online] Available at: https://www.bbc.co.uk/news/world-us-canada-37493165 [Accessed 11 07 2020].

BBC News, 2019. *OK hand sign added to list of hate symbols.* [Online] Available at: https://www.bbc.co.uk/news/newsbeat-49837898 [Accessed 04 11 2023].

BBC News, 2020. *The Kraken: What is it and why has Trump's ex-lawyer released it?.* [Online] Available at: https://www.bbc.co.uk/news/election-us-2020-55090145 [Accessed 26 11 2023].

Benton, B. & Peterka-Benton, D., 2020. Hating in plain sight: The hatejacking by extremist groups. *Public Relations Inquirey,* 9(1), pp. 7–26.

Bhat, P. & Klein, O., 2020. Covert hate speech: White nationalists and dog whistle communication on Twitter. In: *Twitter, the public sphere, and the chaos of online deliberation.* Cham: Palgrave Macmillan, pp. 151–172.

Bogerts, L. & Fielitz, M., 2019. "Do you want meme war?" Understanding the visual memes of the German far right. In: *Post- digital cultures of the far right. Online actions and offline consequences in Europe and the US.* s.l.: s.n., pp. 137–154.

Bouko, C., Van Ostaeyen, P. & Voué, P., 2021. Facebook's policies against extremism: Ten years of struggle for more transparency. *First Monday,* 26(9).

Bowman-Grieve, L., 2013. A psychological perspective on virtual communities supporting terrorist & extremist ideologies as a tool for recruitment. *Security Informatics,* 2(9), pp. 1–5.

Breitbart Store, 2023. *Apparel.* [Online] Available at: https://store.breitbart.com/collections/apparel [Accessed 06 11 2023].

Bruski, P., 2021. *Yellow Gadsden flag, prominent in Capitol takeover, carries a long and shifting history.* [Online] Available at: https://theconversation.com/yellow-gadsden-flag-prominent-in-capitol-takeover-carries-a-long-and-shifting-history-145142 [Accessed 26 11 2023].

Byman, D., 2022. *Spreading hate: The global rise of white supremacist terrorism.* 1st ed. Oxford: Oxford University Press.

Caffier, J., 2017. *Every insult the right uses to troll liberals, explained.* [Online] Available at: https://www.vice.com/en/article/mg9pvx/every-insult-the-right-uses-to-troll-liberals-explained [Accessed 29 11 2023].

Caiani, M. & Parenti, L., 2016. *European and Americian exterme right groups and the internet.* London: Routledge.

CARR, 2020. *A guide to online radical-right symbols, slogans and slurs. s.l.:* CARR.

Colborne, M., 2019. *The far right's secret weapon: Fascist fashion.* [Online] Available at: https://newrepublic.com/article/153161/far-rights-secret-weapon-fascist-fashion [Accessed 05 11 2023].

Colborne, M., 2023. *How (not) to interpret far-right symbols.* [Online] Available at: https://www.bellingcat.com/resources/2023/04/04/how-not-to-interpret-far-right-symbols/ [Accessed 04 11 2023].

Conti, A., 2018. *Learn to spot the secret signals of far-right fashion.* [Online] Available at: https://www.vice.com/en/article/59wjq8/learn-to-spot-the-secret-signals-of-far -right-fashion [Accessed 05 11 2023].

Crawford, B., Keen, F. & Suarez de-Tangil, G., 2020. *Memetic irony and the promotion of. London:* CREST.

D'Antonio, M. & Cohen, M., 2021. *Pay attention to the far right's use of memes to stir extremism.* [Online] Available at: https://edition.cnn.com/2021/09/17/opinions /memes-far-right-extremism-dantonio-cohen/index.html [Accessed 27 11 2023].

Darcy, O., 2022. *Right-wing conspiracy outlet Infowars files for bankruptcy protection as founder Alex Jones faces defamation suits.* [Online] Available at: https://edition .cnn.com/2022/04/18/media/infowars-alex-jones-bankruptcy/index.html [Accessed 06 11 2023].

Darwish, M. et al., 2019. *Selling extremism: Nationalist streetwear and the rise of the far right.* [Online] Available at: https://edition.cnn.com/style/article/right-wing -fashion-streetwear/index.html [Accessed 05 11 2023].

De Cristofaro, E., 2018. *Memes are taking the alt-right's message of hate mainstream.* [Online] Available at: https://theconversation.com/memes-are-taking-the-alt-rights -message-of-hate-mainstream-108196 [Accessed 06 07 2022].

De Saussure, F., 2017 [1966]. Arbitrary social values and the. In: *Social theory: The multicultural, global, and classic readings.* Philadelphia: Westview Press, pp. 119–124.

Denisova, A., 2020. *Internet memes and society. Social, cultural and political context.* London: Routledge.

Dodd, M. & Kinnally, W., 2020. 'Fan publics': An interdisciplinary conceptualisation of external supportive stakeholders. *Prism,* 12(1), pp. 1–12.

Donovan, J., Dreyfuss, E. & Friedberg, B., 2022. *Meme wars.* New York: Bloomsbury Publishing.

Dynel, M. & Messerli, T. C., 2020. On a cross-cultural memescape: Switzerland through nation memes from within and from the outside. *Contrastive Pragmat,* 1, pp. 210–241.

Esposito, J. L. & Kalin, I., 2011. *Islamophobia: The challenge of pluralism in the 21st century.* Oxford: Oxford University Press.

EU Commission, 2021. *Far-right extremists' use of humour, 2021.* [Online] Available at: https://home-affairs.ec.europa.eu/networks/radicalisation-awareness-network -ran/publications/far-right-extremists-use-humour-2021_en [Accessed 24 11 2023].

Evans, R., 2021. *White boy summer, Nazi memes and the mainstreaming of white supremacist violence.* [Online] Available at: https://www.bellingcat.com/news /2021/07/01/white-boy-summer-nazi-memes-and-the-mainstreaming-of-white -supremacist-violence/ [Accessed 27 11 2023].

Farinelli, F., 2021. *Conspiracy theories and right-wing extremism – Insights and recommendations for P/CVE.* Brussels: European Commission.

Fernando, 2021. *The hidden meanings behind the far-right hate symbols on display during the US Capitol riot.* [Online] Available at: https://www.sbs.com.au/news/ article/the-hidden-meanings-behind-the-far-right-hate-symbols-on-display-during -the-us-capitol-riot/keiotibc2 [Accessed 17 08 2023].

Fielitz, M. & Ahmed, R., 2021. *'It's not funny anymore. Far-right extremists' use of humour.* Luxembourg: Publications Office of the European Union.

Fischer, M., 2021. *From memes to race war: How extremists use popular culture to lure recruits.* [Online] Available at: https://www.washingtonpost.com/nation/2021/04/30/extremists-recruiting-culture-community/ [Accessed 27 08 2022].

Gallagher, J., 2020. *Why the extremist 'boogaloo boys' wear Hawaiian shirts.* [Online] Available at: https://www.wsj.com/articles/why-the-extremist-boogaloo-boys-wear-hawaiian-shirts-11591635085 [Accessed 27 08 2022].

Gallagher, R. & Topinka, R., 2023. The politics of the NPC meme: Reactionary subcultural practice and vernacular theory. *Big Data & Society,* 10(1), pp. 1–16.

Gaugele, E., 2019. The new obscurity in style. Alt-right faction, populist normalization, and the cultural war on fashion from the far right. *Fashion Theory,* 23(6), pp. 711–731.

Gault, M., 2017. *Pepe the Frog's creator goes legally nuclear against the alt-right.* [Online] Available at: https://www.vice.com/en/article/8x8gaa/pepe-the-frogs-creator-lawsuits-dmca-matt-furie-alt-right [Accessed 05 11 2023].

Griffin, R., 2013. *The nature of fascism.* London: Routledge.

Grunt Style, 2023. *Men's collection. Patriotic apparel for men.* [Online] Available at: https://www.gruntstyle.com/collections/men?page=5 [Accessed 06 11 2023].

Hals, T. & Stempel, J., 2022. *Alex Jones files for bankruptcy following $1.5 billion Sandy Hook verdicts.* [Online] Available at: https://www.reuters.com/world/us/alex-jones-files-bankruptcy-following-sandy-hook-verdict-court-filing-2022-12-02/ [Accessed 06 11 2023].

Hansted, M., 2023. *Satire om krigen florerer på nettet – og mange har en bagtanke.* [Online] Available at: https://nyheder.tv2.dk/samfund/2023-10-30-satire-om-krigen-florerer-paa-nettet-og-mange-har-en-bagtanke#:~:text=%2D%20Der%20er%20rigtig%20mange%2C%20der,mange%20f%C3%B8lelser%20siger%20Lars%20Konzack.&text=%2D%20De%20taler%20om%20mange%20v%C3%A6rdilade [Accessed 05 11 2023].

Hatmaker, T., 2018. *What we can learn from the 3,500 Russian Facebook Ads meant to stir up U.S. politics.* [Online] Available at: https://techcrunch.com/2018/05/10/russian-facebook-ads-house-intelligence-full-list/ [Accessed 04 11 2023].

Hodge, E. & Hallgrimsdottir, H., 2020. Networks of hate: The alt-right, "troll culture", and the cultural geography of social movement spaces online. *Journal of Borderlands Studies,* 35(4), pp. 563–580.

Hogg, M. A., 2016. Social identity theory. In: *Understanding peace and conflict through social identity theory.* Cham: Springer Natural, pp. 3–18.

Holt, T. J., Bossler, A. M. & Seigfried-Spellar, K., 2022. *Cybercrime and digital forensics. An introduction.* 3rd ed. London: Sage.

IMDb, 2022a. *Magnum P.I. (1980–1988).* [Online] Available at: https://www.imdb.com/title/tt0080240/ [Accessed 27 08 2022].

IMDb, 2022b. *Magnum P.I. (2018–2022).* [Online] Available at: https://www.imdb.com/title/tt7942796/ [Accessed 27 08 2022].

Infowars Store, 2023. *Apparel.* [Online] Available at: https://www.infowarsstore.com/catalog/category/view/s/apparel/id/186/ [Accessed 06 11 2023].

Iqbal, N., 2020. *Fashion ... or fascist? The long tussle over that Fred Perry logo.* [Online] Available at: https://www.theguardian.com/fashion/2020/oct/04/fashion-or-fascist-the-long-tussle-over-that-fred-perry-logo [Accessed 06 11 2023].

ISD, 2023. *Memes & the extreme right-wing.* [Online] Available at: https://www.isdglobal.org/explainers/memes-the-extreme-right-wing/ [Accessed 04 11 2023].

Jones, S. G., 2018. *The rise of far-right extremism in the United States.* [Online] Available at: https://www.csis.org/analysis/rise-far-right-extremism-united-states [Accessed 1 08 2022].

Kansara, V., 2018. *Cambridge analytica weaponised fashion brands to elect trump, says Christopher Wylie.* [Online] Available at: https://www.businessoffashion.com /articles/news-analysis/cambridge-analytica-weaponised-fashion-brands-to-elect -trump-says-christopher-wylie/ [Accessed 04 11 2023].

Kenes, B., 2021. *Boogaloo bois: Violent anti-establishment extremists in festive Hawaiian shirts.* [Online] Available at: https://www.populismstudies.org/boogaloo -bois-violent-anti-establishment-extremists-in-festive-hawaiian-shirts/ [Accessed 27 08 2022].

Khan-Ruf, S., 2021. The European far right and the COVID-19 pandemic. In: *State of hate. Far-right extremism in Europe.* London: Hope not Hate.

Klee, M., 2016. *Pepe the Frog is not a Nazi, no matter what the alt-right says.* [Online] Available at: https://www.dailydot.com/unclick/pepe-the-frog-alt-right-white -supremacist/ [Accessed 11 07 2022].

Knobel, M. & Lankshear, C., 2007. Online memes, affinities, and cultural production. In: *A new literacies sampler.* New York: Peter Lang, pp. 199–227.

Know Your Meme,2020. *Pepe the Frog.* [Online] Available at: https://knowyourmeme .com/memes/pepe-the-frog [Accessed 10 07 2022].

Know Your Meme, 2023. *October 2023 Hamas vs. Israel conflict images.* [Online] Available at: https://knowyourmeme.com/memes/events/october-2023-hamas-vs -israel-conflict/photos [Accessed 05 11 2023].

KnowYourMeme, 2013. *Ordinary Muslim man.* [Online] Available at: https:// knowyourmeme.com/memes/ordinary-muslim-man [Accessed 27 11 2023].

KnowYourMeme, 2018. *It's ok to be white.* [Online] Available at: https:// knowyourmeme.com/memes/its-okay-to-be-white [Accessed 27 11 2023].

KnowYourMeme, 2020a. *Islam is right about women.* [Online] Available at: https:// knowyourmeme.com/memes/islam-is-right-about-women#fn1 [Accessed 27 11 2023].

KnowYourMeme, 2020b. *Judanism.* [Online] Available at: https://knowyourmeme .com/memes/cultures/judaism [Accessed 02 11 2023].

KnowYourMeme, 2021a. *Death of George Floyd.* [Online] Available at: https:// knowyourmeme.com/memes/events/death-of-george-floyd [Accessed 27 11 2023].

KnowYourMeme, 2021b. *White boy summer.* [Online] Available at: https:// knowyourmeme.com/memes/white-boy-summer [Accessed 27 11 2023].

KnowYourMeme, 2023. *BBQ Becky.* [Online] Available at: https://knowyourmeme .com/search?q=BBQ+Becky [Accessed 27 11 2023].

Lee, J., 2018. *"Permit Patty" "BBQ Becky" and the rise of activist memes.* [Online] Available at: https://www.inverse.com/article/46436-permit-patty-and-activism -memes [Accessed 26 11 2023].

Magu, R. & Luo, J., 2018. *Determining code words in euphemistic hate speech using wordembedding networks.* Brussels: Association for Computational Linguistics, pp. 93–100.

Marwick, R. & Lewis, R., 2017. *Media manipulation and disinformation online. s.l.: Data and Society Research Institute.*

Mattheis, A., 2019. *Manifesto memes: The radical right's new dangerous visual rhetorics.* [Online] Available at: https://www.opendemocracy.net/en/countering -radical-right/manifesto-memes-the-radical-rights-new-dangerous-visual-rhetorics/ [Accessed 05 11 2023].

McNeil-Willson, R., 2020. *On the banning of far right groups and symbols, in an online and offline context.* [Online] Available at: https://home-affairs.ec.europa.eu/system /files/2022-02/EUIF%20RWE%20Workshop%20October%202020%20McNeil -Willson%20paper_en.pdf [Accessed 26 11 2023].

Mendelberg, T., 2001. *The race card: Campaign strategy. Implicit messages, and the norm of equality.* Princeton: Princeton University Press.

Meta, 2020. *Banning a violent network in the US. [Online]* Available at: https://about.fb .com/news/2020/06/banning-a-violent-network-in-the-us/ [Accessed 26 11 2023].

Miller-Idriss, C., 2017. *The extreme gone mainstream: Commercialization and far right youth culture in Germany.* Princeton: Princeton University Press.

Miller-Idriss, C., 2019a. *Selling extremism: Nationalist streetwear and the rise of the far right.* [Online] Available at: https://edition.cnn.com/style/article/right-wing -fashion-streetwear/index.html [Accessed 11 08 2022].

Miller-Idriss, C., 2019b. What makes a symbol far right? Co-opted and missed meanings in far-right iconography. In: *Post-digital cultures of the far right. Online actions and offline consequences in Europe and the US.* s.l.: Verlag.

Miller-Idriss, C., 2020. *Hate in the homeland. The new global far right.* Princeton: Princeton University Press.

Molas, B., 2023. *Alt-solutism: Intersections between alt-right memes and monarchism on reddit.* [Online] Available at: https://www.icct.nl/publication/alt-solutism-intersections -between-alt-right-memes-and-monarchism-reddit [Accessed 27 11 2023].

Munk, T., 2024. *Memetic war. Online resistance in Ukraine.* 1st ed. Abingdon: Routledge.

Neiwert, D., 2017. *What is Kek: Explaning the alt-right 'deity' behind their 'meme magic'.* [Online] Available at: https://www.splcenter.org/hatewatch/2017/05/08 /what-kek-explaining-alt-right-deity-behind-their-meme-magic [Accessed 26 11 2023].

Neiwert, D., 2018. *Is that an ok sign? A white power symbol? Or just a right-wing troll?. [Online]* Available at: https://www.splcenter.org/hatewatch/2018/09/18/ok -sign-white-power-symbol-or-just-right-wing-troll [Accessed 04 11 2023].

Noor, P., 2019. *How the alt-right co-opted the OK hand sign to fool the media.* [Online] Available at: https://www.theguardian.com/world/2019/oct/03/ok-sign-gesture -emoji-rightwing-alt-right [Accessed 05 11 2023].

Notopoulos, K. & Broderick, R., 2017. *The far right's most common memes explained for normal people.* [Online] Available at: https://www.buzzfeednews.com/article /katienotopoulos/a-normal-persons-guide-to-how-far-right-trolls-talk-to-each [Accessed 05 11 2023].

Ohlin, J., 2017. Did Russian cyber interference in the 2016 election violate international law. *Texa Law Review, 95*(7), pp. 1579–1598.

Palau, A. S. & Roozenbek, J., 2017. *How an ancient Egyptian god spurred the rise of Trump.* [Online] Available at: https://theconversation.com/how-an-ancient -egyptian-god-spurred-the-rise-of-trump-72598 [Accessed 10 07 2022].

Patrick, W., 2011. *Subcultural theory: Traditions and concepts.* Malden: Polity Press.

Pearson, J., 2017. *People are calling for a shopify Boycott because it hosts Breitbart's store.* [Online] Available at: https://www.vice.com/en/article/ezmyq4/people-are -calling-for-a-shopify-boycott-because-it-hosts-breitbarts-store [Accessed 07 11 2023].

Pemberton, N. T., 2020. *What do you do when extremism comes for the Hawaiian shirt?.* *[Online] Available at: https://www.nytimes.com/2020/06/29/style/ boogaloo-hawaiian-shirt.html?referringSource=articleShare [Accessed 27 08 2022].*

Peters, C. & Allan, S., 2022. Weaponising memes: The journalistic mediation of visual politicization. *Digital Journalism,* 10(2), pp. 217–229.

Peters, J., 2020. *Facebook moves to limit spread of extremist 'boogaloo' pages and groups.* [Online] Available at: https://www.theverge.com/2020/6/5/21282062 /facebook-limit-spread-boogaloo-groups-extremist-anti-government-violence [Accessed 25 11 2023].

Petrow, S., 2017. *The coded lanugage of the alt right is heling to power its rise.* [Online] Available at: https://www.washingtonpost.com/lifestyle/style/the-coded -language-of-the-alt-right-is-helping-to-power-its-rise/2017/04/07/5f269a82-1ba4 -11e7-bcc2-7d1a0973e7b2_story.html [Accessed 29 11 2023].

Phalanx Europa, 2023. *Phalanx Europa.* [Online] Available at: https://phalanx-europa .com/ [Accessed 25 11 2023].

Philips, W., 2015. *Why we can't have nice things: Mapping the relationship between online trolling and mainstream culture.* Cambridge: MIT Press.

Porter, T., 2017. *Snowflake, SJW, cuck: A guide to alt-right ideas and slang.* [Online] Available at: https://www.ibtimes.co.uk/snowflake-sjw-cuck-guide-alt-right-ideas -slang-1605911 [Accessed 29 11 2023].

Postma, F., 2022. *Fascist fashion: How mainstream businesses enable the sale of far- right merchandise.* [Online] Available at: https://www.bellingcat.com/news/2022 /05/24/fascist-fashion-how-mainstream-businesses-enable-the-sale-of-far-right -merchandise/ [Accessed 10 08 2022].

Richardson, J., 2020. *A guide to online radical-right symbols, slogans and slurs. s.l.: Centre for Analysis of the Radical Right.*

Roose, K., 2018. *What is NPC, the pro-Trump internet's new favourite insult?. [Online] Available at: https://www.nytimes.com/2018/10/16/us/politics/npc-twitter-ban.html [Accessed 29 11 2023].*

Ross, A. S. & Rivers, D. J., 2017. Digital cultures of political participation: Internet memes and the discursive delegitimisation of the 2016 US presidential candidates. *Discourse, Context & Media,* 16, pp. 1–11. https://www.sciencedirect.com/science /article/abs/pii/S2211695816301684?via%3Dihub.

Sanchez, J., 2018. Trump, the KKK, and the versatility of white supremacy rhetoric. *Journal of Contemporary Rhetoric,* 8(1), pp. 45–56.

Schori Liang, C. & Cross, M. J., 2020. *White crusade: How to prevent right-wing. s.l.:* GCSP.

Shane, S., 2017. *These are the Ads Russia bought on Facebook in 2016.* [Online] Available at: https://www.nytimes.com/2017/11/01/us/politics/russia-2016 -election-facebook.html [Accessed 04 11 2023].

Shifman, L., 2013. Memes in a digital world: Reconciling with a conceptual troublemaker. *Journal of Computer-Mediated Communication,* 18(3), pp. 251–397.

Simon, M. & Sidner, S., 2021. *Decoding the extremist symbols and groups at the Capitol Hill insurrection.* [Online] Available at: https://edition.cnn.com/2021/01/09/us/capitol-hill-insurrection-extremist-flags-soh/index.html [Accessed 21 08 2023].

Singer, P. & Brookings, E., 2018. *Likewar. The weaponisation of social media.* New York: Mariner Books.

Smith, P. & Brockling, M., 2022. *Here's what we know of the group accused of plotting to overthrow Germany's government.* [Online] Available at: https://www.nbcnews.com/news/world/germany-coup-plot-reichsburger-sovereign-citizens-conspiracy-theories-rcna60492 [Accessed 27 11 2023].

Sommerlad, J., 2018. *What is an NPC? The liberal-bashing meme sweeping social media ahead of the US midterms.* [Online] Available at: https://www.independent.co.uk/tech/npc-meme-right-wing-trolls-liberals-donald-trump-twitter-insults-republicans-a8588036.html [Accessed 28 11 2023].

Spitznagel, E., 2022. *How far-right groups are using fashion symbols to recruit the youth.* [Online] Available at: https://nypost.com/2020/10/31/how-far-right-groups-are-using-fashion-symbols-to-recruit-youth/ [Accessed 11 08 2022].

SPLC, 2023. *Three percenters.* [Online] Available at: https://www.splcenter.org/fighting-hate/extremist-files/group/three-percenters [Accessed 26 11 2023].

Squire, M. & Hayden, M., 2023. *'Absolute bonkers: Inside Infowars' money machine.* [Online] Available at: https://www.splcenter.org/hatewatch/2023/03/08/absolutely-bonkers-inside-infowars-money-machine [Accessed 04 11 2023].

Swinyard, H., 2019. *Pepe the Frog creator wins $15,000 settlement against Infowars.* [Online] Available at: https://www.theguardian.com/books/2019/jun/13/pepe-the-frog-creator-wins-15000-settlement-against-infowars [Accessed 05 11 2023].

Taveria, R. & Balfour, E., 2016. *How Donald Trump won the 2016 meme wars.* [Online] Available at: https://theconversation.com/how-donald-trump-won-the-2016-meme-wars-68580 [Accessed 10 07 2022].

The Washington Post, 2021. *Identifying far-right symbols that.* [Online] Available at: https://www.washingtonpost.com/nation/interactive/2021/far-right-symbols-capitol-riot/ [Accessed 17 08 2023].

Thorleifsson, C., 2021. From cyberfascism to terrorism: On 4chan/pol/ culture and the transnational production of memetic violence. *Nations and Nationalism,* 28(1), pp. 286–301.

Timberg, C., 2017. *Russian operatives used Twitter and Facebook to target veterans and military personnel, study says.* [Online] Available at: https://www.washingtonpost.com/news/the-switch/wp/2017/10/09/russian-operatives-used-twitter-and-facebook-to-target-veterans-and-military-personnel-study-says/ [Accessed 04 11 2023].

Tuters, M., 2019. LARPing & liberal tears. Irony, belief and idiocy in the deep vernacular web. In: *Post-digital cultures of the far right: Online actions and offline consequences in Europe and the US. Bielefeld:* Transcript Verlag, pp. 37–48.

Vera, A. & Ly, L., 2020. *White woman who called police on a black man bird-watching in Central Park has been fired.* [Online] Available at: https://edition.cnn.com/2020/05/26/us/central-park-video-dog-video-african-american-trnd/index.html [Accessed 26 11 2023].

Vice, 2021. *How the far-right weaponised memes.* [Online] Available at: https://www.vice.com/en/article/wx5kdx/how-the-far-right-weaponised-memes [Accessed 18 09 2023].

Walker, R., 2016. *The shifting symbolism of the Gadsden flag.* [Online] Available at: https://www.newyorker.com/news/news-desk/the-shifting-symbolism-of-the -gadsden-flag [Accessed 23 11 2023].

Weale, S., 2022. *Signs of hate: Parental guide to far-right codes, symbols and acronyms.* [Online] Available at: https://www.theguardian.com/world/2022/aug/04 /signs-of-hate-parental-guide-to-far-right-codes-symbols-acronyms-uk [Accessed 27 11 2023].

Weber, P. & Collins, D., 2022. *EXPLAINER: What does Infowars' bankruptcy filing mean?.* [Online] Available at: https://apnews.com/article/alex-jones-infowars -bankruptcy-filing-1a3b51946cb06c5f90c341d3118947cf [Accessed 06 11 2023].

Williams, B., 2020. Black memes matter: #LivingWhileBlack with Becky and Karen. *Social Media + Society,* 6(4), pp. 1–14.

Williams, Z., 2016. *(((Echoes))): Beating the far-right, two triple-brackets at a time.* [Online] Available at: https://www.theguardian.com/technology/shortcuts/2016/ jun/12/echoes-beating-the-far-right-two-triple-brackets-at-a-time [Accessed 26 11 2023].

Wilson, J., 2020. *The neo-Nazi symbol posted by Pete Evans has a strange and dark history.* [Online] Available at: https://www.theguardian.com/world/2020/nov /24/the-neo-nazi-symbol-posted-by-pete-evans-has-a-strange-and-dark-history [Accessed 28 11 2023].

Wipperfürth, A., 2006. *Brand Hijack: Marketing without marketing.* New York: Portfolio.

Woolf, J., 2017. *Fred Perry wants alt-right Bros to stop wearing their polos.* [Online] Available at: https://journals.sagepub.com/doi/10.1177/2046147X19863838 #bibr70-2046147X19863838 [Accessed 26 11 2023].

Yar, M. & Steinmetz, K. F., 2019. *Cybercrime and society.* 3rd ed. London: Sage.

6 Concluding Remarks and Reflections

Understanding Far-Right Extremism in the Digital Era

Events like the Capitol Hill insurrection exemplified the rise of far-right extremism. For a long time, extremist ideologies have been amplified by digital evolution that has enabled a flow of constant communication in a borderless society. The online communications and actions often advocate for political, radical, and societal changes underpinned by neo-Nazi, white supremacist, and ethno-nationalist beliefs (Chapter 1).

This digital propagation has led to a worrying surge in movements advocating violence and societal disturbance (Chapters 3, 4, and 5). This calls for more coordinated efforts by social media companies and tech businesses to ensure their platforms are safe. These platforms offer different access levels and anonymity, with the lesser-regulated areas becoming breeding ground for extremist activities (Chapter 4). The rise of the web has shifted far-right extremism from street marches to digital strategies. Social media tools are now central, employing click-swarming, trolling, and doxing tactics. Symbols and memes have been adapted for in-group recognition, rapid communication, and to circumvent moderation to keep the posts online (Chapter 5) (Albrecht et al., 2019, p. 9) (Table 6.1).

Interplay of Terrorism and Far-Right Extremism

The intersection of terrorism, far-right extremism, and the digital environment forms a multifaceted challenge. Terrorism broadly spreads societal fear, while far-right hate crimes target specific groups, both utilising fear as a tool (Chapter 2). The task of balancing free speech with the protection of online users is made difficult as far-right groups misuse the rights and promote coded messages to target particular groups and individuals in society (Chapter 2 and 5). Digital platforms focused on user engagement unintentionally promote extremist content, highlighting the need for operational changes to prioritise user safety over profit (Chapter 4).

Contemporary terrorism, often associated with religious motives, overshadows the increasing threat of far-right extremism, including subgroups

DOI: 10.4324/9781003297888-6

Table 6.1 Key Themes from this Book

Features	Characteristics
Far-right Extremism and Terrorism have a Broad Impact	Groups and individuals intend to instigate widespread fear for political or ideological goals.
Far-Right Hate Crimes' Targeted Nature	Far-right extremism incites hate crimes focused on specific group identities, leading to localised societal fear.
Digital Echo Chambers	The Internet, particularly social media, amplifies far-right ideologies.
From Online to On-Ground Violence	There is a transition from virtual radicalisation to physical acts of extremism.
Free Speech vs. Hate Speech	There is a thin line between preserving free expression and preventing hate speech propagation.
Exploitation of Free Speech by Extremists	The far-right groups use free speech rights to disseminate divisive content.
Navigating the Post-truth Society	The online environment exacerbates the spread of misinformation, conspiracy theories, and radical views.
Moderation Strategies	There is a lack of uniform methods for digital platforms to mitigate extremist content.
Preserving Freedoms while Preventing Extremism	The digital platforms have an essential role in balancing free speech with the need to curb extremism.
Coded Language and Symbols	Far-right extremist groups employ coded symbols to evade content moderation and convey hidden ideologies.
Fashion as a Propaganda Tool	Fashion is used to spread their ideologies. This use blurs the line between mainstream styles and harmful messages.
Memes and Humour	Memes are used to recruit, communicate and normalise far-right extremist viewpoints by downplaying the seriousness of their beliefs.
Multifaceted Approach	A comprehensive policy, technology, and community strategy should be prioritised.
Protecting Societies from Digital Extremism	There is a need for coordinated action to safeguard against the growing threat of online radicalisation and far-right extremism.

like white supremacists, ethno-nationalists, and anti-government factions, particularly in the West (Schori Liang & Cross, 2020; Koehler, 2016). Their diverse activities, from hate crimes to terrorism, challenge traditional security methods due to their decentralised and elusive nature (Koehler, 2016). Addressing this complex interaction of terrorism, far-right extremism, and hate in the digital world calls for changes to the current approach. This involves rethinking traditional categorisations, redefining free speech and hate speech, revamping online counter-extremism strategies, and modifying digital platform business models (Chapters 2 and 4).

The Internet: A Fertile Ground for Extremism

The Internet, especially its lesser-regulated Deep and Dark Web layers, are instrumental in boosting far-right extremism, as the online environment offers a relatively safe haven from mainstream oversight (Chapter 3). It is clear that far-right extremist groups exploit every loophole in the current online eco-system where the advantages surpass any potential consequences imposed by platform owners and public authorities (Chapter 4 and 5). The online environment and encrypted communications present challenges in tracking and disrupting extremist activities, which are exploiting the borderless spaces without globally agreed regulation (Chapters 3 and 4).

Social media platforms acts as echo chambers, amplifying narratives that align with existing biases, fostering radicalisation and undermining trust in traditional media and democratic institutions (Chapters 3 and 4). The paradox of modern information sharing and communication on these platforms is evident: they can encourage civic engagement and community building while their algorithms potentially create online bubbles that reinforce existing beliefs and deepen societal divides (Albrecht et al., 2019, p. 11; Chadwick & Vaccari, 2019). However, the far-right extremist groups do not operate alone. Politicians from far-right and populist parties maintain strong connections with extremist groups. They spread these groups' ideologies and back their actions, seeking votes in return. Such collaboration normalises these activities, and complicates advocating for government regulation of online platforms (Chapters 3 and 4).

Echo chambers on these digital platforms reinforce biases by limiting the online users' exposure to diverse perspectives. Navigating this complicated digital landscape demands a more detailed approach and understanding of the actors motives, means and methods. This means that both public and private actors need to be engaged in developing proactive responses. Addressing the issues related to the use of encrypted channels, hidden communities, and the widespread dissemination of extremist ideologies in a post-truth era is crucial in effectively countering the threat of digital-fuelled extremism (Chapters 2, 3 and 4). Furthermore, adjusting algorithms to identify and address harmful content proactively - and utilising AI and ML for online fact-checking holds promise for a more secure digital environment. Yet, this opens up new problems concerning censorship, the usefulness of filtering and blocking content, and what type of communication can be curbed.

The Crucial Role of Online Platforms

Social media giants promoting free expression face a complex battle in controlling harmful ideologies (Chapters 1 and 2). Their algorithms are designed to maximise user engagement for profit. To do so, the algorithms amplify divisive content as they generate engagement. This spread of harmful content and communications not only increase societal polarisation but also aids in the spread of extremist ideologies beyond fringe groups. It often mirrors a tit-for-tat situation, with far-right extremist groups and individuals outmanoeuvring law enforcement, technology, and social media companies. They persistently discover and exploit loopholes, while innovating in their communication methods and platform usage (Chapters 3, 4 and 5).

These companies' business structures often prioritise user engagement over content accuracy until the social media companies are called out for not doing enough to secure their platforms. The main focus is not on the users but on advertising revenue. This focus inadvertently creates an environment where sensationalist and polarising content is more likely to be promoted, thus aiding in spreading extremist views (Chapter 4). The concept of free speech absolutism further muddies the waters. Given that users are the primary source of revenue for social media companies, it is essential that their safety is prioritised alongside the platforms' business interests. The challenge for these platforms lies in striking a balance between promoting free speech and managing harmful content to create a secure online environment.

Platforms like chans and gaming environments, often less regulated, provide safe havens for far-right extremist groups. Here, the anonymity and community-driven content moderation allow for the free flow of extremist ideologies. The far-right extremist groups mitigate between the platforms to escape the scrutiny and moderation practices introduced on more mainstream platforms (Chapters 1, 2, and 4). Prioritising the safety of online users over revenue should be paramount. While platforms aim for profitability, safeguarding users from extremist content should take precedence – balancing free speech and protected characteristics. This would ensure a safer online environment based on more robust content moderation strategies prioritising user well-being over financial gains.

Communication through Codes and Symbols

Far-right groups employ coded language, symbols, and humour to spread their ideologies, fostering exclusivity while eluding detection subtly. Online spaces, including anonymous forums and gaming platforms, incubate these ideologies, with online narratives merging into real-world actions, as seen in the Capitol Hill insurrection (Chapters 1, 2, and 4). This clandestine communication, embedding hidden meanings in numbers, symbols, and gestures, proves problematic to decipher. Fashion is utilised as a tool for propaganda, and humour, along with memes, serves to normalise extremist views, particularly among younger audiences (Chapter 5). The use of codes and symbols to circumvent moderation on these platforms is a tactic often employed by far-right extremist groups, as they are typically only understood by insiders. Therefore, they do not trigger the same alarms for themes and considerations that explicit content might. This method allows harmful or extremist content to slip through the cracks of content moderation systems, posing a issue for maintaining a safe online environment.

These ideologies have infiltrated mainstream culture, notably through memes, creating a hostile environment for minorities and transforming mainstream social media into recruitment channels. Far-right extremists engage young audiences by aligning with contemporary trends and language (Grisham, 2021; Mughal, 2022). The Internet hosts these ideologies on both mainstream and alternative platforms like Gab, 4chan, and 8kun, where unmoderated spaces allow for unchecked hate speech (Chapters 3 and 4) (Barlett, 2017; Mughal, 2022; Grisham, 2021). However, on mainstream social media platforms, memes are predominantly considered harmless fun due to their humorous content. This perception can make it difficult to discern when such content serves as a vehicle for harmful ideologies or bypasses moderation under the guise of humour (Chapter 5).

More awareness and education about this tactic are needed to ensure that online users understand these codes and symbols and not repost them to decrease the exposure of far-right extremist ideologies and symbols. Strategies must be developed to manage offensive memes and hidden extremist messages in digital spaces.

Concluding Reflections

A significant shift in tech companies' operational strategies is required to mitigate the radicalising effects of digital platforms. Their business models focused on maximising user engagement often inadvertently promote extremist content, posing a conflict between user safety and revenue generation. These platforms must prioritise responsible content moderation over engagement metrics to curb extremist ideologies. Public and regulatory pressures are vital to driving these proactive changes. The approach to tackling social media challenges encompasses identifying harm, evaluating market dominance, formulating solutions, and navigating implementation hurdles. Central to this is determining who controls the rules and governs public discourse (The Economist, 2020).

Meta's new platform, Threads, struggles with misinformation, particularly regarding the Israel-Hamas war. It quickly became a centre for controversial topics, leading to accusations of censorship (Paul, 2023). In response, Meta has taken steps to improve moderation, especially for Hebrew and Arabic content, and combat misinformation campaigns, such as removing fake accounts linked to Hamas. They have also adjusted algorithms and policies, expanded content removal criteria, restricted specific Instagram hashtags, and limited live features for users with a history of violations (Robins-Early, 2023; Meta, 2023). This situation exemplifies social media companies' broader challenge in balancing business interests with responsibilities toward freedom of speech and user security. But the social media businesses need to show more willingness to manage platforms and content proactively rather than reactively.

Navigating Free Speech

Navigating the fine line between protecting free speech and addressing hate speech is a complex issue, mainly as far-right extremist groups use free speech rights to spread divisive ideologies. Policymakers and online platforms are challenged to define and enforce hate speech policies effectively, requiring public discussions to uphold democratic values while combating extremism. The owner of X/Twitter promotes free speech. However, Musk's approach to free speech on social media is marked by instances of silencing dissent and censoring opposing views, casting doubt on his commitment to free speech principles. A more effective strategy involves open dialogues to balance free expression with harm reduction together with a stronger gatekeeper role to manage content (Brooks & Day, 2022). Under Musk, the platform shifted towards a far-right stance, similar to Truth Social and Parler. Therefore, the platform is losing its unique identity (Warzel, 2023). This intense focus on free speech rights can overshadow other essential rights, such as protecting audiences from abuse, ensuring the freedom to choose content, and promoting truth-seeking by understanding the biases and expertise of information sources (Fellmeth, 2023).

The inconsistent moderation across platforms fails to address the issue of far-right extremism effectively. Far-right groups and individuals frequently switch platforms, using security measures like VPNs and encryption to conceal their activities. This is particularly noticeable on Telegram, where private channels provide autonomy and isolation. A uniform industry approach with consistent enforcement is necessary to address these challenges. For many far-right extremists, being banned from platforms like X/Twitter is seen as a mark of distinction, often leading them to more radical platforms like Telegram (Bump, 2022). Yet. Musk's takeover of X/Twitter has led to increased visibility of far-right extremist content, with a poll favouring the reinstatement of previously banned accounts, including high-profile figures like Ye (Kanye West), the disgraced influencer Tate, and former President Trump (Kleinman, 2023; Morris, 2022). This decision has led to a resurgence of QAnon and other extremist content, further increasing the presence of these ideologies and far-right personalities on the platform (ADL, 2022).

Contemporary Challenges

A 2023 NewsGuard study revealed that most viral misinformation about the Israel-Hamas war on X/Twitter originated from verified users (Weatherbed, 2023; Brewster et al., 2023; Spangler, 2023). This issue extends to platforms like Facebook, Instagram, TikTok, and Telegram, where unverified and false stories about the conflict are widespread. Under Musk, X/Twitter's misinformation issues worsened due to reduced moderation and a greater reliance on automation (Alba & Wagner, 2023; Robins-Early, 2023; Fung, 2023; Paul & Dang, 2022). While X/Twitter uses 'visibility filtering', it now primarily depends on its Community Notes system, where users flag misinformation (Paul & Dang, 2022). However, this method has been inconsistent, with many misleading posts about the conflict remaining unflagged. In September 2023, X/Twitter removed the option to report political misinformation, leaving users without a direct way to report such content. Although X/Twitter has a 'crisis misinformation policy', the absence of a reporting option makes it unclear how users can alert the platform about potential policy violations (ADL, 2023).

Prominent X/Twitter accounts, including those Musk has endorsed, have been known to spread dis- and misinformation about the war, sometimes involving fake videos and anti-Ssemitic content (Robins-Early, 2023). This situation indicates the broader challenge social media platforms face in managing their business objectives with safeguarding their users. However, X/Twitter is not the only company having problems with moderate content on their platform. This issue has attracted global regulatory attention, with the EU investigating X/Twitter, Meta/Facebook, and TikTok for compliance with the Digital Services Act, focusing on the spread of illegal content and false information (Weatherbed, 2023; EU Commission, 2023; Gerken, 2023; Shakir, 2023; Robins-Early, 2023).

The Use of Algorithms and AI

Social media algorithms, designed to enhance user engagement and profit, inadvertently promote extreme far-right movements by fostering societal division and echo chambers. This dynamic leads to increased polarisation, as seen in the spreading and promoting extremist material, including conspiracy theories (Bacigalupo, 2022, p. 162; Miller-Idriss, 2020). For example, YouTube's autoplay feature sometimes leads users to such videos. Studies have connected online hate speech with real-world violence, highlighting the need for platforms to balance free speech with community standards to prevent radicalisation (Müller & Schwatz, 2020; Laub, 2019; Rose, 2018; Berman, 2016).

Platforms like YouTube have shown the ability to modify algorithms for content control, such as prioritising credible news sources during events like the Christchurch attacks (Hern & Waterson, 2019). However, the consistency of these practices across various types of harmful content remains unclear. The challenge intensifies with image and video platforms, where moderating hateful content in visual formats is particularly difficult. Social media companies must enhance algorithmic transparency and make long-term changes to reduce divisive content (Barrett et al., 2021).

Early Days for AI and OCR

Advances in AI and Optical Character Recognition (OCR) have improved content moderation, especially in detecting hate speech in multimedia, but the complexity of this task means human input is still crucial. Facebook uses AI to identify and send suspect content to third-party fact-checkers, helping to address misinformation quickly, yet this process faces difficulties (Meta, 2020). A significant issue with automated moderation is the opacity of the algorithms, commonly described as 'black box' systems, which lack clear insight into their workings. Platforms like YouTube provide limited details about their use of automated flagging (New America, 2023).

AI researchers struggle to develop datasets that capture the subtleties of human language and expression, limiting automated tools' effectiveness across varied cultural contexts (New America, 2023; Ryan-Mosley, 2023). This struggle is exemplified by tech companies like Meta/Facebook, X/Twitter, and Alphabet/Google, who acknowledge the difficulty in contextually interpreting language when addressing Congressional concerns about spreading hate and dis- and misinformation. Meta/Facebook's CEO Zuckerberg has argued that tech companies cannot be solely responsible for resolving global political issues (Ryan-Mosley, 2023), highlighting the complexities of online content moderation.

Initiative Launched to Manage the Risks of Far-right Extremism

Practical solutions to these issues demand a multifaceted approach. Governments, tech companies, and civil society organisations must collaborate on cybersecurity efforts to protect digital spaces from extremist influence. Education and awareness programs should be widespread to empower individuals with the knowledge to recognise and reject extremist narratives. Transnational cooperation among nations and industries is essential to track and counter extremist activities across borders. Additionally, re-evaluating free speech absolutism in the digital age is necessary to find a balanced approach that prevent the proliferation of extremist ideologies. Several effective initiatives have been launched where various stakeholders collaborate, including the Christchurch Call, the Global Internet Forum to Counter-Terrorism (GIFCT), Tech Against Terrorism (TAT), and Terrorist Content Analytics Platform (TCAP). These initiatives demonstrate that collaboration involving public and private actors can be initiated successfully.

Christchurch Calls

Following the 2019 Christchurch attacks, New Zealand's then-PM Ardern and French President Macron led the Christchurch Call to Action. Recognising the global nature of the issue, the Call seeks solutions that transcend borders and platforms. Over 130 international organisations, governments, online service providers and civil society organisations support the Christchurch Call in voluntary commitments to eliminate terrorism and violent extremist content online. Due to the nature of the online environments, the Call must transcend borders and platforms. The issues with far-right terrorism and violent extremist content constitute a global problem which needs a global solution (New Zealand Foreign Affairs and Trade, 2022; Christchurch Call, 2023).

The Global Internet Forum to Counter-terrorism (GIFCT)

The Christchurch Call initiative led to the GIFCT becoming independent and resource-enriched. GIFCT operates on three key pillars: 'Prevent,' which boosts awareness and tools for digital platforms and civil society to disrupt online extremism; 'Respond,' fostering collaboration to mitigate attack impacts; and 'Learn,' backing research into the technology-extremism nexus (GIFCT, 2022, 2021). Since 2017, GIFCT, established by major platforms like Facebook, X/Twitter, and YouTube, alongside NGOs, academics, and governments, has bolstered efforts to counter the misuse of platforms (GIFCT, 2023; Janin & Deverell, 2020).

GIFCT has implemented policies, content moderation strategies, and partnerships to combat Internet terrorism. This includes improved content moderation, machine-learning tools, and a hash-sharing consortium for fast identification and removal of terrorist content. Using a shared database of image hashes, GIFCT swiftly removes extremist content across platforms and works with various stakeholders, including the UN, to advance these efforts (Ganesh & Bright, 2020, p. 11). The importance of robust public-private partnerships in effectively responding to such challenges was particularly highlighted during the COVID-19 crisis (Janin & Deverell, 2020).

Other Initiatives

Tech Against Terrorism (TAT):
    This initiative, launched in 2017 and backed by the UN CTED, supports the tech industry in tackling online terrorism and extremism while respecting human rights. Funded by GIFCT and various governments, it provides essential tools and emphasises the use of Generative AI for content moderation. The focus is on fostering collaboration between governments and the tech sector to manage the threat of online extremism proactively (TAT, 2022; TAT, 2023).

Terrorist Content Analytics Platform (TCAT):
TCAT aims to combat the increasing presence of far-right elements on digital platforms. It creates a digital repository of extremist content, alerting smaller tech companies to its presence on their platforms and assisting in its removal. This initiative highlights the critical need for broad cooperation in the fight against online extremism (Lawson, 2022).

Navigating the Challenges of Digital Extremism

Tackling far-right extremism in the digital sphere demands a sophisticated approach beyond moderating echo chambers and online communications. It is essential to impede the spread of false information, conspiracy theories, and these groups' use of symbols, codes, and memes. This involves scrutinising the business models of digital platforms and their impact on free speech (Chapters 2 and 4). The rise of far-right extremism, enabled by digital platforms, underscores the necessity for vigilant and collaborative responses. The adaptation of these groups to the digital environment, their global influence, and the merging of their online and offline actions pose significant risks to societal cohesion and democratic values. A comprehensive strategy is required, focusing on understanding digital communication dynamics, regulating online content, and building societal resilience against the threats of digital extremism.

The Internet's architecture, the decentralised structure and the interconnectivity are some obstacles to managing the problems of far-right extremism. But there are also other issues. A lack of global cooperation and varying international laws and regulations hinder effective countermeasures. The need for enhanced cybersecurity measures must include cross-border collaboration between law enforcement and the private sector. However, the owners of the different virtual platforms should also be interested in improving the moderation on these platforms to secure their customers' interactions online – and keep the online users safe. Developing public–private partnerships on multiple levels is one way to manage the challenges through dialogue. Additionally, there is a crucial need for public education and awareness to help individuals recognise and reject extremist messaging. Public institutions, educators, and researchers should also be involved in this process.

The societal impact of digital radicalisation is profound, with real-world consequences like the attack on Capitol Hill illustrating the significant influence of online extremism. This poses a threat not only to individual safety but also to the democratic and social fabric of societies (Table 6.2).

Table 6.2 Roles and Responsibilities to Enhance Cybersecurity

Actors	Roles
Governments and Policymakers	Create effective laws to combat online far-righ extremism.
	Focusing on clear definitions of hate speech.
	Ensuring transnational and cross-sectoral cooperation to develop a unified approach.
Law Enforcement and Intelligence Agencies	Develop advanced capabilities to monitor and disrupt extremist networks, especially in less regulated spaces, while respecting privacy rights and the freedom of expression.
	National and international cooperation with relevant partners, including private businesses.
Technology Companies and Digital Platforms	A critical role in developing a uniform approach across the sectors.
	Further developing content moderation policies,
	Manage the algorithm to detect extremist content.
	Collaborate with authorities to develop more proactive processes and practices while balancing user privacy and freedom of speech.
Civil Society and Educational Institutions:	Raising awareness about far-right extremist ideologies.
	Promoting digital literacy and critical thinking.
	Help the public navigate online spaces safely and responsibly.
Researchers and Analysts	Enhance the work in understanding the tactics and psychological aspects of online extremism.
	Engage in research to inform policies and educational programs.
	Cybersecurity should include areas beyond computer science and IT, such as social science, law, business, communication and security studies.
The Public	Online users can help by being vigilant.
	Reporting extremist content.
	Avoiding engagement with far-right extremist material.

References

ADL, 2022. *Extremists, far right figures exploit recent changes to Twitter.* [Online] Available at: https://www.adl.org/resources/blog/extremists-far-right-figures-exploit-recent-changes-twitter [Accessed 12 10 2023].

ADL, 2023. *As war rages, X must curb the spread of misinformation and hate.* [Online] Available at: https://www.adl.org/resources/blog/war-rages-x-must-curb-spread-misinformation-and-hate [Accessed 02 11 2023].

Alba, D. & Wagner, K., 2023. *Twitter cuts more staff overseeing global content moderation.* [Online] Available at: https://www.bloomberg.com/news/articles/2023-01-07/elon-musk-cuts-more-twitter-staff-overseeing-content-moderation?leadSource=uverify%20wall [Accessed 25 11 2023].

Albrecht, S., Fielitz, M. & Thurston, N., 2019. Introduction. In: *Post-digital cultures of the far right.* Bielefeld: Transcript Verlag, pp. 1–22.

Bacigalupo, J., 2022. Responding to cyberhate. In: *Cyberhate. The far right in the digital age.* Lanham: Lexington Books, pp. 159–163.

Barlett, J., 2017. *From hope to hate: How the early internet fed the far right.* [Online] Available at: https://www.theguardian.com/world/2017/aug/31/far-right-alt-right-white-supremacists-rise-online [Accessed 28 08 2022].

Barrett, P., Hendrix, P. & Sims, G., 2021. *How tech platforms fuel U.S. political polarizarion and what government can do about it.* [Online] Available at: https://www.brookings.edu/articles/how-tech-platforms-fuel-u-s-political-polarization-and-what-government-can-do-about-it/ [Accessed 17 08 2023].

Berman, M., 2016. *Prosecutors say Dylann Roof 'self-radicalised' online, wrote another manifesto in jail.* [Online] Available at: https://www.washingtonpost.com/news/post-nation/wp/2016/08/22/prosecutors-say-accused-charleston-church-gunman-self-radicalized-online/ [Accessed 14 10 2023].

Brewster, J., Howard, S. & Schimmel, B., 2023. *Blue-checked, 'Verified' users on X produce 74 percent of the platform's most viral false or unsubstantiated claims relating to the Israel-Hamas War.* [Online] Available at: https://www.newsguardtech.com/misinformation-monitor/october-2023/ [Accessed 25 11 2023].

Brooks, E. & Day, J., 2022. *What is free speech absolutism? Who is a free speech absolutist? Examples, pros and cons.* [Online] Available at: https://www.liberties.eu/en/stories/free-speech-absolutist/44213 [Accessed 03 09 2023].

Bump, P., 2022. *The platform where the right-wing bubble is least likely to pop.* [Online] Available at: https://www.washingtonpost.com/politics/2022/04/23/telegram-platform-right-wing/ [Accessed 01 11 2023].

Chadwick, A. & Vaccari, C., 2019. *News sharing on UK social media: Misinformation, disinformation, and correction.* Loughborough: Loughborough University.

Christchurch Call, 2023. *Our community.* [Online] Available at: https://www.christchurchcall.com/ [Accessed 01 12 2023].

EU Commission, 2023. *The commission sends request for information to X under the Digital Services Act*.* [Online] Available at: https://ec.europa.eu/commission/presscorner/detail/en/IP_23_4953 [Accessed 12 10 2023].

Fellmeth, R., 2023. *Social media must balance 'right of free speech' with audience 'right to know'.* [Online] Available at: https://thehill.com/opinion/technology/3814620-social-media-must-balance-right-of-free-speech-with-audience-right-to-know/ [Accessed 14 10 2023].

Fung, B., 2023. *Twitter loses its top content moderation official at a key moment.* [Online] Available at: https://edition.cnn.com/2023/06/02/tech/twitter-content-moderation-official-eu/index.html [Accessed 23 11 2023].

Ganesh, B. & Bright, J., 2020. Countering extremists on social media: Challenges for strategic communication and content moderation. *Policy & Internet,* 12(1), pp. 6–19.

Gerken, T., 2023. *EU gives Meta and TikTok formal Hamas disinformation deadline.* [Online] Available at: https://www.bbc.co.uk/news/technology-67157733 [Accessed 25 11 2023].

GIFCT, 2021. *Annual report 2021. s.l.:* GIFCT.

GIFCT, 2022. *Preventing terrorists and violent extremists from exploiting digital platforms.* [Online] Available at: https://gifct.org/ [Accessed 13 08 2022].

GIFCT, 2023. *Preventing terrorists and violent extremists from exploiting digital platforms.* [Online] Available at: https://gifct.org/about/ [Accessed 01 11 2023].

Grisham, K., 2021. *Far-right groups move to messaging apps as tech companies crack down on extremist social media.* [Online] Available at: https://theconversation .com/far-right-groups-move-to-messaging-apps-as-tech-companies-crack-down-on -extremist-social-media-153181 [Accessed 28 08 2022].

Hern, A. & Waterson, J., 2019. *Social media firms fight to delete Christchurch shooting footage.* [Online] Available at: https://www.theguardian.com/world/2019/mar/15/ video-of-christchurch-attack-runs-on-social-media-and-news-sites [Accessed 03 09 2022].

Janin, M. & Deverell, F., 2020. *Covid-19: Far right violent extremism and tech platforms' response.* [Online] Available at: https://www.fondapol.org/en/study/ covid-19-far-right-violent-extremism-and-tech-plateforms-response/ [Accessed 01 11 2023].

Kleinman, Z., 2023. *Twitter: Five ways Elon Musk has changed the platform for users.* [Online] Available at: https://www.bbc.co.uk/news/technology-64289251 [Accessed 15 10 2023].

Koehler, D., 2016. Right-wing extremism and terrorism in Europe current developments and issues for the future. *PRISM,* 6(2), pp. 85–99.

Laub, Z., 2019. *Hate speech on social media: Global comparisons.* [Online] Available at: https://www.cfr.org/backgrounder/hate-speech-social-media-global -comparisons [Accessed 14 10 2023].

Lawson, H., 2022. *Bad connections: Countering far-right extremism in online spaces.* [Online] Available at: https://www.munkgc.com/breaking-news/bad-connections -countering-far-right-extremism-in-online-spaces/ [Accessed 13 08 2022].

Meta, 2020. *Here's how we're using AI to help detect misinformation.* [Online] Available at: https://ai.meta.com/blog/heres-how-were-using-ai-to-help-detect -misinformation/ [Accessed 01 12 2023].

Meta, 2023. *Meta's ongoing efforts regarding the Israel-Hamas War.* [Online] Available at: https://about.fb.com/news/2023/10/metas-efforts-regarding-israel -hamas-war/ [Accessed 25 11 2023].

Miller-Idriss, C., 2020. *Hate in the homeland. The new global far right.* Princeton: Princeton University Press.

Morris, C., 2022. *A week of Musk mayhem: Here are all the Twitter changes since Elon took over.* [Online] Available at: https://www.fastcompany.com/90804776/elon -musk-massive-changes-twitter-one-week [Accessed 13 10 2023].

Mughal, S., 2022. *How are people targeted by far right groups online?.* [Online] Available at: https://www.internetmatters.org/hub/question/people-targeted-far -right-groups-online/ [Accessed 16 08 2022].

Müller, K. & Schwatz, C., 2020. Fanning the flames of hate: Social media and hate crime. *SSNR,* pp. 1–84.

New America, 2023. *The limitations of automated tools in content moderation.* [Online] Available at: https://www.newamerica.org/oti/reports/everything-moderation -analysis-how-internet-platforms-are-using-artificial-intelligence-moderate-user -generated-content/the-limitations-of-automated-tools-in-content-moderation/ [Accessed 01 12 2023].

New Zealand Foreign Affairs and Trade, 2022. *Christchurch call.* [Online] Available at: https://www.mfat.govt.nz/en/peace-rights-and-security/international-security/christchurch-call/ [Accessed 13 08 2022].

Paul, K., 2023. *Meta's 'friendly' threads collides with unfriendly internet.* [Online] Available at: https://www.reuters.com/technology/metas-friendly-threads-collides-with-unfriendly-internet-2023-07-07/ [Accessed 25 11 2023].

Paul, K. & Dang, S., 2022. *Exclusive: Twitter leans on automation to moderate content as harmful speech surges.* [Online] Available at: https://www.reuters.com/technology/twitter-exec-says-moving-fast-moderation-harmful-content-surges-2022-12-03/ [Accessed 25 11 2023].

Robins-Early, N., 2023. *Israel-Hamas war poses early disinformation test for Meta's threads.* [Online] Available at: https://www.theguardian.com/technology/2023/oct/13/instagram-threads-misinformation-israel-hamas [Accessed 25 11 2023].

Rose, K., 2018. *On gab, an extremist-friendly site, Pittsburgh shooting suspect aired his hatred in full.* [Online] Available at: https://www.nytimes.com/2018/10/28/us/gab-robert-bowers-pittsburgh-synagogue-shootings.html [Accessed 14 10 2023].

Ryan-Mosley, T., 2023. *Catching bad content in the age of AI.* [Online] Available at: https://www.technologyreview.com/2023/05/15/1073019/catching-bad-content-in-the-age-of-ai/ [Accessed 01 12 2023].

Schori Liang, C. & Cross, M. J., 2020. *White crusade: How to prevent right-wing.* s.l.: GCSP.

Shakir, U., 2023. *EU is formally investigating X over content about the Israel-Hamas war.* [Online] Available at: https://www.theverge.com/2023/10/12/23914862/eu-x-elon-musk-european-commission-probe-dsa-digital-services-act-hamas-israel [Accessed 25 11 2023].

Spangler, T., 2023. *X/Twitter verified blue check-mark users are 'superspreaders' of disinformation about Israel-Hamas War, study says.* [Online] Available at: https://variety.com/2023/digital/news/x-twitter-blue-check-mark-users-superspreaders-disinformation-israel-hamas-war-1235763100/ [Accessed 25 11 2023].

TAT, 2022. *Project background.* [Online] Available at: https://www.techagainstterrorism.org/project-background/ [Accessed 13 08 2022].

TAT, 2023. *Terrorist use of generative AI.* [Online] Available at: https://techagainstterrorism.org/gen-ai# [Accessed 01 12 2023].

The Economist, 2020. *How to deal with free speech on social media.* [Online] Available at: https://www.economist.com/leaders/2020/10/22/how-to-deal-with-free-speech-on-social-media?utm_medium=cpc.adword.pd&utm_source=google&ppccampaignID=18156330227&ppcadID=&utm_campaign=a.22brand_pmax&utm_content=conversion.direct-response.anonymous&gclid=CjwK [Accessed 14 10 2023].

Warzel, C., 2023. *Twitter is a far-right social network.* [Online] Available at: https://www.theatlantic.com/technology/archive/2023/05/elon-musk-ron-desantis-2024-twitter/674149/ [Accessed 03 09 2023].

Weatherbed, J., 2023. *Blue checkmarks on X are 'superspreaders of misinformation' about Israel-Hamas war.* [Online] Available at: https://www.theverge.com/2023/10/20/23925086/x-verified-blue-checkmarks-superspreader-misinformation-israel-hamas-war [Accessed 15 11 2023].

Index

Page numbers in **bold reference tables.

162   *Index*

fashion 117–118
online meme army 127
online platforms 53, 78, 144; digital
extremism 56; role of 145
online proximity, impact of 52–53
online radicalisation 56
online terrorism **40**
online toxicity 110
Operation Google 110
opponents of political correctness 6
Optical Character Recognition
(OCR) 149
Ordinary Muslim Man meme 131
Organisation for Security and
Co-operation in Europe (OSCE),
hate crime **36**
Orlando nightclub attack (2016) 27
OSCE *see* Organisation for Security
and Co-operation in Europe
Oslo and Utøya Island attacks
(2011) 28, **31**

Palmeter, Ryan 30, **33**
Paradox Interactive 97
Parler 87–88
Patriotic Ink 119
peer groups 5
Pepe the Frog **116**, 124–125
Permit Patty memes 132
Pittsburgh synagogue shooting
(2018) **32**
#Pizzagate conspiracy 69
platform governance 41
'/pol/' 124, 130
polarisation 8
political correctness, opponents of 6
pop culture, and online extremism
63–64
populist movements 24
post-truth era: COVID-19 pandemic
60; defining 59–60; summary
of **62**
prejudices 35
privacy, social media 78–80
propaganda **62**
propagating hate 40
Proud Boys 7, 130

prowhite 24
psychology behind, echo
chambers 61

QAnon 4–5, 65, 69–70, **116**, 147
Qassem Brigades 42
Q-drops 70

race traitors 8
racial memes 132
racially motivated attacks 30
radicalisation: online 56;
process of 6
Radix Journal 55
red pill 63–64, **64**
Reddit 78, 87, 90
red-pilling 63
regulating hate speech on social
media 38
Reichsbürger 130
Reichsversand 119
rejection of democracy 5–6
Release the Kraken Flag **116**
Resistance Axis groups 42
rigged elections 68
RIM *see* Russian Imperial
Movement
Robinson, Tommy **84**
role of far-right groups **67**
runes, as codes and symbols **114**
Russia, involvement with European
far-right groups 57
Russian Imperial Movement (RIM) 57
Russian propaganda, memes 126

San Bernardino attack (2015) 27
satire 123–124, 132
secure communication 57–58
Sellner, Martin 27, 119
shadowbanned, X/Twitter 128
shallow fakes 66
Shopify 120
sign of justice 110
SJW *see* social justice warrior
snowflake 129
social belonging 3
Social Identity Theory 13
social justice warrior (SJW) 129

For Product Safety Concerns and Information please contact our EU
representative GPSR@taylorandfrancis.com Taylor & Francis Verlag GmbH,
Kaufingerstraße 24, 80331 München, Germany

Printed and bound by CPI Group (UK) Ltd, Croydon, CR0 4YY
11/06/2025
01899268-0001